T0311631

ROUTLEDGE LIBRARY EDITIONS: URBAN AND REGIONAL ECONOMICS

Volume 24

RURAL RESOURCE DEVELOPMENT

RURAL RESOURCE DEVELOPMENT

An Economic Approach

M. C. WHITBY AND K. G. WILLIS

Routledge
Taylor & Francis Group

LONDON AND NEW YORK

First published in 1978 by Methuen

This edition first published in 2018
by Routledge
2 Park Square, Milton Park, Abingdon, Oxon OX14 4RN

and by Routledge
711 Third Avenue, New York, NY 10017

Routledge is an imprint of the Taylor & Francis Group, an informa business

© 1978 M. C. Whitby and K. G. Willis

British Library Cataloguing in Publication Data
A catalogue record for this book is available from the British Library

ISBN: 978-1-138-09590-8 (Set)
ISBN: 978-1-315-10306-8 (Set) (ebk)
ISBN: 978-1-138-10221-7 (Volume 24) (hbk)
ISBN: 978-1-138-10255-2 (Volume 24) (pbk)
ISBN: 978-1-315-10307-5 (Volume 24) (ebk)

Publisher's Note
The publisher has gone to great lengths to ensure the quality of this reprint but points out that some imperfections in the original copies may be apparent.

Disclaimer
The publisher has made every effort to trace copyright holders and would welcome correspondence from those they have been unable to trace.

Rural Resource Development

An economic approach

SECOND EDITION

M. C. Whitby
and K. G. Willis

METHUEN & CO LTD

First published in 1978
by Methuen & Co Ltd
11 New Fetter Lane
London EC4P 4EE
© *1978 M. C. Whitby and K. G. Willis*
Printed in Great Britain at the
University Press, Cambridge

ISBN 0 416 70730 0 *(hardbound)*
ISBN 0 416 70720 3 *(paperback)*

Contents

Preface

In writing this second edition we have attempted to narrow the scope of the book, making more use of economic analysis as a structural theme. We are therefore glad to acknowledge the contributions of Professor David Robbins and Arthur Tansey to the breadth and scope of the first edition and for generously allowing us to produce this more specialized text from it. In writing this one we have substantially changed the format of the first edition, adding new chapters and completely revising the empirical material presented.

We acknowledge a substantial debt to our colleague, Dr Ian Hodge, who completely reviewed the text in draft and made many useful suggestions. We are also grateful to Janice Price of Methuen, whose entrepreneurial skill led to the publication of the first edition and whose continual encouragement has improved the timeliness of this one. We have also benefitted from the more forthright reviews of the first edition.

Finally we would adhere to the final passage of the preface to the first edition, which stated:

'We expect that readers will find serious omissions of subject from the text. We are equally confident that they would not agree as to which relevant subjects have been omitted. Our main concern is to present ways of analysis which will lead to more effective public decision-making and hence better use of rural resources.'

Martin Whitby
Ken Willis

Part I

1 The setting

In this chapter our main aim is to give a preview of the book as a whole. The chapter starts with a general classification of studies of rural development, in terms of the philosophical position of their authors. It then offers clarification of the focus of the book by defining resources in a rural context. In the third section we set out some indication of the size of the allocation problem we are discussing. The fourth section then summarizes some of the available information relating to rural decision-makers. Finally we present a short résumé of the contents of the book.

Stereotypes

Yet another book about rural Britain has to be justified in terms of its uniqueness of contribution compared with what has been written before. We therefore begin this chapter with an attempt at summarizing the types of writings available on rural affairs. This is done in terms of four stereotypes, which do nevertheless have some bearing on the real world; but, more importantly, they allow us to indicate where this work belongs in the welter of argument relating to the countryside. For ease of reference we have labelled our four stereotypes as follows: the journalist/politician; the scientist-gone-astray; the rationalizing bureaucrat; the market fanatic. We apologize to those readers who find this language too lurid: we overstate here merely to make the point.

4 Rural Resource Development

The journalist/politician is trying to sell something to his reader, be it copy or policies, and as such will take up a value-position which is more or less consistent with that of his party or of his paper. He does not need to justify this value-position and is most likely to take it as given that he will not have to state it. Often such positions become very well known. For example, the farming press in Britain usually supports the short-term farming interest, arguing in favour of what it believes its readers want. Rarely does it argue on behalf of the consumer although, in the long-term, farm incomes are determined by the extent to which food is priced competitively with other goods. To both journalists and politicians, size of audience is critical and this limits the intellectual complexity of the arguments they may use. This lack of sophistication leads them to make quite indefensible statements. Cobbett in his *Rural Rides* (1821–32) provides an excellent example of both the best and the worst a journalist/politician can do. At his best, he provides a very well painted picture of rural Britain. But, in the same work, he comes back over and over to his favourite hobby horses. His distrust of paper money, his scorn for Methodism and his somewhat irrational loathing of speculation are interspersed with many penetrating observations on the state of the countryside.

Scientists who have strayed into the rural development area sometimes find themselves unable to effect the transition from 'objective' scientific work to the murkier normative issues of rural development. This can be seen in many contemporary writings on conservation in which 'scientific interest' (which, of course, brings immediate satisfaction to a small group of scientists and possible or potential benefits to future generations) is frequently equated with the public good. Scientists take such untenable positions because their training does not require them to speculate about or handle social value-judgements. The essential business of science is establishing facts about the universe.

By contrast, in studying rural development we are focusing on a particular set of social problems to which there can be no approved solution without reference to value-judgements. Passmore (1974) makes this distinction very well in the context of defining an ecological problem:

An ecological problem is not, in the first place the same thing as a problem in ecology. A problem in ecology is a purely scientific problem, arising out of the fact that scientists do not understand some particular ecological phenomenon, how, for example, DDT finds its way into the fat of Antarctic birds. Its solution brings them understanding. An ecological problem, in contrast, is a special type of social problem. (We can easily be led to suppose otherwise because most books on ecological problems are written by scientists). To speak of a phenomenon as a 'social problem' is not to suggest merely, or perhaps at all, that we do not understand how it comes about; it is labelled a problem, not because, like a scientific problem, it presents an obstacle to our understanding of the world but rather because – consider alcoholism, crime, deaths on the road – we believe that our society would be better off without it.

Perhaps the largest single source of published studies are the agencies who service rural areas themselves. Many of these will be mentioned by name later in the book: here they are dubbed 'rationalizing bureaucrats' with descriptive, not pejorative, intent. Those employed by agencies have to explain in public what they are doing. Mostly such explanations are *ex poste*: that is to say, they seek to justify past policies rather than to defend future ones. This historic posture is important and pervasive. It means that many studies which could offer useful guidelines for the future fail to do so because they are written with the infinite wisdom of hindsight. When evaluating such source material, it is thus very important to look carefully at its origin and to take account of the problems the agency was facing at the time its findings were published. Agencies exist for particular purposes, which will bias their statements away from objectivity and towards careful selection of arguments and facts. The declared purpose of an agency may be the best single indicator of the bias to be expected from it. Sometimes, as for example with the Ministry of Agriculture, Fisheries and Food, agencies have very basic internal conflicts which surface from time to time. Thus MAFF has to act on behalf of both producers and consumers of food. Usually it justifies policies which offend farmers by stressing its responsibility to consumers, and vice versa. The balance it achieves between these two interests will reflect some particular trade-off established within the ministry. It should not be inferred from these remarks that every word published by agencies is biased. In practice, much of their output is simple, uncontroversial, fact. Nevertheless, the information they publish is often chosen to justify a particular policy stance and this must be borne in mind when interpreting it.

The market fanatic is an animal familiar to economists; indeed he is very likely to have had some economic training. At the crudest, he will argue that market prices are the best possible indicator of social preferences, and that government intervention in economic affairs is an infringement of the liberty of the individual. He may go further and ascribe moral virtue to the outcome of the market and will be instinctively suspicious of attempts to redistribute income. Such dangerous deviations from the true path of righteousness may be threatened with the descent into totalitarianism and the end of the liberal state. Professor Milton Friedman of Chicago is probably the best known protagonist of this view, and he has support from many economists.

This position cannot be brushed aside as easily as policy-makers would like. Undoubtedly Friedman has reminded us of some of the consequences of the economic policies pursued in this country and, we hope, there is a substantial amount of material in this book which he would accept. Perhaps, however, his main contribution relates to the size of the public sector and the extent to which governments should interfere in the economy, and these are not issues we deal with here. Nevertheless, a good deal of the book discusses the problems which have arisen where the market has failed to produce socially desired outputs. To that extent we would part company with the pure market fanatic.

Perhaps we may best sum up our own position *vis-à-vis* these four stereotypes in terms of the passage from Passmore which we quoted above. The journalist/politician is likely to mislead because he will be pursuing some particular set of goals narrower than those of society at large. He will be 'selling' his views to a particular group of supporters and will often appeal to their special interests at the expense of the rest of society. The scientist-gone-astray is most directly dealt with by Passmore. The problem here is that he has gone beyond his particular competence into a world of policy evaluation for which he is not equipped. There is, of course, a technical and factual basis to most policy problems and this could not be adequately identified without scientific measurement. The rationalizing bureaucrat can tell us much that is useful and relevant to a wide range of problems. We must recognize that his terms of reference will oblige him to see (or pretend to see) the world in a particular way and the material he publishes will reflect this vision. The market fanatic provides a useful corrective to the wilder excesses of the policy-makers. He, in common with the other stereotypes, has his own value-configuration, which will influence his conclusions. Insofar as this differs from society's preferences, his views will be irrelevant.

We hope, then, in the ensuing pages, to offer an analysis of rural affairs and problems which will be constructive and analytical. We shall concentrate particularly on the choices to be made, on analysing alternatives and on measuring costs and benefits. Wibberley (1959) made a substantial economic contribution to this area of enquiry and Newby *et al.* (1978) have contributed valuable insights from the sociological point of view. We would approach our subject in the same way as these authors, starting from a social science posture emphasizing logical analysis, but recognizing the vast gaps in our knowledge of the rural scene. We thus find ourselves reading the works of politicians and journalists in the hope of clarifying and identifying social objectives; from the scientists we may learn the technological constraints within which we must operate. The planners and bureaucrats will provide raw information for the analysis and will indicate some of the choices which are worth evaluating. The market fanatic will be the angel sitting on our shoulders, but we shall not allow him free-rein.

Resources

The level of want-satisfaction that an economy can achieve is limited partly by the quantities and qualities of its known resources. Resources are the means for producing goods and services that are used to satisfy wants. Many of the problems in society are caused by the way in which resources are employed with a view to satisfying human wants. It is useful to divide resources into three main groups:

(1) natural resources — all those gifts of nature such as land, air, water, minerals, forests, fish, quiet, pleasant landscape and so on;
(2) labour — all human resources, mental and physical, inherited or acquired;
(3) capital — all equipment, including everything man-made which is not consumed for its own sake, but which may be used up in the process of making other goods.

Some of the most serious confusions arise from a failure to distinguish between resource stocks and resource flows. The best analogy is to think of a bath half full of water with the tap turned on and the plug removed. The level of water in the bath is stock, an amount which is just there. The amount of water coming in through the tap and the amount leaving through the drain are both flows. A flow necessarily has a time dimension: it is so much per period of time. A stock does not have a time dimension, it is just so many kilos, litres, or numbers. The amount of wheat stored up, produced but unsold, in the granaries of the world is a stock: it is just so many million tons of wheat at a point in time. The amount of wheat produced is a flow, calculated at so much per year, or per month. The amount of wheat sold is also a flow, so much per month or year.

Confusion originates deep in history. Ricardo (1817), for example, assumed absolute fixity of 'the original and indestructible properties of the soil' and postulated that man's capacity to enjoy a high standard of living is limited by the fixity of the natural resources available to him, and depends on the number of men relative to the available amount of natural resources. One corollary of this proposition was the conclusion that man can destroy his economic well-being by over-breeding, a deduction early enunciated by Malthus (1798), and coupled with the assumption that man will automatically over-breed when left to his own devices. The avoidance of human disaster would either require self-control (as advocated by Malthus) or strong programmes of population control. The other corollary is the hypothesis that, if a fixed stock of natural resources sets a limit to man's potential economic welfare, and if the present generation has any concern for the economic welfare of its descendents, it has an obligation to preserve, as far as possible, the stock of natural resources for the use of future generations. This corollary has expressed itself in the past in the 'conservation movement', as in the case of J. S. Mill expounding in Parliament in the mid-1860s the urgent need to conserve coal, as a natural resource stock; and, more recently, it has expressed itself in the 'anti-pollution' and 'environment-preservation' movements. In all of these movements, there are elements of the Ricardian assumption that there is something special about the environment that requires keeping it intact in its existing form. However, in the context of contemporary society, natural resources mainly derive their value from the available technology, which is itself a variable alterable by investment in the creation of new technology itself, and from investment in transport and distribution facilities. The environment is a form of social capital stock, with flow characteristics, which society must somehow manage if it is to maximize its welfare.

Contrary to Ricardo, the environment is not 'original and indestructible'. It has built-in tendencies to self-destruction. For example, soils, are eroded by rainfall or wind; the land is eroded by the sea, as in North Humberside where the North Sea bites into the low cliffs of clay, eroding them at the rate of 2 to 7 feet per year; and villages known to exist in medieval times have disappeared completely under this perpetual attack. The economic value of the environment to man may be either enhanced or destroyed by technical progress. Man's whole history has been one of transforming his environment, rather than of accepting its limitations: the draining of the Fens is a good example. This began seriously after the Dissolution of the Monasteries, when the 4th Earl of Bedford, whose family had been given abbey estates in the area, was empowered by Royal Charter to turn the wastelands into good summer grazing grounds. A Dutch engineer, Vermuyden, was engaged to straighten out the rivers and sluice them against tidal flow. The basic idea was simply to assist the downhill dispersal of water over the lower-lying seaward silts or flats. But soon there was no downhill. Paradoxically, the more effective the drainage, the more the spongy peat contracted, so that eventually it was lower than the silts, and the water flowed back. Today, undrained fens kept as nature reserves are higher than the surrounding peatlands. Natural drainage did not work, so hundreds of pumping windmills had to be installed to move the water into the main outlets. Early in the nineteenth century, steam engines began to replace windmills for fen drainage, but today steam engines have been replaced by electric and diesel-powered pumps. The Fens now form some of the most productive agricultural land in Britain. Conversely, pottery technology demands kaolin, and china clay mines have destroyed the landscape around St Austell in Cornwall, where on Carclaze Down, north of the town, huge white mounds of sand and quartz add a weird touch to the landscape. Such land can be restored in the interests of amenity: of particular interest is the Ironstone Restoration Fund, established under the Mineral Workings Act 1951, to assist in the financing of reclamation in the Midlands ironstone field, where working was by opencast methods. Ironstone operators make a contribution to the fund for each ton of ironstone extracted by opencast methods and the Exchequer makes a further contribution. Payments are made from the Fund for old derelict workings and for new workings where the cost of restoration, now a condition of planning permission, exceeds a certain sum.

The economic value of the environment to man can thus either be augmented or destroyed by technical progress. Good social management of the environment may require either deliberate efforts to preserve and augment it (see Chapter 8; an example may be the case of landscape in National Parks and Areas of Outstanding Natural Beauty – see Chapters 5 and 7), or deliberate efforts to transform the wealth that it represents into a more valuable form (for example, conversion of agricultural land for housing — see Chapters 4 and 5). It may be in society's interests at one period of time to transform natural resources into cash, and at another to preserve them as a form of future wealth. Thus, when North Sea oil came on stream, as much production was sought as possible. But in 1977, when Britain's balance of payments problem had improved and oil imports from foreign countries had been substantially reduced, the Secretary of State for Energy ordered one field to shut down production until the natural gas, which was being flared off in the production of oil, could also be brought ashore and fed into the national gas grid. If society possesses depletable natural resources, it may or may not be advantageous to sell them or to allow them to be used up in current production. (A dilemma facing some countries in the Arab world: what level of economic development should they permit now against a possible future energy shortage and consequent increase in the value of the natural resource and, in addition, the risk of alternative energy sources being found?)

With the exception of unique natural features, the depletion of the environment can generally be corrected by subsequent investment. Depleted forests can be replanted, old decaying urban areas rebuilt, polluted waterways revitalized either by oxygenating them or by investment in sewerage treatment works (such as the current Tyneside Sewerage Scheme of the Northumbrian Water Authority which seeks to obturate raw, untreated sewerage disposal directly into the river Tyne), and fish can be farmed instead of caught. New sources of energy (wind, sunlight, nuclear fusion) can be substituted for depletable energy resources such as coal or oil. These considerations are often ignored in systems dynamics (see Forrester, 1971) and in population, resource, and technology models such as that of the Club of Rome (see Meadows, 1972). Naive environmental models have been the subject of fierce attacks, for example by Nordhaus (1973), Surrey and Page (1975), Heal (1975), and Kay and Mirrlees (1975). Conservation and anti-pollution arguments are often weak. They fail to consider the costs and benefits of using environmental resource stocks in terms of the advantages to society. Without some depletion in resource stocks and reduced flows of certain environmental services (clean air, quiet, pleasant scenery), the Industrial Revolution would not have occurred! Conservationists and anti-pollutionists also fail to consider the possibility of reconstituting the environment, or of actually constructing a new environment catering to their environmental desires in terms of investable resources or welfare forgone elsewhere.

It should be stressed at this point that resources must not be confused with the finance necessary to undertake an environmental project. Finance is the provision of money at the time it is wanted. It supplies the means by which people are enabled to consume more (resources) than they produce at certain periods of time. An arable farmer may work himself and pay wages to those whom he employs for many months before receiving a return; it is only when his crop is grown, harvested and sold that he is repaid for his own work and for the wages and expenses he has incurred. Short-term sources of finance are banks, trade creditors, hire purchase, intercompany loans; and long term sources, debenture stock, shares, finance corporations and, for the public sector, the Exchequer. The public sector of the economy denotes the combination of central government, the local authorities, the nationalized industries and other public corporations. The nationalized industries invest some £4000 million per year (1975), about half of which comes from earnings and the remainder by way of loans from the Exchequer. The Exchequer charges interest on such loans.

The allocation, distribution and consumption of resources in society very much depends on the distribution of property rights. Property defines a multiple relationship between man and objects in relation to other men. Property is instrumental in any social structure and has had an important influence on politics (Conservative v. Labour on the distribution of property), and political thought from Machiavelli (property limits political power: i.e. one must not touch other men's wives or there will be trouble) to Locke (property 'should be preserved by the state) and Marx (political structure is erected to protect property). Physical objects cannot be owned by anyone: what a person owns are the rights to use that physical object in a certain way. It is thus more useful to talk of property in terms of the elements comprising property and their corollaries:

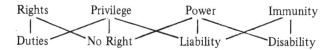

Right is a claim of one person on another, so that the second person has a duty to the first. For example, a landowner has the right that a neighbour should not walk across his land, and the neighbour has a duty not to trespass. Privilege determines whether a man can or cannot perform a right. A man may have the privilege to remonstrate with a trespasser and to sue him in court for any damage; he does not have the privilege of being able to shoot him for trespassing. The corollary of privilege is no right. Power can change rights and privileges. Landowners now do not have the power to change rights and privileges over land as they did in feudal times. The enclosure of commons and the conversion of open fields into privately-owned farms had been a normal practice since the Middle Ages, but the process was vastly extended in the eighteenth century to permit new experiments in agriculture and the extension of farming for a profit. Such changes in rights and privileges were possible when power was in the hands of a Parliament dominated by landowners, and when property formed part of the voting qualification. Parliament is now no longer dominated by the landowners. The National Parks and Access to the Countryside Act 1949, is one example of an Act which changed the rights of access across land. Whereas previously land-owners had exclusive rights to prohibit people from crossing their land (except along rights of way), Parliament decreed that local authorities could make Orders that the public should have access to stretches of open country if a mutual agreement could not be reached with a landowner. The corollary of power is liability and landowners have a liability to accept Access Orders and not to do anything to reduce access. Immunity is the freedom from having legal relation-ships changed, and it is this freedom which landowners enjoyed before parliamentary reform, when Parliament voluntarily re-formed itself. The corollary of immunity is disability to have one's legal relations changed. It is, therefore, possible to have privileges without power, and rights without immunity.

Property rights define (1) the uses to which resources may be put, (2) the uses to which they may not be put, (3) the exclusion of others from use without the owner's consent and (4) the terms under which the rights may be transferred to others. Private property has tended to evolve in western society where it can be enforced reasonably cheaply. However, there is also a lot of common property in western society, usually because there is simply no economic alternative. While, for example, it is possible to imagine a world in which the right to pass sound and light waves or aircraft over private property could attach itself to the private ownership of land, and it is also possible to imagine these rights being bought and sold, it takes little imagination to appreciate the enormous costliness of the procedure of policing and enforcing these rights and the contracts made about them. Transactions costs denote the time, effort and expense employed in arranging an exchange, sale, loan or contract, for example: finding buyers, preparing documents, transferring the cash or other payment, assuring the buyer that he has acquired the property rights he desires in the goods he has bought and policing and enforcing the rights. Transactions costs are clear in the case of sales of property rights in buildings and land, but they are also present, though more difficult to define, in noise, dust, radiation, amenity etc. While (1) and (2) are usually feasible in common property arrangements, (3) and (4) are not. However, the welfare of society depends on common property as well as on private property, and the value of common property to society must be evaluated with that of private property in any resource development scheme, and some judgement must be arrived at concerning the allocation and consumption of common property resources. This issue is taken up and pursued further in Chapters 2, 5 and 7. Rights in property are important because they have allocational implications as well as distributional ones.

Finance

The value of gross domestic product (GDP) at factor cost in 1975 was £93,146 million. It is not possible to define what proportion of GDP is accounted for by rural areas. Indeed, no precise definition exists of a rural area. In everyday usage the word implies pastoral or agricultural land as opposed to 'urban' and 'suburban' areas of towns and cities. Rural areas tend to be thought of as simply those in which agriculture and forestry are the predominant form of productive economic activity. An area which is defined as rural on this basis may house large numbers of people who have no connection with these activities, and the interests and needs of such residents may not coincide with those of the workers in agriculture and forestry and their families. Indeed considerable inter-rural urban flows of income, expenditure and resources exist. People resident in rural areas may work in urban areas; shopping trips to urban centres by rural workers are common; many rural workers and dependents use urban services (hospitals, libraries, cinemas, theatres); while, conversely, urban residents use rural resources, especially recreational and water resources. Some rural-urban flows are accounted for in money transactions at full marginal cost, but other service charges are based on historic costs, average costs, or are enjoyed free of charge. These complex inter-area flows of income and expenditure make the determination of the gross domestic product of rural areas quite difficult.

Despite these reservations, it is clear that for some rural economic activities, resource cost exceeds the benefit (and revenue) produced by them. Such economic activities are only viable on their present scale with the aid of finance in the form of grants and subsidies. Selected economic activities with attendant subsidy levels are set out in Table 1.1. By their very nature and by their terms of reference, these activities are almost exclusively restricted to rural areas. However, this table is by no means comprehensive. Indeed all public corporations engage in cross-subsidy and, with the possible exception of the National Coal Board, tend to subsidize rural areas from profitable urban services and production. Post and telephone services, British Rail, the National Bus Company and its subsidiaries, Electricity Boards, Gas Boards and Area Health Authorities all subsidize rural areas generally. Domestic air routes to remote islands and inland waterways also run at a financial loss. Similarly, local authority costs for the majority of services are higher in rural than in urban areas. This is a result of a combination of large distances and a sparse population, a situation which gives rise to greater transport costs, as in the case of education, and which does not permit economies of scale to be achieved, as in the case of sewerage. It is difficult to obtain figures for the amount of this

Table 1.1   Grants and subsidies to selected economic activities in rural areas

	£ millions (current prices)	
	1974–5	1975–6
Agriculture	494.50*	511.60†
Development Commission	3.73	4.78
Countryside Commission	5.66	6.62
Highlands and Islands Development Board	5.49	6.82
Forestry Commission‡	17.05	26.90

Sources: Annual Review of Agriculture (1977); Development Commission (1977); Countryside Commission (1977); Forestry Commission (1977).

* Of which £169.6 million was received from the European Agricultural Guidance and Guarantee Fund (FEOGA) set up by the EEC to finance the Common Agricultural Policy (CAP)
† Of which £264.00 million was received from FEOGA.
‡ The Forestry Commission is expected to earn 3 per cent on its capital. These subsidies were introduced to:
   (i) record the difference between 3 per cent and the ruling rate of interest;
   (ii) cover new planting and stocking undertaken for social reasons which could not earn the target rate of return; and
   (iii) the provision of recreational facilities for the public for which commercial objectives are not set.

subsidization, partly because of the difficulty of defining rural and urban areas and the boundary between them, and partly because of the difficulty of apportioning capital costs where joint production exists. The complex issue of settlement and service costs is taken up in Chapter 11, but it must be remembered that rural areas are by no means homogeneous: there are many examples within each type of economic activity of production and services which are run at a substantial profit in some rural areas.

However, the welfare of society depends not only on private property resources, which can be valued in monetary terms, but also on common property resources (clean air, pleasant scenery and so on) which are not valued in financial terms and so do not form part of GDP. A methodology to value common property resources, to bring them into commensurable terms with the market valuation of private property resources and to efficiently allocate all resources, is outlined in Chapters 2, 7, and 8. In practice, these resources still have not been evaluated in any consistent manner.

By giving greater discretion to individual agencies, central government has offered them an opportunity of making a more explicit evaluation of common property resources, and of considering effective demand rather than normative need (that which the 'expert' thinks the population should have), or comparative need (everyone must be in receipt of the same service). It also allows greater discretion to be exercised in product distribution or income distribution among families and individuals within areas. Thus equity can be influenced by administratively determined prices, investment and resource ownership. Central government has retracted somewhat from the position of specifying detailed financial criteria of how and on what monies are to be spent, and has allowed more flexibility in spending in order to meet varying demands in different areas. This is significant because total public spending amounted to some £54,465 million in 1975, or 58 per cent of GDP. Expenditure by local authorities amounted to some £14,347 million on current account and £4417 million on capital account or, in total, 20 per cent of GDP and 34 per cent of all public expenditure.

Table 1.2 shows that specific grants to local authorities for such services as roads, housing, police, administration of justice and education, declined from 33.6 per cent of revenue income in 1955 to 6.7 per cent of current income in 1975. A correspondingly greater percentage was provided in the form of general government grants not tied to a specific sector, and the decision as to what such monies should be spent upon was left to the local authority. Greater discretion in expenditure matters is gradually being given to local authorities in most sectors. For example, Transport Policies and Programmes inaugurated in 1974 left to local authorities the decision as to how they should spend their transport grants, i.e.: how many resources they should devote to public or private transport, the modes of public and private transport and the extent of development in each, and in what areas of the local authority resources were to be devoted. In 1977, the Department of the Environment set up a similar scheme with regard to housing. Housing Investment Programmes are to be drawn up at the local authority's discretion and are to provide details of the allocation of a block grant of finance for housing between new buildings,

Table 1.2 Sources of revenue finance (current account) of all local authorities

£ millions (current prices)

	1955		1965		1975	
	Amount	*Percentage ‡*	*Amount*	*Percentage ‡*	*Amount*	*Percentage ‡*
Rates	475	39.2	1,228	38.8	3,893	27.1
General government grants	83	6.9	968	30.6	6,902	48.1
Specific government grants*	407	33.6	281	8.9	966	6.7
Miscellaneous†	246	20.3	691	21.8	2,586	18.0
Total local authority receipts	1,211		3,168		14,347	
GDP	16,873		31,221		93,146	

Source: Central Statistical Office (1976a).

* Includes roads, housing, police, administration of justice, education, other.
† Comprising trading income, rents from houses and land, interest on money.
‡ Addition does not always equal 100 per cent due to rounding errors.

modernization of existing housing, tenure sectors, housing type, spatial area etc. A consistent methodology is required to allocate such resources in a scientific rather than an emotive manner.

The decision environment

Greater discretion will allow resource allocation and distribution to be changed if the control of the local authority passes to another party. Greater discretion may have allocational and distributional consequences: local government has greater freedom to pursue goals of economic efficiency, greater freedom to determine its own pattern of equity and, consequently, greater responsibility to establish trade-offs between efficiency and equity goals itself, rather than rely on central government direction. Other agencies operating in rural areas who likewise have discretionary powers, face many similar problems. How much this will affect rural areas is open to debate. The Committee on the Management of Local Government (1967) pointed out that rural councillors were in general older than the average, more likely to own their own houses and consequently less likely to live in council houses, more likely to be retired from work, less likely to be manual workers and, predictably, many more were farmers. Thirty-five per cent of rural district councillors were farmers, compared with 15 per cent of all councillors. The report shows that 55 per cent of rural district councillors were elected un-opposed at their first election, compared with 34 per cent for county council and 31 per cent for all councils. Rural councillors were much older on average than other councillors. Perhaps the sharpest difference of all was the method of appointment at their last election: no fewer than 69 per cent of rural district councillors were returned unopposed, compared with 38 per cent from all councils and county councils. The situation will now have changed somewhat with local government reorganization in 1974, but the picture of rural society as being essentially conservative in nature still remains true.

Newby *et al.* (1978) found, in the autumn of 1973 (just before local government reorganization), that 21 per cent of those replying to a questionnaire survey sent to all East Anglia local authority members were farmers. This proportion rose to 31 per cent among rural district councillors. A further 9 per cent of all councillors were either part-time farmers or had some close commercial or professional connection with agriculture. Furthermore, they report that, in the key council roles such as committee and council chairmanships, farmers were more prominent than their share of council seats would suggest. These authors then go on to describe in some detail the way in which farmers are effective in representing their own interests in local government in Suffolk. This is achieved partly by combining with 'conservation' interests, and is made much easier because the farm worker acquiesces in the process.

There is neither time nor space here to do more than sketch out the lines and roles of agencies and pressure groups. The problem for rural areas lies in discerning who shall play what role according to which rules. The parties in the who bit are numerous, ranging from rural dwellers to potential urban dweller beneficiaries such as recreationalists, and encompassing pressure groups such as the Country Landowners Association, the National Farmers' Union, the National Trust for Places of Historic or Natural Beauty, the Council for the Preservation of Rural England, the Friends of the Earth, The Ramblers Association, the Society for the Protection of Ancient Buildings, the Georgian Group, The Victorian Society, the Ancient Monuments Society, the Commons Open Spaces and Footpaths Preservation Society, The Civic Trust, the Botanical Society, the British Ecological Society, the Council for Nature, the Holiday Fellowship, the Youth Hostels Association, the Womens Institute, the Rural Community Councils etc. In addition, many local pressure groups exist, for example: the Dartmoor Preservation Society, the Newcastle and Northumberland Society, the Yorkshire Naturalists' Trust and so on. Other parties voicing opinions are the 'experts', planners, agriculturalists, botanists, foresters, and so on; politicians, and the electorate at large.

The roles played by these parties are various. Some act as advisers (Nature Conservancy, Agricultural Development Advisory Service), others as situation analysts (NFU), or as researchers (Countryside Commission), or priority-setters (Countryside Commission). Many pressure groups or agencies fulfil more than one role, and specific multiple objective development agencies have been created, such as the Highlands and Islands Development Board which was set up for the purpose of assisting the people of the Highlands and Islands to improve their economic and social conditions and to enable the Highlands and Islands to play a more effective part in the economic and social development of the nation. The HIDB Act of 1965 gives the Board special powers to finance and make grants and loans to private individuals, and to carry out projects itself. Grants and loans are given to all sectors, from fisheries to manufacturing and processing, tourism, transport, agriculture and horticulture, and to service industries. It is thus wider in scope than the Development Commission, which is restricted to factory provision in rural areas.

The rules consist of the terms of reference of the agencies and statutory bodies such as the HIDB, the Countryside Commission, the Planning Committees, and the behavioural norms of the pressure groups. Some pressure groups, such as those concerned with motorway proposals in some urban and rural areas have become very militant and disruptive at official inquiries. The arguments of pressure groups are frequently expounded in emotive terms, with emphasis being placed on the uniqueness of the case, implying that it is an all or nothing decision with no trade-offs possible. The rules and criteria by which such pressure groups present their case are such as to make comparison with other objectives difficult, and evaluation subjective.

These organizations have arisen because free exchange and the price mechanism have broken down.[1] Common property cannot be traded because property rights do not exist. Society has had a long history of allocating resources other than by the price mechanism, for example: allocating rare princesses to knights who slay the most dragons, queuing, or allocating political office to candidates most willing to exhaust themselves by serving society or by attending trade union or political party meetings. The pressure group system works in rural areas in the same way, the greatest weight being attached to the preferences of those prepared to expend most effort and resources in demonstrating their concern. However, the present difficulty is that there are so many conflicting and tangled roles, that scorn is usually poured on any judgement or outcome. It is extremely difficult to know how the judgement was arrived at and if it was obtained in any consistent and scientific manner. The heaviest burden of responsibility falls on 'policy makers' whose unenviable task is to detect, clarify and give operational context to the wishes to society. The proper discharge of their responsibilities is made extremely difficult by the fact that many of the judgements they should make are usurped by others, and the information at their

[1] Of course, the possibility exists that pressure groups may be set up to subvert the price mechanism.

disposal is biased accordingly. For example, practically all development plans present three alternative strategies for the development of the area. But these are drawn up by planners and are often variations along a similar theme – the theme currently in vogue, such as high rise buildings in the 1960s or continuous urban renewal in the 1970s. Politicians are thus encouraged, often all too readily, to shuffle off their responsibilities to the 'experts', even though these experts are not experts in the relevant matters. Of course the 'experts' frequently reply that politicians are usually unwilling to make decisions at this stage and someone (the expert himself) has to decide society's wishes. This is a weak answer. 'Experts' are the servants of society, not its masters. There is every justification for experts standing firm and forcing politicians to discharge their responsibilities and representative functions, so that the decisions of politicians are made clear to the electorate to whom they are responsible.

One of the purposes of this book is to re-emphasize a theory to which all agencies and pressure groups can relate, to offer criteria through which competing arguments, claims, and opinions can be tested and measured, and to provide a common methodological evaluation or language through which all agencies and pressure groups, whatever role they are playing, can communicate intelligently with each other.

An outline of the book

The thirteen chapters have been grouped together in two parts. Part I deals with topics of wide general and methodological relevance. In Part II the chapters are concerned with single applied subject areas. The final chapter attempts a synthesis of these two approaches, presenting a case study of one particular past public decision.

The four remaining chapters of Part I aim to provide an introduction to applied economic analysis and an account of the institutional basis of public decisions in rural areas, through the planning system. Chapter 2 contains a review of the minimum of economics required to analyse public decisions at the local level. This chapter seeks to combine theory and practice: some students will find that they will need to read an introductory economics text before they can understand this chapter, others will feel inclined to skip the introductory sections and go straight to the applied part. Chapter 3 then takes a more quantitative approach, introducing the various models which are available for rural planning purposes. The next two chapters (4 and 5) deal in turn with the planning procedures applicable in rural areas, and the measures and institutions aimed at regulating the use of the countryside.

In Part II several issues are dealt with in turn. Chapter 6 presents a survey of the existing pattern of land use and then discusses the complex policy question of land use conversion. Following this, Chapter 7 discusses analytically the questions of recreation and amenity and Chapter 8 reviews economic aspects of resource and environmental conservation. Chapter 9 deals with the analysis of rural depopulation, concentrating on the demographic models available. Chapter 10 reviews some of the issues of farm policy. Chapters 11 and 12 are related in that the first deals with rural transport and the second with the pattern of rural settlement which it attempts to modify. Finally, in Chapter 13, we present a case study of a particular rural resource allocation decision, which summarizes some of the main themes of the book and allows us to indicate ways in which the techniques and approaches discussed here might have improved a particular decision.

2 The economics of public choice

Most economic decisions are taken in the private sector, that is to say by private individuals pursuing their own private interests. Economics began as a study of such decisions and it has since been adapted to incorporate the important collective decisions taken by groups either on behalf of themselves, or of other sections of society. Economic theories of public choice have been built on these individualistic foundations, which perhaps explains why they have only recently become sufficiently sophisticated to reflect the greater complexity of the public sector.

From the study of individual choices came the early influential statement that an efficient situation is one in which no person's welfare can be improved without someone else losing. Such a situation is sometimes referred to as Pareto-optimal or Pareto-efficient, after the Italian economist of that name. The necessary conditions which would identify it are that producers shall be combining the best available technology to minimize costs with a use of productive factors, such that the marginal cost[1] of each factor is just equal to its earnings, and further, that consumers will allocate their incomes so that their marginal utility per unit of expenditure on all

[1] Those unfamiliar with marginal analysis might well consult an elementary economics textbook for a fuller treatment. Samuelson (1976) and Lipsey (1975) are highly recommended.

goods is (as they perceive it) equal. In brief, these conditions provide answers to the *what?, how?* and *for whom?* questions in a society.

In a fully decentralized economy, it is argued, such a situation would be brought about by the unfettered operation of free markets for goods, services and factors. However, it is most unlikely that such a situation will arise in practice, partly because perfect competition will not necessarily bring about an ideal distribution of welfare – its operation might impoverish the poor and enrich the wealthy to an extent generally thought undesirable – or because it is very difficult, if not impossible, to establish veritably perfect competition.

Such competition requires that all goods and services shall be identified in terms of exclusive property rights, so that no person's production or consumption interferes with anyone else's, and so that monopolistic pricing of goods or factors does not occur. It is thus extremely unlikely that either mixed or market economies will be in an optimal state in terms of the efficiency with which they produce, consume and distribute. However, even if they were at an efficiency optimum, it is still likely that welfare would be shared between individuals or groups comprising the society in a less than optimal way.

Although we have indicated that the so-called free market will theoretically bring the economy to an efficient situation by the simultaneous responses of producers, consumers and factory owners to changing prices, it must be noted that this is not the only way in which an efficiency optimum may be sought. Thus, in a society where all allocation and production decisions were taken by public officials and, furthermore, each individual's consumption of all available goods was similarly controlled, these officials would use the same criteria if they were seeking to maximize efficiency. Whether a society seeks efficiency, using the 'hidden hand' of the competitive process or the interventionist agency, does not affect the conditions which would define an efficient situation.

There is, however, one important proviso that must be added to this statement. It is likely, some would say inevitable, that a very large bureaucracy would be needed to completely replace the competitive system. The price system may be seen as a very subtle control mechanism which rapidly transmits information from one economic agent to another. Such a system could only be fully replaced by a man-made mechanism at enormous cost. Hence the criteria by which an optimum will be identified, will only yield the same result for the two systems if the *transactions cost* of arriving at the optimum is the same in both cases. Most economists would assert that the transactions cost of a bureaucratic allocation system will be larger than that incurred by the price system. However this, almost instinctive, line of argument may owe much of its appeal to the fact that it is usually used in defence of an already existing market against some bureaucratic intervention. It might be defensible, then, to ignore the past costs of setting up the market system in the first place, although the current costs of operating the market should not be overlooked. But there will be situations where there is no market; perhaps where a new good (or bad) commodity has just been developed. Under those conditions the free market-versus-bureaucratic mechanisms question may have to be decided on the basis of transactions cost.

This brief introduction has indicated a number of elements which together define the public allocation problem. They include the question of social objectives and the constraints within which they are pursued, together with the problems of measuring progress towards these objectives and of developing criteria by which attempted or proposed improvements may be judged; the extent to which policies may be pursued by more sophisticated regulation techniques, including taxes and subsidies or by more precisely defining property rights and, finally, some of the more difficult problems of economic analysis are reviewed.

Objectives and constraints

Few human actions are completely motiveless: furthermore, most actions are undertaken for more than one reason. When the actor, or the decision-maker has a collective identity – a committee, council, board or some other group – the likelihood of many different objectives being pursued increases. In considering group actions, it is essential to specify objectives, so that progress towards them can be measured.

However, simply to list objectives may not help, particularly where there are many, because the choice problem would then require identification of the extent to which one objective could be traded-off against another. One way of reducing the problem is to define objectives at an aggregated level, so that they can embrace a number of elements all expressed in common units. In the case of a private firm the objective might be to maximize profits, defined as the difference between receipts and expenditures, the size of which can be measured because all elements are valued in common money units. To measure profit in this way is to assume that £1 worth of expenditure causes as much dissatisfaction to the firm as would £1 less of receipts. However, suppose the owner of the firm also wishes to minimize the number of hours he works per week, perhaps to have the longest possible annual holiday. In order to rank the alternative combinations of profit and leisure available to him, we should have to have some means of translating profit into leisure, or vice versa, or a means of expressing both profit and leisure in terms of a common unit of account which might be satisfaction, happiness, or some similar concept.

In addition to the problem of objectives, there is the related problem of constraints. Any firm has a limited amount of factors at its disposal, and the ways in which they can be productively combined will be limited by the available technology. This aspect of the choice problem can perhaps best be explained by a farming example. Suppose a farmer has 100 hectares of land, £100,000 working capital and employs two workers. Soil and climatic conditions may combine with the quality of his other factors – his own and his workers' skills, for example – to limit the possible number of enterprises he might operate, to six. He then has the problem of chosing how much of each of these to establish. If he pursues the objective of profit maximization, then the best combination of enterprises he could aim for becomes a question of optimizing the use of each of his constrained resources. The way in which the constraints operate is an integral part of the problem. If there were no constraints, he would have no problem: the existence of constraints is as important in the public sector as in the private sector.

Some objectives can be expressed in the form of constraints. For example: a farmer might adopt an objective of obtaining a stated amount of leisure time. This could be incorporated into the optimization problem as a constraint on the amount of labour available to the firm. In the public sector, too, one way of handling objectives is to convert them into constraints. However, this expedient is not often undertaken because it requires precision about the size of the constraints.

For public activities objectives may be combined together in a

Social Welfare Function (SWF), which states the relationship between progress towards each of a society's objectives and its total welfare. Most readers of this book will not have seen an actual SWF because they are essentially a theoretical construct relating to the processes which take place in a politician's mind. One of the controversies in welfare economics relates to the form of the SWF (see Nath, 1973, for a useful summary) – the way in which the welfare of individuals is combined to give total welfare – but for this text we shall adopt a more pragmatic approach regarding it merely as a list of objectives.

This conveniently allows us to separate the functions of economist and politician. The economist needs to know the list of variables which are included on the right-hand side of the SWF, but he may leave the politician to combine the variables together. Of course, this distinction may prove difficult to sustain, because the politician may well ask for advice about the way in which the variables should be combined. Thus, following our earlier discussion we might propose a SWF such as:

$$SW = f(E, D)$$

which states that aggregate social welfare is determined by the level of economic efficiency of the system (E) and the way in which the output of the system is distributed between groups (D). We deal later with problems of measuring E and D: here we concentrate on the form of the SWF.

Why can we not simply write down an equation – such as:

$$SW = 32 + 7.6E + 0.3D + 1.9ED$$

which would tell us precisely how social welfare is determined from E and D? We could do this in practice either by estimating the coefficients from knowledge about a set of past decisions, or by choosing a set of coefficients which seem appropriate and obtaining validation of them through the political system. However, although both approaches have been followed (Weisbrod, 1968; McGuire and Garn, 1969), neither has been widely adopted. Indeed McGuire and Garn, who put forward a proposed SWF for selecting regional development projects in the USA, were criticized for doing so by Mathur (1971), on the grounds that they could not, as professionals, either know or decide how society would relate or trade-off progress towards different objectives. Such trade-offs should be determined by the politician and he should not be confused with the complexities of explicit ranking functions. McGuire and Garn replied in practical terms that an agency with a large budget and many hundreds of possible projects on which to spend it, must develop precise criteria which should realistically incorporate relevant value-judgements.

Weisbrod's study was also interesting in this context. He developed the approach of examining past decisions as a means of measuring implicit weights given to different objectives in selecting water development projects in the USA. His study focused especially on the weights given to the way in which benefits were shared amongst four groups – poor and rich whites and poor and rich non-whites. The results he obtained enabled him to write down the SWF implicit in past decisions as:

$$SW = -1.3Y_1 + 2.2Y_2 + 9.3Y_3 - 2.0Y_4$$

where the Y_i are the shares of benefit obtained by each group. To take these results at face value would imply that social welfare was enhanced by transmitting benefits to rich whites and poor non-whites, and reduced by distributing them to poor whites and rich non-whites.

Weisbrod says little about the implication of these results, perhaps because his paper is mainly concerned with methodology for estimating the weights. The results are, in fact, based on four decisions in the USA and these are the weights which precisely fit the facts. However, an alternative would be to take a larger number of decisions and use a more elaborate statistical estimation technique. This might allow errors on individual decisions to cancel each other out and produce a more 'central' estimate of the weights applied.

But, even if the difficulties of measurement of weights could be overcome, questions of their applicability to other situations would remain. In effect, it would be reasonable to assert that the weights should reflect the political consensus of the government ruling during a period. Obviously a change of government would be likely to bring a new consensus and hence a new set of weights. But a change of government, of itself, implies a change in the balance of views within the electorate, part of which may be attributable to changes on the relative weight given to efficiency and distribution by individual voters. As such shifts in opinions can occur at varying speeds, there is an obvious danger that weights determined for some past period, even a recent one, will no longer represent the present views of the electorate. The possibility of obtaining the weights direct from politicians also exists, though obviously it would be difficult to achieve in practice. We might thus summarize alternatives:

> *either*: allow politicians to set the weights, or trade-off objectives one against the other, feeding them the best possible information on the contribution of possible policies to each objective in the SWF.
> *or*: attempt to express all of the differences between policies on a single (welfare) scale, using weights determined by some past political process, or from an explicit statement of weights obtained direct from the politicians.

Generally the first alternative is least radical in terms of the procedures followed in developed countries. There may, nevertheless, be particular situations where officials will wish to involve themselves more deeply in the trading-off process, as in the McGuire and Garn example. There is also a growing tide of opinion in favour of the second alternative, notably in the developing countries (e.g. Squire and Van der Tak, 1976).

Perhaps this approach is more defensible in such situations, due to the overloading of the political systems of these countries, where the turmoil of the development process confronts politicians, who may well be completely untrained and inexperienced, with a multitude of complex issues to resolve. As these cases are generally outside the scope of this book, from here onwards we proceed on the assumption that the object of the analysis is to measure the impact of policies on each term in the SWF, leaving to the politician the task of relating these impacts one to another. His job is thus to aggregate and respond to the demands and preferences of his electorate when making decisions on its behalf. In some cases, where 'leadership' is needed, he may feel constrained to give his own preferences more weight than those of his electors. The scope for such leadership may well be limited by the proximity of the next public reckoning, when he has to stand for re-election.

Constraints are of two essential types. First there are constraints which dictate what relationships between resources and outputs are possible, in the same way as the production function does for the firm. These delimit the feasible range of options and we therefore call them feasibility constraints. Second there are resource constraints on the public decision-maker. These may be quite similar to those which apply in the private sector as, for example, where any agency's activities are limited by a fixed annual budget. They may also arise from the finite nature of particular resources in the economy or, equally important to the agency, from firmly held convictions in society as to how much of a resource should be publicly controlled.

Feasibility constraints may arise in the public sector from technical or physical relationships which determine the response of output to changes in the use of inputs. An example would be the number of cases or problems that can be handled by an individual clerical officer and the extent to which his output could be increased, say, by computerizing the work he does. Feasibility constraints may also arise from particular regulations which apply to the public sector, e.g. regulations governing accountability for public money spent may well prevent such money from being distributed in many small units while allowing it to be distributed in larger sums. This might arise from the transactions cost of the two distribution patterns which would obviously be very different in each case. Perhaps the most important class of feasibility constraints binding individual agencies are those incorporated in their terms of reference. Organizations set up to grow trees profitably may, for example, have some difficulty in persuading their paymasters that they should also combine this with other activities, including recreation and sporting use of the land, and many other land management functions. It is appropriate that agencies set up in the public sector for a particular purpose should have clearly defined terms of reference, but it must equally be recognized that such terms may prove restrictive and prevent the agency performing effectively in terms of resource use.

Measuring progress: efficiency

Having described the related problems of objectives and constraints, we now turn to the question of measuring progress towards these objectives. At the beginning of this chapter we defined the efficient situation, in rather a narrow sense, as one where no one could be made better off without someone else being made worse off. However, this is a very conservative and restrictive criterion for measuring progress, as a number of writers (e.g. Rowley & Peacock, 1975; Nath, 1973) have pointed out, because it very rarely occurs that one person's welfare can be enhanced at zero cost to everyone else.

Thus a pure Paretian definition of efficiency would rule out most acts of public intervention! However, Hicks and Kaldor both proposed modifications to the Pareto criterion: namely that if the gainers could profitably compensate the losers from a policy, then that policy could in principle be desirable, even if no compensation was actually paid. They thus introduced the notion of a net increase in efficiency as a criterion. The quest for an ideal criterion does not end there, however, as Scitovsky (1941) has pointed out. It would be possible for a policy to be adopted on a Hicks-Kaldor modified Pareto principle, but it could then be appropriate for the losers to bribe the gainers to reverse the policy. But perhaps a more serious line of attack on the Pareto principle comes from authors such as Nath (1973), who challenge the basic assumption that everyone is deemed to be the best judge of his own welfare, and argue for a more frankly normative approach to establishing the relationship between objectives. Nath attempts to reinstate the earlier welfare propositions of Pigou, which were explicitly based on an utilitarian moral philosophy. He prefers these bases to the Paretian value-judgement which, he claims, represents a logically mistaken attempt to provide economics with value-free prescriptive power.

At a more pragmatic level, while the theoretical and philosophical questions of Paretian welfare economics have been debated, the application of economics to problems of policy analysis and project appraisal had proceeded apace. At this practical level of work we require a working definition of efficiency. From Pareto, supplemented by Hicks and Kaldor, comes the notion of a net increase in efficiency where benefits from a decision exceed the costs. To make this general concept more useful, we must settle a number of empirical questions: first a group of questions relating to measurement of efficiency, and second the problem of condensing this information to provide decision criteria.

The first problems to be settled are those of defining benefits and costs and, of these, the first is to define the boundaries of the economic system to which the decision relates. This could be straightforward as, for example, where a major item of physical capital is under consideration. The benefits might consist of a single item of output (e.g. water from a dam) and the costs would be evaluated in terms of the resources tied up in the system.

An essential principle, in defining the system, is that we are usually trying to measure the effects of the policy or project *at the margin*. We are trying to compare the situation *with* the project with the situation *without* it. This is sometimes quite difficult to do, requiring more than the usual before-and-after data which may be readily available. The marginal approach assumes that all past benefits and costs are irrelevant – they have been produced or incurred and no policy or project can undo that. It is common fallacy that the decision whether to market a new product or not, should be influenced by the level of past research and development expenditure devoted to it. Such views are conspicuous in discussions on defence expenditures, where the level of development expenditure on a weapon system which has become obsolete before being brought into use, is discussed as if it had some bearing on the decision to put it into production. Of course, past expenditures are important and we should learn what we can from them, but mostly they will tell us about our mistakes and certainly, once incurred, they do not provide a sound argument for further expenditure on in-efficient projects.

However, it is a very well-known phenomenon that where competitive markets for consumption goods exist, prices will tend to a common level. Nevertheless some consumers of these goods might be willing to pay more to consume them than the market price requires. This phenomenon of 'consumers' surplus' and its analogous 'producers' surplus' (or economic rent), is widely accepted to be an important component of the benefit flowing from an activity, though one which will not be picked up if market revenues alone are used as the measure of benefit. These concepts are illustrated in Fig. 2.1:

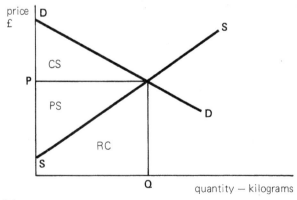

Figure 2.1

The consumers' response to price changes is indicated by the downward sloping demand curve DD in Fig. 2.1. The slope indicates that consumers will respond to rising prices by reducing the quantity they buy and to falling prices by increasing their purchases. Under competitive conditions the price of all that is consumed will be determined by the price paid for the last (or marginal) unit bought. The producers will generally respond in the opposite way, by increasing production directly with prices along the supply schedule SS. SS and DD intersect at point (P,Q), which is the equilibrium where quantity demanded at price P is just equal to quantity supplied at price P. At this point consumer expenditure is the product $P.Q$, equal to producer revenue. At the equilibrium point there are some consumers who would have purchased a smaller amount of the good at a higher price. These consumers are thus obliged to spend *less* than they are prepared to on this good. A moment's reflection should convince the reader that this will be true at any point on the demand curve, except where it intersects the price axis. Consumers are thus held to benefit by more than the amount they are required to spend by the market. This extra benefit is called 'consumers' surplus' and it is labelled CS in Fig. 2.1. Similarly, it can be shown that the real cost of resources used in production is equal to the area below their supply schedule. The producers thus achieve a revenue which exceeds their costs by an amount equivalent to the area above SS, but below the price line. This is called producers' surplus or economic rent.

Strictly for purposes of measuring benefits and costs, these economic surpluses should be brought into account. Social benefit should include changes in consumer surplus while producer surplus should not be included in social cost. This prescription is somewhat utopian: in practice, it is often found that analytical studies ignore economic surpluses by simply measuring benefits and costs at the ruling market prices. This is obviously much easier than bringing surpluses into the argument, as it avoids the requirement of estimating demand and supply schedules.

Apart from the problem of economic surpluses there is a more basic question as to the appropriateness and even the availability of price information. Where project inputs and outputs may be bought and sold in competitive markets, it will usually be possible to ascertain the relevant prices. However, where markets are monopolistic or are distorted by other forces (perhaps by government policies, perhaps through lack of information), it is likely that prices will not accurately reflect social opportunity costs or social benefits at the margin. Where that is the case, we may have to correct the market price data in order to arrive at the relevant prices. These problems can perhaps best be illustrated by reference to examples.

Where the existence of monopoly causes output prices to be higher than they would normally be, we could argue that the valuation of costs and benefits should be adjusted to bring them to free market levels. However, our enthusiasm for tampering with the data should be abated by the thought that perhaps the monopoly will be present whether or not the policy is adopted and, if that is so, then perhaps monopolistic prices will be no more misleading than estimated free market prices.

A more serious case arises where resources are unemployed. Here there is perhaps more of a consensus as to the appropriateness of adjusting prices. If we know that a worker would have been unemployed had he not been hired through a particular project, then it can be argued that the social opportunity cost of his services is less than the wage he earns. The problem then is 'how much less?'. We could adopt a formula for calculating this *shadow wage*:

$$W_t^* = W_t(1 - p_t)$$

where W_t^* = the shadow wage rate

W_t = the market wage rate

p_t = the probability that such workers would be unemployed.

However, we must be clear what is meant by unemployment here. Where the unemployment arises because of a cyclical reduction in business activity – the so-called deficient demand unemployment – it can be argued that it should be ignored in calculating the shadow wage. If the unemployment is structural in origin, due say, to the decline of a particular industry, then it would be appropriate to bring it into the calculation. Obviously, the distinction between structural and deficient demand unemployment may be difficult to sustain in practice, but it is nevertheless important to do so. Another item which might seem relevant to the calculation of shadow wage rates is the social security payments made to the unemployed. It is clear that by taking the unemployed into employment, the government's financial obligations are reduced. However, it may be argued that, from the point of view of society, such payments do not affect the allocation of resources and hence should not enter into the determination of social opportunity costs or shadow wages. It is emphasized that we are considering efficiency here: if the distribution of income was of concern, a different form of analysis, focusing on actual incomes, would be required.

An interesting case where corrections to market prices probably are justified, arises in the context of converting land from agriculture to forestry in Britain. The details of the debate are dealt with in Chapter 6; here we will use one particular aspect of it – as an example of the complexities of estimating shadow prices. Full details of the calculations referred to will be found in Whitby (1977). Most of the land converted to forestry in Britain is taken out of livestock rearing. Such farming activities have for decades been influenced by the availability of subsidies, a notable example being the 'headage payments' made annually to hill sheep and hill cattle. Hill farmers receive these subsidies and, it is argued in the official literature, they should be removed from the farm revenues used in calculating the social opportunity cost of land under agriculture. Hill farmers sell their lambs and beef animals in 'store' condition: that is, they are sold to other farmers who fatten them further before they are ready for slaughter. There is also a subsidy on fat lambs, and it is argued that this will enhance the prices received by hill farmers for store lambs. What, then, is the 'true' social opportunity cost of store sheep production?

Fig. 2.2. represents this situation in diagrammatic terms. Undisturbed, hill farmers would sell their store sheep along a supply schedule $S_m S_m$ and fatteners' demand for store lambs would be indicated by $D_m D_m$. The introduction of the hill sheep subsidy would cause the supply schedule to 'shift' to $S_s S_s$, indicating that there will be more store sheep sold at any given price in the subsidized situation than without the subsidy. Further, a demand shift, to $D_s D_s$ from $D_m D_m$, is induced by the fat lamb subsidy and this will also add to the revenue of hill farmers. Thus, with both subsidies in existence, the social opportunity cost of hill sheep production will be $P_1.Q_1$. To calculate this from hill farm revenue data, we would need to deduct the hill sheep subsidy and an amount equivalent to $(P_3.Q_3 - P_1.Q_1)$. Clearly such complex calculations will often be quite impossible in an operational context. Simpler

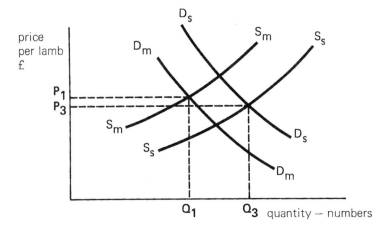

Figure 2.2

expedients of the kind which have been adopted in the agriculture/forestry calculations will be unavoidable in practice. At an early stage in the estimation of shadow prices, it becomes necessary to consider the cost of obtaining the information. McKean (1968), in a seminal paper on shadow pricing, urges that as much use as possible should be made of market prices, and that elaborate calculations should only be made where it is clear that the benefits obtained from improving the information available will exceed the costs.

The extreme case where shadow prices are neeeded arises where no market exists for project inputs or outputs. This may be, as for example with a recreational facility, where the output is not sold to consumers, and access to the facility is rationed by congestion or by travel costs. A related set of cases arises in the context of what are called technological externalities, usually defined as the effects of one economic unit on another which are not transmitted through markets. The classic technological externality is pollution – where, for example, the effluent from one plant affects the production costs of another. If a project under consideration would inflict substantial costs on other producers or consumers, then this would have to be brought into the reckoning by estimating the value of these costs. A number of ingenious techniques have been evolved over the years and there is now an extensive literature on the subject (Layard, 1972, presents a useful collection). McKean (1968) summarizes the possible sources as:

(1) the implied prices emerging from other economic calculations, for example from the 'dual' of linear programming solutions;
(2) prices from similar markets or from markets for the same good in other countries;
(3) the prices implicit in other government decisions.

He is not optimistic about any of these possible expedients. Those obtained from (1) will only be appropriate if the assumptions underlying the economic model (for example the objective function) are the same. (2) raises the difficult question of what markets may be judged 'similar'. (3) is similar to Weisbrod's approach of measuring the weights of the SWF and raises similar difficulties. It is quite unlikely that public decisions will be consistent over a wide range of activities and at different times. They may nevertheless be better than no guidance at all as to the implicit social valuations of resources and goods.

Another operational problem which arises with prices is that there may be widely divergent trends within the structure of prices relevant to a project. For example, if the benefits and costs of a project accrue over a fifty-year period and there is a tendency for the cost of the project inputs to rise more rapidly than the price of its outputs, this would affect the desirability of the project. The analyst could be accused of complete unreality if he did not take account of such divergent price trends but, on the other hand, it may be very difficult to prepare realistic forecasts of prices beyond the immediate future. By contrast, inflation, defined as a general rise in the level of all prices, should be ignored in appraising future cost and benefits.

Many government projects commit resources for long periods of time and involve revenue or benefits accumulating over several decades. Where this occurs some account must be taken of the way in which costs and benefits are distributed over time and this is generally done by discounting. The technique of discounting is well described in many texts; briefly it involves summing future (or past) streams of income (or cost) to a value at some point in time. It involves a choice as to the length of time over which benefits or costs will be accumulated and the rate at which they are to be discounted. These two factors – time horizon and discount rate – interact, in that choice of a high rate of discount reduces the present value of cash streams beyond a few years to negligible amounts. On the other hand, if a low discount rate is used then the aggregate benefits and costs of a project may be very sensitive to the time horizon over which they are summed; and the choice of time horizon, which may be arbitrary, can become a critical factor in selecting projects.

Clearly the rate at which benefits and costs are discounted will have a major impact on the selection of projects and policies. High discount rates will favour activities which produce benefits early rather than late, and work against projects with high initial capital cost and low operating (recurring) costs. What level of discount rate should then be used? Unfortunately there is little agreement amongst economists either as to the rate which should be used or how it should be determined. In the operational world, agencies with particular types of activity will naturally advocate discount rates which favour the easing of their budget constraint. The choice of social discount rate (SDR) is thus very important in determining which agencies and activities will grow and which will not. In such a situation, there is a strong case for one rate of SDR being chosen and applied across the board in the public sector. Naturally the SDR will have to be revised occasionally, as the availability of funds and the demand for public projects changes, and at such stages, those with an interest in investing funds may participate in the debate as to the appropriate SDR (see for example Price, 1973, or Wolfe and Caborn, 1973, on this problem in the context of forestry).

Broadly speaking, these arguments arise from two separate considerations: first, the Social Time Preference rate (STP) is advocated as being the rate which reflects society's preference as between present and future consumption. There is no simple and obvious way of measuring STP, however, although a number of ingenious suggestions have been made (see Pearce, 1971, for a useful review). The alternative to STP is the Social Opportunity Cost rate of discount, which reflects the opportunity cost of investment funds in terms of the rate of return on marginal investments. The problem here is that of choosing what is the opportunity cost from amongst a complex structure of existing discount rates in the money market. Some workers argue in favour of either STP or SOC, as if the two schools of thought were not reconcilable. Another possibility (which is discussed by Pearce) is that some form of synthetic rate of discount, embodying components of both STP and SOC principles, should be calculated. The argument here is essentially concerned with what society foregoes in order to make the public investment. If it could be shown that only consumption was postponed, then the STP rate would be appropriate: if only other investment was foregone then the SOC rate would apply. Since most public expenditure decisions involve postponement of both consumption and investment, the notion of a synthetic rate has appeal.

If the system was at a Pareto-optimum, equilibrium in capital markets would equate SOC and STP rates of discount, but in practice such equilibria are rare. The common state of affairs is that SOC rates of discount exceed STP rates. This means that budgets in the public sector are sufficiently constrained to hold SOC rates above equilibrium levels. Under such conditions, there is bound to be uncertainty and debate about the SDR. The final level of SDR used will thus reflect a consensus between the various schools of thought.

As the time-span over which benefits and costs are being measured extends, so too does the risk and uncertainty attaching to the predictions. Up to now we have discussed the problems of measuring benefits and costs as if they could take only one value which is known. This is rarely the case, and economists have classified such forecasting errors into two types: risk and uncertainty. Risk is usually defined so as to include those divergences from the expected outcome which are *actuarially* predictable. Uncertainty includes all such divergences which are not predictable: it thus refers to an absence of information.

The essence of risky situations is that information could in principle be obtained to state the probability of any forecast outcome occurring. Ideally, this would allow the analyst to state the most likely value (the arithmetic mean of the probability distribution) of the outcome, and to give some indication of the probable range of variation (variance) of outcomes about the mean.

Uncertainty, by contrast, is more difficult to handle analytically. The approaches to dealing with uncertainty in decision-making are derived from mathematical game theory. Each of the several different models (Dasgupta and Pearce, 1972, compare four) available, requires an initial assumption as to the decision-maker's preferences for different outcomes. Would he prefer the best of the worst possible set of outcomes, or the worst of the best possible set? Or does his preference take some other form? Clearly the problem is more severe in the public sector where collective choices are being made.

In some contexts approximate rules have been adopted, such as adding a 'risk-premium' to the discount rate, shortening time horizons, or discounting benefits at a higher rate than costs. Such expedients are, however, as arbitrary as they are crude: they seem more likely to bias the selection process than anything else. However, it would be defensible for the analyst to look at each prediction and give it an explicit error-rating. These ratings could then be used to apply standard risk-loadings – perhaps by adding proportionately to discount rates. As long as the ratings were allocated consistently, this would provide an acceptable means of allowing for risk, without adding unduly to the computational complexity of the procedure.

A final word on risk and its relation to the subject of sensitivity analysis is necessary. This technique, which involves changing the value of project parameters in turn and observing the effect on the outcome, is widely used in cost benefit analysis although its usefulness is severely limited for two reasons. First, if there are several parameters, which are independently determined, within any project, simply to vary them one at a time and observe the effect is unrealistic. In practice, it is likely that several parameters will have been incorrectly specified and we should therefore test the sensitivity of the outcome to changes in value using groups of parameters. But proceeding on this basis would confront us with the problem of assessing the meaningfulness of several sets of possible solutions. Secondly, sensitivity analysis can tell us no more than which assumptions or parameters were important in determining the outcome. It tells us *nothing* about the appropriateness of the assigned value or the assumption made. Thus, at best, sensitivity analysis may offer some guidance on which project parameter is worth estimating most carefully.

Having discounted the time streams of benefit and cost to a single point in time, there is one more stage required to complete the efficiency analysis. This is the calculation of efficiency criteria. Up to this point the analysis has produced two magnitudes: present value of benefits ($PV(B)$) and present value of costs ($PV(C)$). Algebraically these are obtained from:

$$(1) \quad PV(B) = \sum_{t=1}^{T} \frac{B_t}{(1 + i)^t}$$

where B_t = benefit in year t

T = project time horizon

i = the discount rate

and

(2) $PV(C) = \sum_{t=1}^{T} \dfrac{C_t}{(1+i)^t}$

where C_t = cost in year t.

These magnitudes are now manipulated further in order to produce criteria which will allow comparison of different projects. Note that in preparing criteria, we shall be losing some information and, further, that there are different criteria available which involve the loss of different amounts of information. Clearly one of the criteria for choosing investment criteria will be the amount of relevant information it retains. The three criteria commonly used are:

Cost-benefit ratio $= \dfrac{PV(B)}{PV(C)}$

Net Present Value or Benefit minus Cost $= PV(B) - PV(C)$

Internal rate of Return, $= r$

where $\sum_{t=1}^{T} \dfrac{B_t}{(1+r)^t} = \sum_{t=1}^{T} \dfrac{C_t}{(1+r)^t}$

Jensen (1969) presents a useful comparison of the operating characteristics of these criteria. He shows that the three will all coincide at one point, where

$$\frac{PV(B)}{PV(C)} = 1.0$$

$$PV(B) - PV(C) = 0$$

$$\text{and}\quad r = i$$

The situation is also shown diagrammatically, for one project, in Fig. 2.3, which illustrates the relationship between $PV(B)$, $PV(C)$ and i. As noted above, increases in the discount rate reduces the present value of future streams of benefit and cost. In the example, $PV(B)$ exceeds $PV(C)$ at low discount rates, and they cross over at the point where the discount rate equals the internal rate of return. This is also the point at which the curve of $PV(B) - PV(C)$ (the Net Present Value Curve) cuts the i-axis; this is where $PV(B)/PV(C) = 1.0$. A set of curves such as this could be drawn for

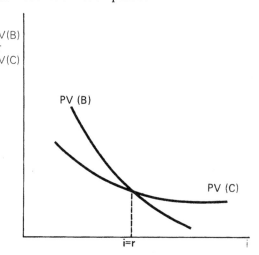

Figure 2.3

any project, and they would summarize for us the characteristics of
the investment under consideration. In Fig. 2.4 a set of *NPV* curves
for four projects (**A–D**) is drawn:

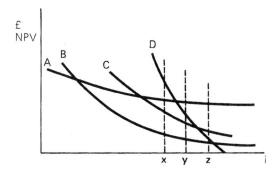

Figure 2.4

These curves cross each other frequently, and each time this
happens their ranking on an *NPV* criterion will change. As it is the
changes in the discount rate which bring this about, we may say that
project ranking will be sensitive to the discount rate. The rankings

for three different values of i are tabulated as follows:

$$i = x \quad y \quad z$$

	D	A	A
ranking	A	D	C
	C	C	D
	B	B	B

Other criteria are similarly sensitive to i and it is therefore not surprising that the SDR is the subject of much controversy. For example, if we were to extrapolate the *NPV* curves and use an internal rate of return criterion, we would find that the projects would be ranked **A**, **B**, **C**, **D**, in descending order of preference.

Jensen's detailed study leads him to the conclusion that $PV(B)$ — $PV(C)$ is the most useful criterion, being sensitive to scale and timing of the project and having only one value for a given SDR.

The effects of different discount rates and time horizons on possible criteria can be illustrated by reference to an hypothetical example. This will also serve to bring out some important operational points. Table 2.1 sets out the annual cash flows for five projects. The first point to note is that casual inspection gives no idea at all as to which, if any, of the projects would have a positive *NPV* at normal rates of discount. The projects have deliberately been given strikingly different streams of cost and benefit. Project **A**, which might be a clean air programme, incurs a large expenditure in the first year and makes a constant surplus over operating cost thereafter. The first year's investment is smaller for project **B**, but further investment is incurred for the next four years and, again, a constant stream of benefits ensues. This project might be a road which requires land purchase first, then construction outlays before benefits begin to flow. Project **C** is a small-scale flood control programme. After some initial investment in the first year, the annual operating costs are constant, but are offset by comparatively large sporadic benefits every five or ten years. D_{46} and D_{50} are alternative ways of managing trees on the same piece of land. In D_{46}, the production period is somewhat shortened by incurring a small extra expenditure in year 15. This outlay has the effect of bringing both thinning and felling forward a few years.

Table 2.1   Annual flows of costs and benefits for five hypothetical projects

	Project									
	A		**B**		**C**		**D$_{46}$**		**D$_{50}$**	
Year	Cost	Benefit	Cost	Benefit	Cost	Benefit	Cost	Benefit	Cost	Benefit
0	800	0	100	0	200	0	1,000	0	1,000	0
1	10	100	100	0	10	0	10	0	10	0
2	10	100	100	0	10	0	10	0	10	0
3	10	100	100	100	10	0	10	0	10	0
4	10	100	100	100	10	200	10	0	10	0
5	10	100	30	100	10	0	10	0	10	0
6	10	100	30	100	10	0	0	0	0	0
7	10	100	30	100	10	0	0	0	0	0
8	10	100	30	100	10	0	0	0	0	0
9	10	100	30	100	10	100	0	0	0	0
10	10	100	30	100	10	0	0	0	0	0
11	10	100	30	100	10	0	0	0	0	0
12	10	100	30	100	10	0	0	0	0	0
13	10	100	30	100	10	0	0	0	0	0
14	10	100	30	100	10	200	0	0	0	0
15	10	100	30	100	10	0	50	0	0	0
16	10	100	30	100	10	0	0	0	0	0
17	10	100	30	100	10	0	0	0	0	0
18	10	100	30	100	10	0	0	0	0	0
19	10	100	30	100	10	100	0	0	0	0
20	10	100	30	100	10	0	0	0	0	0
21	10	100	30	100	10	0	0	0	0	0
22	10	100	30	100	10	0	0	0	0	0
23	10	100	30	100	10	0	0	0	0	0
24	10	100	30	100	10	200	0	0	0	0
25	10	100	30	100	10	0	0	0	0	0
26	10	100	30	100	10	0	20	100	0	0
27	10	100	30	100	10	0	0	0	0	0
28	10	100	30	100	10	0	0	0	0	0
29	10	100	30	100	10	100	0	0	0	0
30	10	100	30	100	10	0	0	0	0	0
31	10	100	30	100	10	0	0	0	20	100
32	10	100	30	100	10	0	0	0	0	0
33	10	100	30	100	10	0	0	0	0	0
34	10	100	30	100	10	200	0	0	0	0
35	10	100	30	100	10	0	0	0	0	0
36	10	100	30	100	10	0	0	0	0	0
37	10	100	30	100	10	0	0	0	0	0
38	10	100	30	100	10	0	0	0	0	0
39	10	100	30	100	10	100	0	0	0	0
40	10	100	30	100	10	0	0	0	0	0
41	10	100	30	100	10	0	0	0	0	0
42	10	100	30	100	10	0	0	0	0	0
43	10	100	30	100	10	0	0	0	0	0
44	10	100	30	100	10	200	0	0	0	0
45	10	100	30	100	10	0	0	0	0	0
46	10	100	30	100	10	0	200	12,000	0	0
47	10	100	30	100	10	0	0	0	0	0
48	10	100	30	100	10	0	0	0	0	0
49	10	100	30	100	10	100	0	0	0	0
50	10	100	30	100	10	0	0	0	200	12,000

Table 2.2   Discounted costs and benefits, $^B/C$ ratio, *NPV* and *IRR* for five hypothetical projects

Item	Project in £s				
	A	**B**	**C**	**D_{46}**	**D_{50}**
PV(C)	899	619	299	154	141
PV(B)	991	818	289	174	108
PV(B)/PV(C)	1.103	1.321	0.966	1.126	0.767
PV(B)-PV(C)	92	199	−10	20	−33
IRR	11.19	15.15	9.49	10.32	9.38

In Table 2.2, the five projects are compared on different criteria obtained by discounting the streams at 10 per cent. If the projects were being considered as possible investments by a local authority, the estimates in Table 2.2 should assist in making the choice. First D_{46} and D_{50} should be compared as they are *mutually exclusive* projects – they cannot both be undertaken. In fact D_{46} is superior on all of the three criteria under consideration so, presumably, it would be chosen. This leaves the problem of selecting the projects to be undertaken from **A**, **B**, **C** and D_{46}. Following Jensen, we might use *PV(B)-PV(C)* as the criterion, in which case the projects would be adopted in order **B**, **A**, D_{46}, **C**. This coincides with *IRR* ranking, but differs from the ranking on *PV(B)/PC(C)*, which is **B**, D_{46}, **A**, **C**.

How many of the projects were to be undertaken would depend upon whether funds were constrained or not. If unlimited funds were available, then projects in which $B/C \geqslant 1.0$ or in which $IRR \geqslant i$ would be chosen: in this case **A**, **B** and D_{46}. However, where the budget is constrained, the form of constraint would have to be taken into account. Most commonly the constraint would only relate to the first year's costs. In that case reference to Table 2.1 (line 0) will show that a budget of £1900 would allow all three justifiable projects. However, note that this would commit substantially more resources – from Table 2.2 we can see that the total *PV(C)* for justifiable projects amounts to £1672. Similarly, if the budget constraint related to five years, rather than one, then the actual cash outlay for these three projects would be £2380, although this would be abated by £600 if the benefits in Table 2.1 are actual cash receipts obtained by the authority which may be re-invested.

Measuring distribution

It was argued above that distribution was an important social objective which should be included in the social welfare function. One way of incorporating distribution – by using a distribution-weighted SWF – has already been discussed. In this section we discuss the problems of measuring progress towards society's distributional objectives. First, however, we should note that such objectives are rarely clearly stated, and hence progress towards them may not be easy to measure. Generally, we need to know whether society wishes to have a more or a less equal distribution of welfare. In the UK, and the majority of developed countries, we might take the existence of progressive income taxes, and the range of social welfare benefits offered, as evidence of enthusiasm for removing inequalities. However, there are always a few who will argue against such equalizing tendencies, and such voices might dominate the scene from time to time. Thus, although we might assume a general preference for more rather than less equality, economists must bear in mind that this direction will be pursued with varying enthusiasm over time. Although policies aimed at redistribution of income have been applied for a long time, economists have been very slow to build distribution into their models. This is partly because of the inadequate development of theories to explain distribution and partly because the concept of distribution is difficult to analyse and measure. In this section, problems of measuring income distribution are briefly discussed.

Methods of measuring distribution range in complexity from simple frequency distribution to statistical measures known as inequality coefficients. An example of an attempt to compare distributions from two populations illustrates the frequency distribution approach. Here, the household incomes of sailing club members are compared with those of the population at large. The extreme dissimilarity between the two distributions was of interest in that it demonstrated the predominance of relatively high incomes amongst members of the sailing club.

However, two aspects of this tabulation are also important. First it relates to incomes *before* tax, and the individual's welfare is more closely determined by his income *after* tax. We should therefore either correct this distribution for tax or, at least, bear in mind that the effect of the tax system would be to even out the inequalities implied by the table. Secondly, to simply compare the income of club

Table 2.3 Distribution of income of members of a sailing club
compared with the national pattern

Range of household income, before tax	Sailing club members (1971)	UK households (1967–68)
£1000 or under	2.3 per cent	59.1 per cent
£1001 − £2000	18.0	34.2
£2001 − £3000	27.4	4.7
£3001 − £4000	20.9	1.3
£4001 − £5000	9.5	1.3
Over £5000	21.9	0.7
	100	100

Sources: Lewis and Whitby (1972); the sailing club income data is taken from a sample survey of club members; the UK data comes from Central Statistical Office (1969).

Note: Due to rounding errors, percentages may not add up to 100 per cent.

members with those of the population at large tells us little about the way in which the benefits of membership are distributed across income groups. In the study from which it was taken it was found that, within the membership, the lower income groups sailed more frequently than the higher income groups. They thus acquired more than their share of benefits and, to that extent, the sailing club will have contributed to a more equal distribution of welfare.

Much can be learned from simple cross-tabulations of benefits against income groups, but these require careful interpretation and it is often quite unclear whether one distribution is more or less equal than another. For this reason, general mathematical measures of inequality have been developed which summarize cross-sectional information. One such measure is the Gini ratio or inequality coefficient which is calculated from the Lorenz curve, illustrated in Fig. 2.5. Along the horizontal axis, the percentage of population achieving a given level of income is recorded, and on the vertical axis, their share of aggregate income is measured. Generally the more unequal the income distribution, the more the curve sags; for a completely equal distribution it will lie on the line, passing through the origin, at 45° to the axis The Gini ratio measures the relationship between the area above the curve but below the 45° line (A) and the whole area underneath the 45° line $(A + B)$.

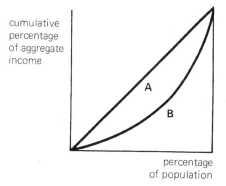

Figure 2.5

In a recent application of this measurement technique, Josling and Hammway (1972) measured the redistributive effects of British agricultural policy. In this case, the authors calculated inequality coefficients for farm income, including and excluding various subsidies, and hence were able to examine the effect of subsidies on the overall distribution. This study was based, however, on incomes before tax and thus did not reveal the *net* effect of subsidies on disposable incomes. This is an important general problem – whether to analyse incomes before or after tax. If the redistributive effects are under consideration, then income after tax is more appropriate; on the other hand, if it is the allocative aspect which is under consideration, incomes before tax may be the appropriate focus of analysis. If we are concerned with equity, then the main policy instrument for achieving this – the income tax system – may well be powerful enough to outweigh any adverse distributional effects of a policy.

A more serious problem with such studies is that they do not measure the effects of policies on expected incomes over a whole career. People are not motivated by, nor do they derive all of their satisfaction from, their income in one year. Decisions such as those involved in transferring employment from one industry to another, would be based on expectations extending over a number of years and possibly over a whole lifetime. To that extent, the proper focus of a distribution analysis might be the present value of expected future incomes. A related problem is that farmers and other self-employed people may not evaluate their success in terms of income alone – many of them will be seeking to accumulate assets as well. Indeed, in agriculture, redistributive policies may have as important an effect on assets, through inflated land values, as they have on incomes. The intricate analytical problems encountered in demonstrating the size of such an effect will, however, be beyond the scope of this work.

The advantage of Gini ratios is that they allow us to condense a lot of information down to one number, and we can use such a number to rank policy options in precisely the same way as the efficiency criteria discussed above. As a ranking function, the Gini ratio will have greatest appeal in situations where large numbers of different policy options or projects are being compared. Where only a few projects are under consideration, it may be quite acceptable to present the distributional impact data in the form of a cross-tabulation.

The example of agricultural subsidies raises further interesting problems of distributional measurement, which are also of quite general occurrence. It is well known that one effect of raising agricultural prices, through subsidies, is to make farm land more expensive. This is obviously advantageous to the few who can cash in on the valuation increase by selling their land, but disadvantageous to the young would-be entrant into farming. Similar effects, where the value of a subsidy is passed on to others, have already been mentioned in relation to the hill sheep subsidy and the guaranteed price of fat sheep in Britain. Farmers have been aware of the benefit of price subsidies to their input suppliers, although the size of this effect has not been measured. The essential point is that the initial recipients of a subsidy may be unable to retain the benefit it apparently conveys, because of the operation of market forces.

One possible means of coping with this problem of value transmitted from one economic unit to another, is through the branch of economics developed by Boulding (1973), called 'grants economics'. This school emphasizes the distinction between *exchange transactions*, in which one person typically buys a good or service in exchange for money, and a *grant* which is a one-way flow of value. The essential distinction is that the net worths of the participants in an exchange remains unaltered by the transaction, whereas a grant does change the net worth of both donor and recipient. Exchange transactions are, of course, the bread and butter of economics, but grants are clearly of major importance in the public sector. The usefulness of the grant concept is that it emphasizes the distributional aspect of public sector activities and offers a framework for their measurement.

Regulatory problems

The analysis presented so far has been developed in the context of public agencies undertaking investments on behalf of society. However, there are many governmental activities which require no investment, although their economic implications may be profound. These activities are described as 'regulatory' here, for want of a better word: the essential point is that they are activities which have slight investment implications. Thus the issues they raise are not similar to those found in the private sector, which is dominated by individuals pursuing their own private interest as they identify it. The most common source of regulatory issues come from the important class of economic problems labelled 'technological externalities' which have already been mentioned. They arise where the activities of one actor in the economic scene conflict with those of another, and the two sets of decision are not linked through a market. Thus *A* produces a good (or bad) which reduces (or increases) *B*'s cost of production, but because there is no market in which the good (or bad) can be traded, *A* has no incentive to produce at an optimal level. Note that we are talking here about *production* of an externality – this excludes pecuniary externalities which arise when one unit's activities sway the prices affecting another's. The situation can be represented diagrammatically as in Fig. 2.6:

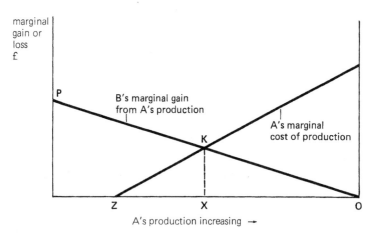

Figure 2.6

On the horizontal axis, A's production of the technological externality increases as we proceed from left to right. After point Z further increases in production involve him in extra cost. Moving along the same axis B's marginal gain declines, to reach zero at O. Clearly A would prefer to produce at point Z – as far as he is concerned, greater production imposes costs but brings no benefit. By contrast, B's most preferred position is at O, where he can gain no more from further increases in A's production.

However, if we consider the problem from the point of view of society as a whole, we can say on efficiency grounds, that the optimal level of production will be at X. This is because no further net increase in the surplus (B's gain minus A's cost) is possible with production greater than X, and with production less than this a net gain is possible. How, then, we do reconcile the inherent conflict between A and B?

There are four possible ways. First we could bring A and B into contact through a market, so that they can influence each other's decisions. Secondly, we could impose a tax on B's consumption of the good so that, in effect, he pays for what he consumes. Thirdly, we could subsidize A's production so that he will produce more of the good. Finally and fourthly, we could issue an administrative fiat instructing A to produce at the desired level and B to limit his consumption to that level. These possible ways of dealing with a technological externality will be considered first in the absence of transactions cost and from the point of view of efficiency alone. Later the problems of transactions cost and distribution will be introduced into the argument.

Establishing a market where none exists is essentially a matter of defining the good to be traded and identifying its initial owners. Once that has been achieved, there may then be further costs incurred, by the owner or by the state, in protecting the ownership of these rights. In developed countries, much effort has gone into the establishment of a basic system of property rights, but such systems are never static, requiring continual redefinition as new goods and bads emerge. The existence of a system of property rights enables an individual to buy or sell such rights, and the owner of such rights will be able to prevent others from using them in any way. These characteristics are obvious in the case of a tube of toothpaste, but less so in the case of land ownership, which may bring rights to cultivate a plot, but may or may not include the right to build on it and is unlikely to enable the owner to exclude others from enjoying its visual aspect, even if he can prevent access to it.

According to Demsetz (1966), a fully defined system of property rights, in a situation where policing and transactions costs were zero, would produce three results:

(1) the value of all harmful and beneficial effects of alternative uses of property rights will be brought to bear on the owners;
(2) to the extent that owners of property rights are utility maximizers property rights will be used efficiently; and
(3) the mix of output that is produced will be independent of the distribution of property rights among persons except insofar as changes in the distribution of wealth affect demand patterns.

The first of these propositions implies that a complete system of property rights would preclude externalities and the second underlines their role in the market. The third proposition emphasizes the effect of a well-defined system of rights in enabling the control of resources to be concentrated in the hands of those able to make the most efficient use of them.

If definition of property rights is so powerful an economic tool, what are its limitations? Clearly they will depend upon the restrictiveness of assuming zero police and transactions costs, and of ignoring the distributional implications of different configurations of rights. Violation of these assumptions will weaken the conclusions reached by Demsetz, and hence reduce the benefits from fully defining the system of rights. Nevertheless these costs are, in principle, measurable and could therefore be brought into the calculations. Increasing the scope of the system of property rights does therefore offer a solution to problems of externalities. Its attractiveness will depend partly on the losses arising from the externality and partly on the costs of establishing and maintaining rights.

The policy options of taxing B's consumption or subsidizing A's production are illustrated in Fig. 2.7.

A subsidy to A will, in effect, shift his marginal cost curve to the right, so that it now cuts the axis at X, which becomes his preferred position. In inducing this change in A's behaviour, B gains an aggregate benefit equivalent to area $PK.XZ$, compared with his position with production at Z. The cost of bringing this about will be $XK.ZX$, that is: the unit ratio of subsidy multiplied by the volume

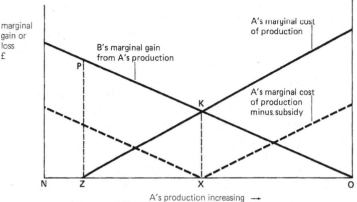

Figure 2.7

of production over which it is paid. Whether such a payment should be regarded as a social cost, to be brought into the reckoning, or a transfer payment, to be ignored, would depend upon the circumstances. The alternative of taxing *B*'s consumption (at rate KX per unit) would induce *B* to content himself with attaining point X, rather than striving for O. If the tax was at a flat rate it would produce revenue equal to $XK.ZX$, although, because the gain and cost curves are not quite symmetrical, there would be a small extra tax gain ($NZ.KX$) if every unit of consumption, including those produced at zero marginal cost between N and Z, were taxed. Such a minor asymmetry between the effects of a tax and of a subsidy might indicate which was to be preferred. Otherwise, the efficiency gains and losses might well be similar and characteristics such as transactions cost, or the distributional effects of the policies under consideration, might decide the issue.

The fourth alternative – determining production and consumption by administrative fiat – may well be the preferred option under certain circumstances. If administration was costless, this would obviously be an attractive way of taking the system to equilibrium at X. However, where administrative costs were substantial, they would have to be incorporated. The magnitude of administrative costs, which are worth incurring in order to achieve point X by fiat, can be seen in Fig. 2.7. The net social gain of moving from Z to X is PKZ (that is: *B*'s gain minus *A*'s loss). Therefore, if the choice was whether to stay at Z or move to X, we could say that it would be worth moving to X, as long as administrative or transactions costs did not exceed PKZ.

If we represent the (unknown) transactions cost in this case as T_f, and those associated with subsidies and taxes as T_s and T_t respectively, then we can immediately indicate the preferred policy option as being the one which takes us to X for the smallest T. In the real world, with many producers and consumers, the transactions costs of these various policies may be very different for each option. In many cases, it will not be possible for administrators to take the system to equilibrium without incurring enormous costs in locating it. For many amenities produced as externalities, it would be virtually impossible (prohibitively costly) to tax consumers in relation to their enjoyment of the good. It might also be costly to reimburse large numbers of small producers who all contribute (perhaps in varying amounts) to an amenity. If the transactions costs in all of these cases exceeded the possible net benefits from reaching equilibrium, and establishing a market for the good was similarly costly, then perhaps the amenity should, rationally, be 'written off'. The only consideration which might be brought into the argument to save it would be distributional aspects, and the trade-off here would require political validation.

Conclusion: does economic analysis help?

Having reviewed the issues that arise in the economic analysis of public issues involving resources, we are now in a position to consider whether it does provide worthwhile answers to the questions raised. At various points in the chapter, limitations of the analysis have been pointed out and the assumptions on which it rests have been stated. We therefore end the chapter by examining the economics of economic analysis: in effect asking, 'is it worth it?'

As with any other allocative problem, we are essentially asking whether the benefits flowing from different ways of using resources exceed the costs. In this particular case, we are concerned with the benefits generated by improving decisions together with the costs of doing so. Strictly speaking, benefits should be measured in terms of the decision outcomes following from economic analysis, compared with those following from other kinds of analysis, including informed judgment. If we were able to make such a comparison we should be fortunate indeed, because it would settle some very awkward questions once and for all. It might be possible to do this from a careful *ex poste* analysis of the outcome of a decision, with the *ex ante* advice offered from contending sources. As far as we are aware, such a study has not been undertaken, though *ex poste* analysis has been used by Haveman (1972) in the more limited role of checking the predictions of *ex ante* economic analysis of water resource projects in the USA.

In the absence of an objective comparison between economic analysis and other disciplinary approaches, we can only state what we believe to be the advantages of an economic approach. The dissenting reader, seeking support, might try Self (1975) as an alternative. Self's book is in two sections: the first half is a lengthy critique of the theoretical foundations of cost-benefit analysis, covering familiar ground. The second half then compares various models of the political democratic decision process with CBA *as if they were mutually exclusive alternatives.* This erroneous view of economic analysis as a black box into which data is fed and from which decisions emerge, is one for which economists themselves are partly responsible. Economists should recognize, indeed most do, that their role is to assist the decision process by providing information. In that role, we contend, economic analysis has a great deal to offer by helping to explore the contribution of policies and projects to social objectives. Some of the limitations of economic analysis have already been spelt out in this chapter. The two remaining problems which may not be overlooked at this stage are the theory of the second best and the question of intangibles.

The theory of the second-best was first put forward by Lipsey and Lancaster (1956) who pointed out that if any one of the conditions for a Pareto-optimum was not met, then the optimal level of all other variables changes. Nath (1973) summarizes the essential dilemma this poses for policy-makers by underlining the point that most taxes and subsidies, designed to 'improve' the distribution of income, would, in fact, violate the Paretian conditions, hence the introduction of such measures would lead to a need a redefine the optimal efficiency situation. Other important violations of 'first-best' necessary conditions include externalities and imperfections in factor and product markets. Nath suggests some ways round second-best problems which may be used in practice. First, if it is found that the constraint on achieving a first-best situation is in an isolated sector which does not have strong links with the rest of the economy, then first-best conditions would still hold for the rest of the economy. Secondly, it may prove possible to remove the constraint by legislation; such might be the purpose of anti-monopoly legislation and of attempts to constrain the activities of trade unions. Thirdly, there are possibilities of adjusting prices charged in the public sector to allow for second-best constraints. It must be recognized that second-best problems are a considerable limitation on the applicability of economic analysis to many situations, but their effect is to add an element of uncertainty to the conclusions reached, rather than to invalidate them completely.

The problem of intangibles arises from the difficulty of measuring and evaluating all the consequences of an activity. Critics will say, 'it's not all a matter of economics' or 'you cannot put a price on this or that resource'. In a sense these propositions are acceptable – it is of course true that there is no *market price* for many things, but they do nevertheless have an implied shadow price. Furthermore, to pretend that something does not have such a price, difficult to measure as it may be, is mere self-deception. It is important to recognize that there will be some aspects of projects which are beyond measurement and they must not be overlooked in appraisal. When the analysis is presented to the policy-maker, it is essential that all factors not taken fully into account should be listed. Such a schedule of 'intangibles' should be exhaustive. Naturally, the longer the list becomes, the less attention should be paid to the economic evaluation.

It is sometimes alleged that intangibles, because their existence cannot be quantitatively acknowledged, are automatically given less weight than the estimated costs and benefits of the project. This is, indeed, a danger and should be recognised by economists. The danger, however, does not necessarily argue a case for forgoing economic analysis: rather, it provides a reason for presenting intangibles, and all obtainable information about them, as carefully as possible.

To return to the question raised at the beginning of this section, we would argue that there are many public decisions in rural areas which would be improved by economic analysis. Thus our answer to the question 'is it worth it?' is, for such issues, affirmative.

3 Quantitative planning models

Many quantitative models in rural areas have been mainly concerned with the systematic exploration of technical possibilities. The system, whether ecological, agricultural, or social, which is the focus of attention, is described or simulated or modelled at some level of abstraction in a quantitative way, and the effects of various feasible changes in any controllable variable or input are then explored with respect to the behaviour or output of the system. Inputs need not be commensurable with each other, and neither need inputs be commensurable with outputs.

Much of this type of work is essential, and a prerequisite to any prescriptive technique such as operations research or cost-benefit analysis. It is designed to facilitate understanding and is necessary in rural areas – as Dye (1973) has pointed out – because of the complexities arising from the multisectoral economic interests, the multisectoral social and economic interests, and the multidimensional planning criteria. Multisectoral economic interests include agriculture, forestry and recreational interests competing for available land, rural labour and development finance. Multisectoral social and economic interests include private investment by individual landowners and public investment, including grants and subsidies. Social overhead capital may also be affected where major development results in changes in rural social structure. Multidimensional planning criteria are financial, economic, and welfare orientated, including the physical, biological and aesthetic effects of the plan on the environment, and other factors affecting the amenity value of the area.

The resolution of the conflicting interests in a rural region presents a formidable task to the planner, even assuming the availability of adequate data. Dye (1973) attempted a partial solution of the problem by quantifying all relevant elements in the rural situation in terms of a computer simulation model. This would leave the politician free to exercise his judgement on the desirability of alternative planning possibilities from the competing environmental and other viewpoints. Changes were made in input variables, such as agricultural prices, to show the considerable interaction in practice, and the changes in net benefit accruing to owners of property rights in land, the labour implications of changes in land-use, the effects on the size of agricultural holdings, and livestock numbers etc.

Rural development plans under the Town and Country Planning Acts have been less ambitious. Essentially, they are descriptive, relying on subjective appraisal rather than on any rigorous, quantitative, methodological framework. This has been the case whether the development plans were formulated under the Town and Country Planning Act 1947, or the more recent Town and Country Planning Act 1968,[1] with its emphasis on policy and strategic issues in structure plans, and the detailed elaboration of policy proposals in local plans. One only has to look at development plans for rural areas such as Northumberland County Council, 1967, 1969; Nottinghamshire County Council, 1966, 1969; and Lindsey County Council, 1973; to see that, while covering a wide range of matters such as population, employment, housing, industry and commerce, transport, shopping, education, social and community services, recreation and leisure, conservation of landscape, public utility services, and so on, they lack any kind of anlytical substance, despite a prescriptive orientation. They neither provide an adequate management framework for planning in the broadest sense, nor do they show any awareness of the deep substantive developments within the individual disciplines which aim to study aspects of our society. Rural plans can thus be criticized on two main counts; they lack any procedural theory of planning, and they are unaware of progress

[1] Subsequently consolidated into the Town and Country Planning Act 1971. These Acts are documented in Chapter 4.

within individual disciplines of the social sciences. This chapter will concentrate on developments within individual disciplines and appraise how these might be used in quantitative planning.

Development plans usually appear as a catalogue of ideas covering aspects of society, with a statement proposing an ideal situation, and they rarely contain any explanation as to how objectives are arrived at and distilled from the many divergent and often strong feelings about the countryside. The analysis of objectives and problems is not undertaken in terms of a commensurable unit of measurement, so comparisons are difficult and it is almost impossible to assess the consequence of any trade-off between one objective and another. Costs and benefits are rarely mentioned or related, and there is little or no analysis of the interaction between changes in instrument variables[1] and target variables,[2] or the simultaneous changes elsewhere in the system.

In contrast, when the quantitative analyst has formulated the model of his understanding and the goals it serves, he is still nearer the beginning of his analysis than the end. He must still particularize his model by estimating the values of the various 'given' parameters that enter into it. For this purpose, he usually employs more or less advanced statistical methods. Then he must solve the model, that is: he must find explicit relationships between, on the one hand, the parameters under the control of the local authority, and the measure of utility on the other. When this has been done, he is in a position to determine the optimal values of the decision parameters, to make his recommendations and to try to persuade policy makers/councillors to adopt them.

Quantitative and mathematical formulation does not ensure that a model will necessarily be a good one, but it does offer an easier means of checking the logical consistency of many non-mathematical models. Methodological foundations that have been laid bare and discussed are safer things on which to build than those which have not been scrutinized, because the risks involved are apparent. It is sometimes argued that mathematical models in the social sciences involve precisely defined variables that have no counterpart in the real world. Of course, similar problems arise in non-mathematical analysis of such variables, and this is not a strong

[1] Instrument variables are the means available to the policy-maker.
[2] Target variables or goals which are to be purposefully (though indirectly) influenced by the policy-maker.

argument against quantitative models. Moreover, the process of having to define and measure these variables is a source of progress to the field of study. Another argument points to the complexity of socio-economic systems as a reason for being pessimistic about the scientific approach. But to say that a problem is too complex for scientific methodology is saying nothing more than that ignorance exists. More observational evidence and additional thought leading to new concepts and models are required.

The basic structure of the policy problem can be represented diagrammatically, as in Fig. 3.1. There are a number of basic sequential steps in this policy model. First, the definition of objectives and goals: the socio-economic objectives and criteria by which a problem (if any) is deemed to exist. Chadwick (1971) argued that goal formulation is the most important, but also the most neglected, part of the planning process. Chadwick sees goal formulation as the very crux and hinge pin of the rational process, and believes that if goals are inconsistent with social preferences, then the plan must be wrong. In so far as structure and local planning are procedures for identifying and carrying out public policy, the effectiveness of the exercise very much rests on the validity of its axioms. Secondly, an explanation of the actual situation is required, through the building of a quantitative model, to assess the operation

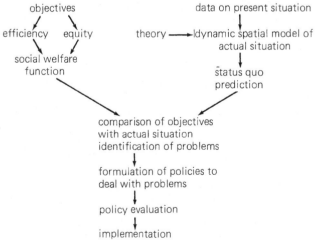

Figure 3.1

of the system, to identify difficulties and constraints, and to assess the power of the available policy instruments. Thirdly, problems must be identified in terms of equity and efficiency criteria based on differences between objectives and the actual situation, and these problems must be defined in areal terms on the ground. Fourthly, the range of possible solutions must be proposed in the light of available policy instruments and the formulation of alternative approaches which might produce end-results compatible with the forces, limitations, and constraints identified by the model of the actual situation. Finally, the different solutions must be evaluated according to some criterion, such as net present value, in relation to their effectiveness in meeting objectives, the resources which they consume, their effect on different sub-groups in the population, and the implications of uncertainty about the future.

This chapter is mainly concerned with models of the actual situation, although prediction and policy evaluation are mentioned.

Input-output models

If we want to express the impact of an economic policy – for example, a policy which increased the demand for outdoor recreation in rural areas – we must convert the formulation of the objective function (an increase in the final demand for recreation) into a formulation in terms of the total output of all industries in the economy. If a policy of increasing recreational demand in rural areas is adopted, employment and income will be generated in the area by:

(1) direct increases in factor incomes generated within businesses which receive tourist expenditure;
(2) indirect increases in factor incomes generated in other businesses whose turnover is augmented with purchases made by the original businesses;
(3) induced increases in factor incomes generated as a result of expenditure by residents of the region whose income has previously been increased through direct or indirect income generated by tourism.

Thus, for example, increases in direct tourist spending may lead to more hotel accommodation being built. If this happens, then the construction industry will expand its output and hence require more machines and materials. This situation will, in turn, necessitate more inputs of steel, copper, electricity, crude oil and so on. These industries will therefore have to expand their outputs, perhaps even making demands back again on the oil and coal industries for more fuel for their generators, blast furnaces etc. The initial decision to build more hotels will lead to increases in the outputs of a large number of industries. If we calculate the effects of all these inter-dependencies, we would obtain figures showing the increases in the total outputs of the different industries which are needed in order to make the original increase in the output of hotel accommodation possible. Having completed this stage, we could then calculate the increases in labour and capital requirements which would be required by the different industries. If these amounts were less than the amounts of unemployed labour and under-utilized capital, then no further calculations would be necessary, and we could conclude that the country could produce more hotel accommodation without having to reduce the output of something else.

Input-output deals with this stage of the calculation, but if trade-offs exist, and if we seek the most efficient way of relating the gross outputs to the inputs of labour and capital which would be needed, we require some operations research technique, such as linear programming, or perhaps to further extend the analysis with a more appropriate optimizing technique, like cost-benefit analysis.

Let us assume that the economy can be divided into industries or sectors that produce goods and services. Apart from the sectors of the economic system producing goods and services, there is a house-hold sector which supplies factor services and demands private consumer goods, and a trade sector which demands exports and supplies imports.

We can show the relationship in any year in the past between final demands for industries' products and the total outputs which they had to produce to meet these demands, by using an input-output table, as in Table 3.1.

Reading across the second row, for example, the table tells us that to enable the three industry groups to produce the goods which went to final demand, the industrial group produced a total of 40 units, of which 22 were sold to final demand (13 to consumers and the go-vernment, 5 to capital formation for investment, and 4 to foreigners), while the remaining 18 were sold to other industries (5 to agriculture – tractors, fertilizers, etc. – and 13 to services). Reading down the second column shows how total output of industry was produced. Industry used 8 units of the products of agriculture (timber, food for

Table 3.1   Typical input—output table

Sales by	Purchases by						
	Production						
	Agricul-ture	Indus-try	Ser-vices	Appro-pria-tion	Accumu-lation	Exports	Total output
Production							
Agriculture		8	1	5	0	1	15
Industry	5		13	13	5	4	40
Services	2	15		22	0	11	50
Appropriation	6	15	36		0	3	60
Accumulation	0	0	0	19		1	20
Imports	2	2	0	1	15		20
Total input	**15**	**40**	**50**	**60**	**20**	**20**	

processing, textiles, etc.) and 15 units of the products of the service industries. It also used 15 units of other inputs, for which it paid wages, salaries, interest, and profits, and 2 units of imports. When examining the relationship between total outputs of industries and their contributions to final demand, we are usually more interested in the total of final demand and in the contribution made by each industry towards it, rather than in the division of final demand into consumption, investment and imports. For this reason, the I-O table is often compressed so that the parts in which we are not interested disappear. Thus, an alternative way to express an input-output matrix is as in Table 3.2:

Table 3.2   Input—output matrix

Sales by	Purchases by				
	Agricul-ture	Industry	Services	Final demand	Gross output
Agriculture		8	1	6	15
Industry	5		13	22	40
Services	2	15		33	50
Value added	8	17	36		
Gross input	15	40	50		

Two assumptions are required to calculate, from Table 3.2, the gross outputs which will be needed to make possible any particular level and composition of final demand. The assumptions are:

(1) industries operate under conditions of constant returns to scale, that is, if, for example, their outputs double, then they will need twice as many inputs of all kinds;
(2) proportions in which industries use their inputs will remain unchanged over time, whatever changes take place in their output, thus, for example, agriculture will always need two-fifths as many units of services as units of manufacturing industries.

These assumptions are not a limitation to the technique if only short periods of time or small changes in outputs are considered.

The total output of industry $i - (X_i)$ – is equal to the output of industry i which is sold to industry, $j - (X_{ij})$ – and the output of industry, i sold to final demand $- (Y_i)$:

$$X_i = \sum_{j=1}^{n} X_{ij} + Y_i \quad i = 1, \ldots, n \tag{1}$$

If we ask what determines an industry's demand for the product of another industry, the simplest answer is that it is proportionate to the demanding industry's output. In other words, industry j's demand for the output of industry i is proportionate to the total output of industry j:

$$X_{ij} = a_{ij}X_j \tag{2}$$

where a_{ij} is the coefficient of proportionality, or input-output coefficient, or technical coefficient, and

$$0 \leqslant a_{ij} \leqslant 1 \tag{3}$$

Substituting the expression $a_{ij} X_j$ for X_{ij} in equations (1), gives simultaneous equations:

$$X_i = \sum_{j=1}^{n} a_{ij}X_j + Y_i \quad i = 1, \ldots, n \tag{4}$$

which may be rewritten as:

$$X_i - \sum_{j=1}^{n} a_{ij}X_j = Y_i \quad i = 1, \ldots, n \tag{5}$$

In matrix notation, this may be written as:

$$X - AX = Y \tag{6}$$

If an identity matrix I (equivalent to a unit multiplier in ordinary mathematics), is then introduced:

$$IX - AX = Y \tag{7}$$

thus:

$$(I - A)X = Y \tag{8}$$

If matrix $(I - A)$ has an inverse, we may multiply both sides of equation (8) by this inverse:

$$(I - A)^{-1}(I - A)X = (I - A)^{-1} Y \tag{9}$$

but:

$$(I - A)^{-1}(I - A) = I \tag{10}$$

thus:

$$IX = (I - A)^{-1} Y \tag{11}$$

and

$$X = (I - A)^{-1} Y \tag{12}$$

Input-output can be made clearer by considering an example for the United Kingdom economy in 1963:

X_{ij} =	Agriculture	Industry	Services
Agriculture		443	15
Industry	537		3,208
Services	286	3,098	
Gross input	1,667	16,436	20,837
from which a_{ij} =	0.0	0.026953	0.000720
	0.322136	0.0	0.153957
	0.171566	0.188489	0.0
and $(I - A)^{-1}$ =	1.009942	0.028174	0.005064
	0.362534	1.039998	0.160374
	0.241605	0.200861	1.031095

Given that the values of the technical coefficients are assumed to remain constant, it is now possible to use the inverse matrix to estimate the effect of change in final demand on gross output as a whole. Suppose, then, that the final demand for agricultural goods increases by £100 million (i.e. about 8 per cent from a total final demand of £1209 million in 1963), then the effect on the economy as a whole would be:

$$\begin{bmatrix} 1.009942 & 0.028174 & 0.005064 \\ 0.362534 & 1.039998 & 0.160374 \\ 0.241605 & 0.200861 & 1.031095 \end{bmatrix} \cdot \begin{bmatrix} 100 \\ 0 \\ 0 \end{bmatrix} = \begin{bmatrix} 101 \\ 36 \\ 24 \end{bmatrix}$$

In this case, an increase in the final demand for agricultural products of £100 million, would result in an overall increase in output of £161 million, of which £101 million would be for agricultural goods (i.e. £1 million in addition to the initial £100 million in final demand), £36 million for manufactured goods, and £24 million for services. The crude multiplier for the agricultural sector would thus be 1.61 (that is: total output divided by initial expenditure, or 161/100).

If, on the other hand, there was an increase of £100 million in the final demand for manufactured goods, then, in this case, there would be an overall increase in output of £152 million (i.e. £4 million in addition to the initial £100 million in final demand for manufactured goods), £28 million for agricultural goods, and £20 million for services. The crude multiplier for the manufacturing sector would thus be 1.52 (that is: 152/100).

Thus a greater expansion in total output would result if the final demand for agriculture's output increased by an absolute amount, than would result from an equivalent absolute increase in final demand for industry's output. From hypothetical data, a similar conclusion is reached by Masser (1972), who argues that it might be expected that this would be reflected in policies relating to public authority expenditure. A more refined version of this argument was earlier presented by Fox (1963) and Sengupta (1963). They used a 2×2 matrix of the agricultural sector and the rest of the economy, for both an advanced industrial country and an underdeveloped country, to look at the consequences of a policy of growth. Their main conclusion was that in underdeveloped countries, or in under-privileged regions of large industrialized economies, current political thought on growth policies should be the reverse of those in the highly industrialized parts of the world. To maintain or improve the British, American or French current rate of growth, these input-output results suggest that the best policy would be to support the agricultural complex. Whereas, for example, the Indian or Brazilian rate of growth could, according to Sengupta, be best increased by supporting industrialization.

Such conclusions appear naive: they ignore gains from trade and specialization according to comparative advantage, which make it possible to produce more of all goods if both areas are producing some of both commodities (Lipsey, 1975). Input-output analysis is capable of quantifying the increase in income and employment, resulting from an injection of expenditure in any one sector of the economy in an area. But if the economy does not possess unused resources of land, labour, and capital, input-output cannot take account of the opportunity cost of this expenditure, i.e. benefit forgone. The extra production of agricultural products may confer no benefit at all. Thus, input-output is not a method of appraising projects and policies to indicate those which are economically and socially worthwhile: it is a systems analysis method to assess impact only, and it is not an optimizing technique. Moreover, input-output analysis, while it may quantify externalities, such as pollution generated, cannot value the social costs and benefits which may arise from such factors as congestion, pollution, environmental despoilation, amenity, improvements in landscape and so on. Finally, expanding agricultural production in rural areas in advanced economies – for example, the Mezzogiorno in Italy – may not benefit these areas, since service and industry sectors supplying agriculture are frequently not located within them to any great extent. This is frequently overlooked by regional scientists such as Boudeville (1966).

A number of input-output studies have been undertaken (Bourque and Cox, 1970), principally in the USA, of single region areas. Kalter (1968) undertook an inter-industry analysis of the central New York (state) region, based on data gathered by questionnaires from local firms, and this was used to estimate the goods and services sold by each industry group to all other groups (transactions matrix). Kalter and Allee (1967), in an earlier study, applied the same technique to a study of a recreation area on Long Island, New York, while the Isard et al. (1966) Philadelphia input-output study was one of the earliest attempts at using the technique on a regional scale. In Britain, an input-output model of Anglesey was used by Archer (1973) to assess the economic impact of spending by different categories of tourists on the local economy.

Many problems are encountered with the use of input-output

models and Robinson (1972) provides a very useful account of them in detail. Briefly, they involve problems of industrial classification in the input-output matrix, the problem of by-products, statistical rounding errors when dealing with large input-output systems, problems of simultaneity if returns to scale are encountered, technical change if the model is to be used on a predictive basis with resulting possible changes in the input-output coefficients over time, and the question of predicting any relative price changes.

Interactive regional input-output models are rare. For a two-region, three-industry system, such a model would have the form:

$$
\begin{bmatrix} X_1^1 \\ X_2^1 \\ X_3^1 \\ \hline X_1^2 \\ X_2^2 \\ X_3^2 \end{bmatrix}
-
\begin{bmatrix}
a_{11}^{11} & a_{12}^{11} & a_{13}^{11} & a_{11}^{12} & a_{12}^{12} & a_{13}^{12} \\
a_{21}^{11} & a_{22}^{11} & a_{23}^{11} & a_{21}^{12} & a_{22}^{12} & a_{23}^{12} \\
a_{31}^{11} & a_{32}^{11} & a_{33}^{11} & a_{31}^{12} & a_{32}^{12} & a_{33}^{12} \\
\hline
a_{11}^{21} & a_{12}^{21} & a_{13}^{21} & a_{11}^{22} & a_{12}^{22} & a_{13}^{22} \\
a_{21}^{21} & a_{22}^{21} & a_{23}^{21} & a_{21}^{22} & a_{22}^{22} & a_{23}^{22} \\
a_{31}^{21} & a_{32}^{21} & a_{33}^{21} & a_{31}^{22} & a_{32}^{22} & a_{33}^{22}
\end{bmatrix}
\cdot
\begin{bmatrix} X_1^1 \\ X_2^1 \\ X_3^1 \\ \hline X_1^2 \\ X_2^2 \\ X_3^2 \end{bmatrix}
=
\begin{bmatrix} Y_1^1 \\ Y_2^1 \\ Y_3^1 \\ \hline Y_1^2 \\ Y_2^2 \\ Y_3^2 \end{bmatrix}
$$

with superscripts denoting regions and subscripts indicating sectors. This example is limited to three sectors. In matrix form with partitioned matrices and vectors it appears as:

$$
\begin{bmatrix} X^1 \\ \hline X^2 \end{bmatrix}
=
\left[I - \begin{bmatrix} A^{11} & A^{12} \\ \hline A^{21} & A^{22} \end{bmatrix} \right]^{-1}
\cdot
\begin{bmatrix} Y^1 \\ \hline Y^2 \end{bmatrix}
$$

Econometric models

Econometric models provide a useful set of planning techniques. A major drawback to the use of input-output methods is the difficulty of obtaining information on transactions between all the sectors of the economy. The standard of accuracy and the detail required, make the collection of this information a difficult and highly expensive task. An alternative approach to the assessment of the economic impact of a project or policy, is to construct an econometric model or a series of mathematical equations to show the general relationships between relevant factors. Thus, for example, an adopted form of the Keynsian multiplier (as follows) has been used by Greig (1971, 1972) for an investigation into the income-employment multiplier effects of setting up a new pulp mill in Lochaber, and of investment by the Highlands and Islands Development Board into the fishing industries of the Scottish Highlands.

$$kr = \frac{1}{1 - c(1 - t_d - u)(1 - m - t_i)}$$

where kr = the regional income multiplier

c = the fraction of additional income which is consumed

t_d = direct tax

u = the percentage decline in transfer payments (such as, social security)

m = the proportion of spending which is on goods imported into the region

t_i = indirect tax rate.

Browrigg (1973) conducted a similar study into the impact of a new university on Stirling and, more recently, Henderson (1975) attempted to measure the economic effects, in terms of income and jobs, of tourist expenditure in Tayside, based on the economic concept of the multiplier. Currently, Hodge and Whitby are using a neo-Keynsian multiplier model to estimate the impact of a Development Commission-sponsored factory programme on regional income and employment in the eastern borders of England and Scotland.

Examples of simultaneous models of income and economic activity rates in rural areas and agricultural labour supply and demand are given in Chapters 9 and 10. These types of models could be extended to cover other fields of the rural economy. For example, Bell (1967) has proposed a regional econometric model for Massachusetts with seventeen endogenous variables: export income, local service income, total income received, total produced income, total capital stock, manufacturing capital stock, non-manufacturing capital stock, investment in manufacturing sector, investment in non-manufacturing sector, employment, labour supply (actual), expected labour supply (natural increase), population (actual), expected population (natural increase), annual wage per employee, migration and unemployment. He also proposes six exogenous variables: gross national product, birth rate (per 1000) minus death rate (per 1000), prospective unemployment (difference between natural increase in the labour force and labour demand), capital stock in manufacturing, capital stock in non-manufacturing and time. Bell's model is essentially recursive,[1] and individual equations are evaluated by ordinary least squares (OLS) or two-stage least-squares. In the evaluation of an extended simultaneous system, the models must be restrictive enough so that, given sufficiently large samples, the values of parameters can be determined. This is a problem of identification after which the most appropriate estimator of structural coefficients must be chosen to give consistent and efficient estimates (Christ, 1966). Glickman (1971) developed an econometric model to give annual forecasts for a region. The model is a macro-economic structure consisting of twenty-six inter-dependent equations arranged in two blocks. The first block consists of the manufacturing sector, the service sector, and all other sectors. For these three sectors equations are specified for output, employment, average annual wage, gross regional product, personal income, consumer prices, labour force and population. In the second block, equations allow the estimation of local government revenues and expenditures. The blocks are recursive with causality flows from the private sector block to the government block, but no feedback occurs.

More recently, Czamanski (1972) developed an econometric model which was used by the Nova Scotia Voluntary Planning Board in 1968 and 1969, in connection with work on a long-run development plan for the province. The model contained target variables (such as per capita income, out-migration etc.); intermediate variables, covering the description and operation of the model, but which are of no immediate interest by themselves (total population of Nova Scotia, total wage income and personal savings); instrument variables which may be influenced by policy-makers (such as direct investments by government, defence spending in Nova Scotia); data variables determined outside the model (for example, average yearly wage income per worker in Canada, rate of interest on loans and Canadian GNP) and lagged endogenous variables. The whole model was composed of seven sub-models covering (1) the iron and steel industry, (2) manufacturing and employment, (3) output and investments, (4) households, (5) govern-

---

[1] Recursive implies a relation of precedence in which the objective function depends upon the solution of the preceding problems in the sequence.

ments and trade deficit, (6) population and migrations, and (7) welfare. Available data had an important influence on the structure of the model. Some econometricians would claim that a description of real world phenomena would ordinarily result in interdependent systems. However, the Nova Scotia model had to be developed as a recursive and not interdependent model, even at the risk of over-simplifying some of the relationships and violating some preconceived notions about economic behaviour. This arose because the model was estimated on the basis of time series data covering sixteen years. Hence estimating the model, even on an equation by equation basis, leaves very few degrees of freedom and introduces some awkward problems associated with small samples. With an interdependent system, resort would have to be made to some simultaneous estimating procedures, such as two-stage least-squares or limited information – maximum likelihood methods, and the number of variables involved, even in a small interdependent sub-system, would quickly exhaust the degrees of freedom. Lagged relationships lead to a loss of additional degrees of freedom, and these also had to be avoided as far as possible, in view of the limited number of observations available.

Discriminant analysis can be a useful method of estimation, among other econometric techniques. Discriminant analysis provides a means of testing classifactory schemes, identifying the 'most important' variables and tidying up the scheme by assigning uncertain cases to their most likely groups. Multiple discriminant analysis has been used to evaluate economic models for rural planning in two ways:

(1) by discerning the subset of feasible alternatives for a group of rural communities;
(2) by testing the statistical significance of rural development programmes.

Before illustrating how discriminant analysis can be of use in resource development planning, it is worthwhile to describe briefly the essence of discriminant analysis.

Discriminant analysis has grown out of interest associated with assigning an unknown object to one of G mutually exclusive groups, on the basis of a set of n measurements on that object. This is done by finding a linear function of the differences of the means:

$$y = v_1 x_1 + v_2 x_2 + \ldots + v_m x_m$$

which discriminates most successfully among the groups (Anderson, 1958; Tintner, 1952). The coefficients (v_i) of the linear function y are computed so that the ratio of the sums-of squares between groups means, to sum-of-squares within group means, is maximized. Assume there are two groups **A** and **B**, containing N_j ($j = 1, 2, \ldots, k$) objects each, with each object being scored on each of n characteristics. Upon computing the discriminant function for this set of objects[1] at least two interesting analyses can be carried out. One possibility is to measure these same variables on an object of uncertain group identity, substitute these values into the discriminant function and, based upon whether $y \geqslant y^*$,[2] place the object in the appropriate group **A** or **B**. If $y > y^*$, the object most resembles those in group **A**; while if $y < y^*$, it most resembles those in group **B**. The second possibility is to compute the coefficients in order to discern the relative importance of the variables x_1, x_2, $\ldots$, x_n in discriminating between membership in group **A** or **B**. Thus, it is possible to rank the n variables in descending order of their relative contribution to determine proper group membership.

The fact that marginal costs and marginal revenues vary between areas, means that gains can be effected by moving towards a competitive equilibrium, i.e. where marginal costs and returns are equated between areas. Ricardo, Mill and Marshall developed the principle of comparative advantage, according to which total output (welfare) is increased by specialization. Simply stated: a rural parish has a comparative advantage *vis-à-vis* a second parish, in the production of a commodity or service in which it has a lower opportunity cost. If two parishes are each producing the same pair of commodities, then the total output of both commodities can be increased, if each parish transfers resources into the production of the commodity in which it has a comparative advantage. This theoretical economic framework has been used by Bromley (1971) and Willis (1973) to choose a rural development policy for Wisconsin and the northern Pennines respectively. For the northern Pennines, analysis was concerned with rural development between agriculture, industry, or recreation, and it was initially assumed to depend upon the average income from each of these activities in the

[1] There is always one less discriminant function(s) than there are groups to discriminate among.
[2] y^* is the critical value of the discriminant function. For three groups there are two discriminant functions and two critical values.

parish. Each parish was, therefore, scored with respect to average income from each of the three activities, and categorized as suitable for agricultural, industrial, or recreational development depending upon which generated the highest average income. Unfortunately, the income variables measure average revenue product to labour, whereas optimality is achieved where marginal revenue products are equated. Therefore, the rather restrictive assumption had to be made, in the absence of any marginal revenue data, that equilibrium pertained with respect to labour within each broad sector group (agriculture, industry, tertiary) in each parish. Transfer of resources is possible, therefore, between activities within a parish and between parishes according to different rates of return. The assumption of a perfectly competitive situation with regard to labour within each activity within a parish, means that marginal revenue equals average revenue. Sixteen other variables were used from the agricultural and population censuses which could be hypothesized as influencing future rural development. Discriminant analysis revealed that income data was the best discriminatory variable to indicate the appropriate development strategy. Nevertheless, some areas were reclassified when all variables were taken into consideration (see Table 3.3).

Discriminant analysis was also used to test the statistical significance of Northumberland County Council's (1969) rural development plan. The plan essentially involves growth in some settlements and no growth, or actual decline, in others. Northumberland County Council (1968) undertook a survey to provide information about some of the villages in rural Northumberland, which would subsequently help in the task of working out detailed proposals for the implementation of their rural development policies. Of the sixteen villages surveyed, five were designated as 'supporting growth points' and the other eleven either as consolidation points, or as villages not designated for development. No methodology is presented to substantiate this classification, and one can only suppose it was undertaken in a subjective manner. The sixteen villages were scored with respect to those variables stated by Northumberland as being important in determining growth or no growth, and a discriminant analysis undertaken on Northumberland's classification. Table 3.4 indicates that, while most villages were correctly identified on the basis of the data used, a certain amount of reclassification did take place.

Table 3.3   Classification of selected parishes for development in the northern Pennines

Parish	Group with largest probability		Probability for group		
	A priori*	A posteriori †	A	I	R
Allendale	R	A	0.687	0.010	0.304
Bewcastle		A	0.999	0.000	0.001
Burtholme		A	0.984	0.004	0.012
Solport		A	1.000	0.000	0.000
Hexhamshire		A	1.000	0.000	0.000
Edmondbyers		A	1.000	0.000	0.000
Blanchland		A	0.990	0.000	0.010
Kirkwhelpington		A	0.571	0.003	0.426
Slaggyford		A	0.632	0.363	0.006
West Allen		A	0.787	0.000	0.212
Stapleton	R	A	0.552	0.001	0.447
Humshaugh	R	A	0.583	0.090	0.327
Brampton		I	0.000	1.000	0.000
Stanhope		I	0.000	1.000	0.000
Middleton-in-Teesdale		I	0.032	0.646	0.322
Long Marton	A	I	0.279	0.444	0.277
Haydon	R	I	0.001	0.821	0.178
Wolsington	R	I	0.002	0.810	0.188
Appleby	I	R	0.003	0.240	0.757
Falstone	A	R	0.305	0.000	0.694
Bardon Mill		R	0.110	0.007	0.883
Bellingham		R	0.011	0.002	0.987
Brough		R	0.005	0.075	0.920
Rothbury		R	0.003	0.002	0.995
Otterburn		R	0.002	0.000	0.998
Slaley	A	R	0.302	0.016	0.682

Source: Willis (1973).

* Classification based on average income to agriculture (*A*), industry (*I*), service (*R*), before discriminant analysis was undertaken. Except where indicated, a priori classification was the same as a posteriori.

† A posteriori classification after discriminant analysis was undertaken on all explanatory variables (income variables plus sixteen other variables).

Table 3.4   Discriminant analysis reclassification of growth and non-growth centres in Northumberland's Rural Plan

		Revised classification by discriminant analysis		
		Growth	*Others*	**Totals**
County	Growth	4	1	**5**
Council classification	Others	2	9	**11**
	Totals	**6**	**10**	**16**

Source: Willis (1973).

Until more time series and cross section data become available, regional econometric models will continue to be relatively simple, but reasonable predictions are often possible with models in this form.

The relative advantages and disadvantages of input-output and econometric stochastic models as used in regional studies, are not easily weighed. The choice is between a highly disaggregated, but extremely simple model, based on a rigid set of assumptions, and a sophisticated analytical tool. The great weakness of input-output, and other simple multipliers, is that there is almost nothing in these models to indicate any basic divergence between the particular hypothesis upon which they are based and empirical fact. Econometric stochastic models, on the other hand, permit theories and observations to be related, statements to be made as to the extent to which observations support a belief in the theories, and the estimation of the strength of the influence of one variable on another.

Mathematical programming – optimizing techniques

One problem which is too easily ignored in physical planning, but which for many areas is the most critical, is the problem of how to put a limited set of resources to best use. Input-output and econometric models emphasize general interdependence: they are concerned primarily with system modelling and play a scientific role. However, since a land-use development plan should be a prescriptive document, and many other plans fall into this category (for example, farm plans, agricultural policy and so on), techniques ought to be considered which will help a client or a society to improve his or its position.

Linear programming is one optimizing technique: it is an operations research technique, and it gives a practical rule for calculating the solution to the problem we pose. Linear programming is the simplest and most widely used of the mathematical programming techniques. It is a technique for solving maximization or minimization problems confronting decision-making agencies, subject to certain side conditions, or constraints, that limit what the agencies are able to do. Linear programming techniques provide little information regarding the operation of the economy beyond what is provided by the conventional theory of the firm. An example of a simple linear programming model is given in Chapter 12 so, to avoid duplication, an example is not provided here. Instead we shall concentrate on the role of this technique in planning.

Linear programming has proved a flexible and useful tool in the economic planning of agricultural production and resource use (Heady, 1957), because many processes in farming do involve linear relationships, i.e. one added acre ploughed generally requires an equal input and can be considered to add an equal increment to output. However, the extension of linear programming to planning whole areas has proved more difficult.

Ben-Shahar, Mazor and Pines (1969) suggest plans should be sought which maximize social welfare objectives under a given set of constraints. In view of the complexities of the data, constraints and criteria, a solution of efficient plans is advocated by mathematical programming. They developed a theoretical linear programming model which offers a simultaneous solution for future sub-periods of land-use for residence, employment and also transportation. Costs are discounted, and shadow prices used to value activities where appropriate. Some preference criteria are measured in money terms but others, which are difficult to measure in money terms, are measured on the basis of ordinal criteria.

Operationalizing such models had not proved easy. The model developed by Spiegelman, Baum and Talbert (1965) overcomes many of the technical problems associated with input-output and linear programming. It contains a highly disaggregated foreign trade sector that permits competitive comparisons between local and foreign industries, as well as technological change and detailed analysis of labour demand and supply. This planning model was developed for small rural areas and applied to a five county area in south central Kentucky and is, in effect, a disaggregated form of linear programming. It was designed to determine the amount of outside financing needed to achieve income and consumption targets, the least cost mix of new manufacturing and agricultural activities promoted by outside financing, the techniques of production to be employed, the degree of technical change required and the rate of local capital formation. The optimal solution is made to conform to the competitive solution by simulating the trade pattern of a free economy. The model also takes into account external economies resulting from the simultaneous expansion of sources of supply, markets, services and labour supply.

In Britain, operational effort has been influenced to a considerable extent by the approach of Friend and Jessop (1969) to evolve a 'technology of choice' for the planning process. The approach of AIDA (Analysis of Interconnected Decision Areas) is suggested to find solutions where there are many combinations of choice to be considered. In the AIDA approach, the problem is expressed as a set of 'decision areas', each with one or more mutually exclusive 'options'. Incompatible options are defined by 'option bars'. All feasible combinations of decisions are then identified and the solutions ranked by alternative sets of weights. This approach was illustrated by Friend and Jessop (1969) by means of two case studies, one of urban renewal in a limited area close to the centre of a town, and a second case depicting the problem of priorities concerning different types of public development, including housing, schools, shopping and drainage.

Openshaw and Whitehead (1975, 1977) argue that AIDA works well on small, well defined problems, but that larger problems would produce a great number of feasible solutions, unless there were a substantial increase in the amount of option bars, or constraints, present. Openshaw and Whitehead tried to overcome the short-comings and to extend the AIDA approach by re-expressing it as an integer linear programming problem. Thus their decision optimizing technique (DOT) is an integer programming generalization of AIDA, and AIDA and DOT are seen as contributing to the development of an effective decision-orientated paradigm for planning, in that they satisfy a need for an explicit and reasonably objective methodology.

There are still, however, practical difficulties associated with the technique as it has been applied. Subjectivity plays a considerable part in specifying constraints or option bars: for example, a car park may be allowed to locate on one site, but this would preclude other sites being used for car parks. In their study of problems and strategic policy in Morpeth town centre, Openshaw and Whitehead (1975) propose six evaluative criteria which were (1) cost to district ratepayers, (2) cost to county ratepayers, (3) income to district council, (4) number of car parking spaces created, (5) an indicator of environmental improvement, a subjective assessment between —5 and +5, and (6) amount of shopping floorspace created. However, these are not optimal, but rather suboptimal criteria, since they do not even begin to encompass all the results of policy changes which could be relevant to the welfare of individuals in a particular area. In addition, the difficulty for evaluation is that many of these are non-commensurable: how is an environmental index to be rated against cost to district ratepayers? Future studies using this programming approach will be more useful if elements are measured in commensurate terms and, in addition, if some effort is made to quantitify benefits, for example, the number of car parking spaces provided and amount of shopping floor space created, not in terms of physical units, but in terms commensurable to costs, such as the willingness to pay. Another omission is that of time. The idea that a given expenditure arising in five years' time may be preferable to the same expenditure arising today, because money can be reinvested with profit in the meantime, is a familiar one in economic analysis. Similarly, the idea that social benefit today may be preferable to the same benefit in five years' time is accepted intuitively by all politicians, particularly if they have to stand for re-election in the intervening period. Of course, there are great problems in deciding the appropriate discount rate. The controversy between the Social Time Preference and Social Opportunity Cost rate was reviewed in the previous chapter and need not be repeated here, except to point out that it cannot be ignored and that it is as inappropriate to assume a zero discount rate, as Friend and Jessop (1969) did in looking at priorities within a changing town, as it is to assume an infinite discount rate after a certain period, such as by shortening the planning or time horizon from twenty to ten years, to deal with the problem of future risk and uncertainty.

Both AIDA and DOT are concerned with the analysis of interconnected decision areas, yet estimates for the evaluation of alternatives have been obtained (Friend and Jessop, 1969; Openshaw and Whitehead, 1975, 1977) by the simple addition of appropriate items. However, due to the interdependence in the location of some important activities, each site needs to be recosted if any change takes place elsewhere in the system, because the costs and benefits of the development of each site are likely to vary according to the development permitted on other sites. The simple linear additive solution will be incorrect if there are services that are common to any two of the specified areas, or if there are economies of scale in providing services for sites. In other words, the practical application of these programming techniques has not been to study interconnected decision areas in the true sense of the word at all. The problem which is common to these types of programming and studies (such as that by Warford, 1969, on settlement relocation, Chapter 11), is that there is no means by which it is possible to declare, within the self-imposed constraints, that the options are in any way optimal, since to know the optimal alternative would require a knowledge of the magnitudes the study is designed to provide! But although Warford begins with an arbitrary selection of relocation sites, which may not be optimal, each planning alternative is reappraised and new costs and benefits are estimated for each site as the planning alternatives change: the effects of changes elsewhere on the first site are estimated.

Nevertheless, despite shortcomings in application, decision optimizing techniques provide a worthwhile addition to the development of planning models. The further development of programming models along the lines suggested by Funck (1970) would be worthwhile. Funck constructed a model for the optimum solution of welfare systems and regional policy decisions, but looking at only two individuals, goods and production factors. This simple model includes externalities in production and consumption, and political constraints. Within the restricted set of assumptions, the results of the model describe relations between regional welfare, production, markets, and regional economic policy, in an optimum situation. In reality, the problem is more complex: transportation must be introduced, so that the neoclassical approach of Funck would quickly approach its limits and other techniques, such as non-linear programming, would need to be applied. Optimality conditions are extremely complex expressions and are difficult to handle within the normal range of computational effort. Maximization of welfare is a true second-best problem and Funck's model is based on the second-best theorem put forward by Lipsey and Lancaster (1956) (see Chapter 2).

Forecasting

There are several possible objectives in time series analysis: these may be description, explanation, prediction, and control. Time series may be analysed for any one, a combination, or all of these reasons. Traditional methods of time series are mainly concerned with decomposing a series into a trend, cyclical fluctuation, seasonal effects, or other irregular fluctuations. Forecasting the future values of an observed time-series, is an important problem in many areas of rural development. However, there is no universally applicable forecasting procedure: the correct procedure is the one which is most appropriate for a given set of conditions. The many types of forecasting procedure can be classified into three broad categories: subjective, univariate and multivariate.

Forecasts can be made on a subjective basis using judgement, intuition, commercial knowledge and any other relevant information. Procedures of this type, such as panelling, the Delphi model, or scenario writing, have been described by Bayliss (1968).

Univariate forecasts can be based entirely on past observation in a given time series, by fitting a model to the data and extrapolating. Forecasts of future sales of a product are often based entirely on past sales, and population is also frequently forecast by this projection method. Moving averages, polynomial (see Tintner, 1952), exponential (Rodgers, 1974) and other functions fall into this category. A series of at least ten previous observations is required, and it is unwise to project forward to a period longer than half of the number of past years for which data is available. There is no logical basis for choosing among the different curves, except by goodness-of-fit, and often it is possible to find several curves which fit a given set of data almost equally well but which, when projected forward, give widely different forecasts.

Recently, Box and Jenkins (1968, 1970) have provided a general strategy for time series forecasting. This forecasting procedure consists basically of fitting a mixed autoregressive integrated moving average (ARIMA) model to a given set of data, and then taking conditional expectations. It is first necessary to examine the data in order to see which member of the class of ARIMA processes appears to be most appropriate, before estimating the parameters of the model by least squares. Residuals are then examined to see if the fitted model is adequate, and if not, then other ARIMA models may be tried until a satisfactory model is found. The Box-Jenkins procedure involves a subjective element which allows choice from a wide variety of models. This is an advantage yet, at the same time, requires considerable expertise: many people understand ideas of trend and seasonality, but are completely baffled by ARIMA models. When variation is dominated by trend and seasonality, the effectiveness of the ARIMA model is mainly determined by the differencing procedure and some other way of measuring trend and seasonality may be more appropriate. In any case, statistical forecasts are more likely to be accepted if their derivation is understood. Nevertheless, Box-Jenkins is of considerable interest to the statistician in forecasting.

Multivariate forecasting procedures use a multiple regression model to relate y to present and past values of other variables $(x_1 \ldots x_m)$ and also possibly to past values of y. Multiple regression models sometimes work well in economics, but there are several dangers in the method. First, the ready availability of computer programmes has resulted in a tendency to put more and more explanatory variables into the model with dubious results. For example, if X_3 was believed to be unrelated to Y but it was suggested it should be tried, there is a 5 per cent chance of finding a significant statistical relationship (at a 95 per cent level), even though, in reality, no such relationship exists. When many variables are included just to see if there are any relationships, the probability of no error is $(.95)_k$. Thus Tarver (1961) used 24 independent variables to explain migration with a probability of no error of $.95^{24}$ or .29 and an error probability of .71. When n is greater than 13, the probability of error exceeds that of no error. The probability of drawing a false conclusion, therefore, increases dramatically as more variables are included. It can be kept small by reducing the level of error for each variable tried on from 5 per cent to 1 per cent, or by restricting the number of independent variables to 6 or 7. Secondly, some independent variables are usually not independent at all, and while it is unnecessary for the explanatory variables to be completely independent, large correlations should be avoided, since there may be singularity problems. Thirdly, some crucial explanatory variables may have been held more or less constant in the past, and it is then impossible to assess their effect and include them in the model in a qualitative way. Finally, error terms are sometimes not independent and this may lead to disappointing results in multiple regression.

Econometric models, in the form of sets of simultaneous equations, fall into this multivariate category. An introduction to econometrics is given by Walters (1970). Box and Jenkins (1968, 1970) also consider multivariate forecasting, as well as univariate, in a class of models which they call transfer function models and which are a natural extension to the ARIMA class.

When choosing a forecasting procedure, consideration must be given to the purpose of the forecast, the degree of accuracy required and the amount of money available etc. Univariate forecasts are mainly intended to act as a norm and if forecasts are required for planning or decision making, then ideally one should set up a multi-variate model. However, these are relatively difficult and expensive to build, especially econometric models and transfer function models, and they sometimes have poor predictive powers. Considerable controversy exists. Naylor *et al.* (1972) showed that univariate Box-Jenkins forecasts were better than forecasts obtained using the Wharton econometric model; Wagle *et al.* (1968) quotes examples where hand forecasts were much better than objective statistical forecasts; and Armstrong and Grohman (1972) cite an example where econometric forecasts are better than univariate fore-casts, which in turn are better than subjective forecasts. Rodgers (1974) shows the superiority of the Box-Jenkins process over an exponential smoothing model. She prefers the Box-Jenkins model to an econometric model for forecasting wool prices because of the necessity of predicting explanatory variables, the errors of which will be reflected in wool price predictions, and the strong multi-collinearity between income and supply of substitutes, which results in predictions which have large variances associated with them.

Conclusion

This chapter has attempted to illustrate the main types of models and techniques, although the coverage is by no means comprehensive. A good set of models and techniques already exist for rural and regional analysis which serve a wide variety of purposes and problems. The application of such techniques would permit planning problems to be analysed in a scientific way. Models have the advantage of requiring assumptions to be explicit and evidence to be presented, and they rely on types of evidence and analytical methods which can be challenged, validated or rejected by others. In practice, of course, slipshod and incompetent work is found. Yet properly executed, the appropriate techniques produce precise answers so far as the data will allow. The major problem is that techniques are frequently not applied in planning studies at a regional, county or district level. Indeed, rarely is any part of the quantitative planning model outlined in Fig. 3.1 adopted with any rigour. This has led to a yawning credibility gap in town and country planning, and comments such as that by Geddes (1971) on the Yorkshire and Humberside Regional Strategy can all too easily be made:

this is the basic difficulty with the present report and others like it. It never gets down to the nitty gritty. Its well-intentioned ideals are seldom translated into precise, quantified policies and programmes. Public investment implications are dismissed in a derisory three paragraphs. The need for priorities to be determined among possible conflicting objectives competing for limited resources is glossed over with a smooth assumption about 'balanced progress' towards all objectives at once.

4 Town and country planning procedures

The statutory system of land-use planning in Britain has its origins mainly in remedies devised for the relief of urban congestion in the nineteenth century (Ashworth, 1954). It arose out of the implicit, if not explicit, recognition of the external diseconomies associated with urban growth and of ill defined property rights. Indeed, the history of rural planning can be seen largely as a by-product of new demands made upon rural areas by urban populations. A part, therefore, of the essential objective of the machinery of rural planning, is the resolution of conflict between urban demands on land use and the traditional primary rural economy. This can be seen as early as 1580, when Elizabeth I proclaimed a green belt out of a recognition that the inhabitants of London must be provided 'of sustenation of victuall, foods and other like necessities'. With the development of modern transport, the need for a belt of productive farmland adjacent to a city is no longer imperative, although some conceive the problem as still remaining!

The complementarity of rural and urban areas was very much embodied in Ebenezer Howard's garden city concept which was a reaction to the ugliness of the Industrial Revolution. To bring the city dweller closer to the country, Howard proposed a series of garden cities, each to be surrounded by a green belt ring. Green belts are conceived as rough rings of land, usually several miles wide, around a number of developed areas. Within green belts no further urban development is permitted, and in this way the expansion of cities and urban conglomerations is to be halted. Howard saw no conflict between town and countryside. He thought that the disutilities of urban growth were imposed upon urban dwellers, while the countryside's lack of accessibility imposed costs on rural dwellers. He argued that the garden city concept resolved both problems in that the green belt restricted the growth of the urban area and provided the countryside with a large, and close, urban market. The green belt was envisaged as no more than two miles wide to separate each town (of up to a 60,000 population) from the next. This green belt-garden city-new town concept would have resulted in a grouping of urban development in clusters surrounded by countryside. The idea was thus to maximize accessibility and environmental quality simultaneously. Ebenezer Howard envisaged the concepts of green belts and new towns in the countryside as interrelated solutions to urban problems.

Howard was at pains to point out that although he developed the idea in 1898, he did not invent the idea of new towns any more than he invented green belts. Perhaps the true originator of the new town concept (and the father of town planning!) as an answer to the problems of urban growth was the great Victorian economist, Alfred Marshall. Marshall (1884) had a very clear idea of the costs and benefits of such a policy and argued that 'the removal of large classes of the population of London into the country would be in the long run economically advantageous' for reasons of location economics; the fact that industry does not take external costs into account and that the social costs paid by the community would be higher in large cities than in smaller communities; and that there are many workers in footloose manufacturing industries where 'the supply of labour is determined by the character of the population, and the demand follows the supply'. Howard specifically acknowledged the ideas and sound economic reasoning of Marshall, who described economics as 'man in the ordinary business of life'. Today, however, town planners have an all too unhealthy disregard for the fundamentals of economics. This anti-economic cult is worshipped with almost innate depravity by the planning profession.

Specification of plans — structure plans

A land-use plan is (in theory) a prescriptive document: it is designed to help society improve its position. In practice, a land-use plan may be nothing of the sort: there is little in present day town planning work, and in the techniques used to prepare plans, to inspire much confidence in the prescriptive notion of welfare increase. Nevertheless, the formal status of a plan is derived from the legal requirement of the Secretary of State for the Environment, that development plans be formulated by the local planning authorities and submitted to him for approval. Their preparation is not merely authorized, but is compulsory. Planning procedures and development plans are, for better or worse, important policy instruments, backed by law and possible economic sanctions. For this reason alone, town and country planning is worthy of consideration.

The original development plans of local authorities were made under the Town and Country Planning Act 1947. The authority had to submit to the Minister of Town and Country Planning (subsequently the Minister of Housing and Local Government, and now the Secretary of State for the Environment) a development plan indicating the manner in which it was proposed that land in the area should be used, and the stages by which any development should be carried out.

Current legislation under the Town and Country Planning Act 1968 (subsequently incorporated within the Town and Country Planning Act 1971) provides for new types of development plan. The procedure is much the same as the 1947 system: survey, analysis and plan.

Every planning authority must make a survey of its area covering:

(1) the principal physical and economic characteristics of the area, including the principle purposes for which land is used, and the same characteristics of any neighbouring area if they affect the area surveyed;
(2) the size, composition and distribution of population;
(3) communications, transport system and traffic of the area;
(4) any other considerations likely to affect these matters;
(5) any changes in these matters and the effect these changes are likely to have on the development of the area.

Every local planning authority must prepare and send to the Secretary of State a structure plan for its area. This plan must be in the form of a written statement and must formulate the authority's policy and general proposals, including those for the improvement of the physical environment and the management of traffic. It should link these proposals, if necessary, with the general proposals for the development and other land use in neighbouring areas. The policy and general proposals formulated under the plan must be justified by the results of the survey, and by any other information which may have been obtained and must have regard to current policies with respect to the economic planning and development of the region as a whole, to the resources likely to be available for carrying out the proposals, and to such other matters as the Secretary of State may ask the authority to take into account.

A number of structure plans have been submitted such as the Oxfordshire Structure Plan (1976) and some have been approved by the Secretary of State, for example: the Staffordshire County Structure Plan (1973), the Leicester and Leicestershire Structure Plan (1974), the East Sussex County Structure Plan (1975) and the Worcestershire County Structure Plan (1975). The policy formulated in a structure plan for each respective area must relate to such appropriate matters as population, employment, housing, industry and commerce, transportation, shopping, education, other social and community services, recreation and leisure, conservation of townscape and landscape, utility services and any other relevant matters. In addition to these general requirements, a structure plan must contain indications of the following items considered appropriate by the planning authority:

(1) the present needs and opportunities for change in the area;
(2) any projected or likely changes which may affect matters dealt with in the plan;
(3) the extent (if any) of development under the New Town Acts;
(4) the size, composition and distribution of the population in the area, and the state of employment and industry, together with assumptions on which estimates are based (the information must relate both to the existing situation and to the expected situation in the future at a time appropriate to the plan);
(5) current policies in the economic planning and development of the region;
(6) social policies and considerations;
(7) resources likely to be available to carry out policy and general proposals formulated in the plan:
(8) the control of development in the area;

    (9) the relationship between the various policies formulated in the plan;

    (10) any other relevant matters.

Adequate publicity must be given to the report of the survey made in preparation for the plan, and to the matters which it is proposed to include in the structure plan. Those who may be expected to want an opportunity of making representations about the proposed plan, must be made aware that they have a right to such an opportunity, and those wishing to make representations must be given an adequate opportunity of doing so. The structure plan, when submitted to the Secretary of State for approval, must be accompanied by a statement giving particulars of the steps taken to obtain the views of the public and an account of any consultations with other persons. Before deciding whether to approve or reject a structure plan, the Secretary of State, must consider any objections lodged against it and must order a public examination of such matters affecting his consideration of the plan as, in his opinion, ought to be so examined. An account of the examination of structure plans in public, originated by the Town and Country Planning (Amendment) Act 1972, is provided by Dunlop (1976).

The Department of the Environment's advice to authorities preparing structure plans (Circular 98/74) is to:

    (1) make explicit the assumptions (and reasons for those assumptions) on which the structure plan is based;

    (2) concentrate on essentials, i.e. key issues, especially the location and scale of employment, the location and scale of housing, the transportation system, and then conservation, recreation and tourism, location and scale of shopping centres, and location and scale of land reclamation;

    (3) plan for about fifteen years ahead.

The financial implications of structure plans

In a narrow sense, local government finance is concerned with raising the resources necessary to meet the expenditure needed to provide local government services, allocating those resources between the various services and ensuring that value for money is being obtained. The financial implications of structure plans cannot be ignored, yet this is one of the most neglected areas in town and country planning. The Town and Country Planning Act (1971), Section 7 (4), refers to resources in the following way: 'In formulating their policy and general proposals . . . . . . the local planning authority shall . . . . . . have regard . . . . . . to the resources likely to be available for the carrying out of the proposals of the structure plan'. This general statement has been augmented by various Structure Plan Notes of advice to local planning authorities from the Department of the Environment. What burden on local finances is acceptable is essentially a matter for the local authority concerned. However, Structure Plan Note 6/72 on Resource Aspects of Structure Plans, points out that the documentation made available at the submission of the plan to the Secretary of State, should be sufficient to show that the implications to local authority finances have been made clear to the elected members of the local authority concerned and have been found acceptable to them. For this purpose, the local authority will doubtless wish to take account of:

(1) loan charges consequent upon capital expenditure;
(2) the scale of other recurrent expenditure which is implied by the capital expenditure;
(3) the prospective level of the Rate Support Grant and other relevant grants from the Central Government;
(4) the prospective growth in rateable values, both domestic and non-domestic, implied in the plan.

Resource implications also arise in plan evaluation aspects of structure plans. Thus Structure Plan Note 7/72 on Evaluating Alternatives in Structure Plan Making, suggests that local authorities should give explicit consideration to the following four aspects of alternative policies and general proposals in structure plans:

(1) their effectiveness in meeting aims;
(2) the resources consumed by policies which do this;
(3) the incidence or distributional effects of those policies on different subgroups in the population;
(4) the implication for policies of uncertainty about the future.

In pursuit of its aims the structure plan uses resources. The volume of resources to be consumed is of special interest to central government, since the claim on national resources and the way in which they are consumed is a primary factor in managing the economy. The local planning authorities are more concerned with the financial revenue and expenditure implications of the plan, particularly the likely growth in rate income and the running or variable costs, as well as the cost of servicing additional debts arising from new capital expenditure or fixed costs. For specific projects included in plans requiring public investment, especially those carried out in the short-medium term, Structure Plan Note 7/72 advises the desirability of knowing if the benefits to be derived from the projects represent a reasonable return on resources.

The resource implications of plans continue to be emphasized with DoE Draft Structure Plan Note No. 6 (1975) on the generation of alternative strategies in structure planning. Here again the advice is that the keynote of any strategy must be its realism, and that only those alternatives which are demonstrably feasible in terms of likely availability of resources, should be worked up to the detail required for final evaluation.

Do structure plans meet these obligations in any meaningful sense? A consideration of the attention given to resources in a selection of plans shows that, all too often, there is not only a complete lack of analysis, but also a complete lack of understanding.

Typical of several is the Staffordshire Structure Plan (1973) which has a mere four-and-a-half pages devoted to the problem and is chiefly composed of naive statements such as:

> . . . . . . the local authorities are committed to a hard core of consequential capital and continuing revenue expenditure. The absolute size of this hard core is unimportant, it has to be met given the population to be served and the standard of service to be provided. It will be of substantially the same amount whatever the distribution of the planned population; that is whatever strategy is adopted. There is, therefore, little or no purpose in embarking upon extensive detailed calculations to ascertain the total amount of expenditure, either capital or revenue, on local government services likely to be generated by the Structure Plan.

The Plan also suggest that enough resources can always be found, and that they will always be sufficient to finance the necessary expenditure because no financial constraint exists: 'there is no limit to the local rate which can be levied other than its political acceptability'. It is then suggested that financial evaluation at any stage of the Plan is unrealistic since local authority services never reach complete development, and that financial evaluation should not be attempted when long-run local authority objectives continue to change with changing social conditions.

In contrast, the Draft Structure Plan for Oxfordshire (1976) points out that the effect of some of the strategies considered would be a cost in excess of the expected rate of financial growth during the period, and seems to suggest that the preferred plan evolved partly in consideration of this. The Draft Structure Plan for North Yorkshire (North Riding County Council, 1973) estimates the capital costs sector by sector (for example: education, highways, housing, recreation, sewerage, land reclamation) over the period 1971–91. The estimated annual capital expenditure by local authorities in North Yorkshire was £14 between 1960 and 1970, but the proposed expenditure for 1971–81 was £27 per head, falling to £12 per head per year between 1981 and 1991 (in 1971 prices).

One of the most detailed financial appraisals was undertaken by the South Hampshire Structure Plan (1973) which tried to maximize environmental standards with minimum costs. The financial assessment was made in the light of capital expenditure, the effect on loan charges and on the general rate fund etc., and came out in favour of alternative strategies C,D,B,A in order of preference, C being preferred because it seemed to offer the best prospects of economical phasing, its operational costs were lower and it was least likely to involve heavy initiating expenditure on development.

Thus, so far the performance of local authorities in structure planning has been somewhat variable. The plans published to date show wide variations in methods of financial analysis, from dangerous naiveté to some professional sophistication. It is to be hoped that, in future, sound academic and professional financial analysis and evaluation will be conducted according to some standard, common format or criterion.

Plan evaluation

Like financial assessment, plan evaluation is weak in the British planning process. Methods and theory have been applied haphazardly and sporadically. Lichfield's Planning Balance Sheet underlies the proposals for the expansion of Peterborough (Lichfield, 1969). Cost-benefit analysis has been applied occasionally (Flowerdew, 1971), while other methods of plan evaluation, such as the goals achievement matrix (Hill, 1968), have been proposed.

DoE Structure Plan Note 7/72 states that it will no longer suffice for decisions to be reached by means of a feeling for the right answer once all the seemingly relevant facts are known. It urges the evaluation of alternative plans, with special emphasis on their effectiveness in meeting aims, their use of resources, the incidence or distribution of their costs and benefits within the community, and what implications uncertainty about the future holds for them. If structure plans are to act as a framework or strategy, evaluation is clearly fundamental to the 1968 development plan system for guiding development through more detailed measures, in particular, local plans and capital investment programmes.

DoE Structure Plan Note. 8/72 proposes a matrix approach to evaluation incorporating elements of cost-benefit analysis, cost-effectiveness analysis, the planning balance sheet and the goals-achievement matrix, with aims cross-tabulated by alternatives. It advocates that the aims should be sufficiently broad to ensure that no major alternatives are excluded, but in sufficient detail for them to lead explicitly to evaluation criteria, and that alternatives should be distinct, i.e. likely to produce noticeable differences in their consequences, while being feasible in terms of satisfying constraints.

It is advocated that among the alternative plans, costs and benefits should be distinguished. But benefits include all the consequences of the alternatives, whether advantageous (benefit) or disadvantageous (disbenefit), while the costs include all resources committed in each alternative, though valued only at market prices in financial terms and excluding social costs. It is also argued that costs and benefits should be quantified as much as possible, but then it is suggested that, for benefits, market values should be used and non-monetary measures used where market values are not appropriate, for example: accessibility indices, house condition indices, landscape quality indices etc., and that, for intangibles, there is no substitute for subjective arguing (see Table 4.1). This kind of valuation thus raises all the problems of commensurability. Finally, it is suggested that the shorter and longer term consequences of alternative policies should be distinguished and valued differently. Costs and benefits will have different flows over time and these must be weighed against each other. The value of both costs and benefits depends on when they occur: the earlier they occur the more significant they will be. However, since not all costs and benefits in the evaluation matrix are expressed in monetary terms, discounting

Table 4.1 Typical proposal for an evaluation matrix for structure plans

Aims	Alternatives								
	A		B		C		D		
	Costs	benefits	Costs	benefits	Costs	benefits	Costs	benefits	
a		VERY GOOD		GOOD		BAD		GOOD	Subjective statement
b		80		82		75		90	Quantitative measure
c	£	22	£	19	£	30	£	28	Index
d	£	£	£	£	£	£	£	£	Monetary valuation
e		GOOD		VERY GOOD		BAD		FAIR	Subjective statement

Source: DoE (1973).

cannot be applied, thus commensurability in time cannot be established, nor time evaluated, except in a very crude way.

Structure Plan Note 8/72 eventually turns to the interpretation of the evaluation matrix. Examination is advocated under the three headings of effectiveness: resource effects, distributional effects and response to uncertainty. Effectiveness is concerned with the degree to which each of the plan's aims or objectives is achieved. Where common measures of performance, such as money are used, then the weighing of aims is implicit in the unit costs and benefits. Since aims are not all measured in commensurate terms (such as monetary units) weighing is suggested as a means of measuring the plan's relative performance, or effectiveness of meeting each aim. It is recognized that establishing weights will not be easy, but various methods are suggested including asking planners, politicians or the public to choose weights, or undertaking public attitude or behaviour surveys, or interpreting viewpoints expressed in public participation exercises. In this way, presumably trade-offs will be established and alternatives compared in terms of differences between the so-called 'benefits' and 'costs'. Resource effects cited include determining whether alternative projects present a reasonable rate of return and, therefore, an efficient use of resources. This now merely involves what was stated to be impossible before: valuing the flows of benefits and costs arising from the project in money terms, discounting them at the Treasury Test Rate and comparing net present values. Distributional effects are interpreted by disaggregating the matrix and establishing separate matrices to show the effects on different sub-groups of the population. Sub-group matrices can indicate whether any section of society bears costs or receives benefits greatly different from the average, a situation which may or may not be desirable. Sensitivity analysis is advocated to assess the importance of uncertainty in some variables.

Planners have not applied micro-economic theory to plan evaluation in any rigorous way. Planners have rejected the application of the tenets of theoretical welfare economics to actual decision making, arguing that it contains inherent methodological difficulties. As a consequence, the baby has often been thrown out with the bathwater, so that many useful economic theorems – ideas and techniques which would have helped society improve its position – have not been used. Planning no longer faithfully reflects the prevailing ideas of micro-economics and this is where planning practice diverges from orthodox economic theory. Planning has not evolved an alternative, conceptually rigorous method to describe, analyse and evaluate urban and rural problems and planning objectives, and to identify the interactions and conflicts between them. Planning practice is evolving pragmatic and conceptually limited procedures which aspire to help the community to make a conscious choice of planning strategy with reference to aims and objectives. It has yet to prove that such planning procedures are capable of determining whether one social state is or is not to be preferred to another.

Specification of plans — local plans

Whereas structure plans deal with policy and strategic issues, the local planning authority also has to deal with local issues within the framework of the ministerially approved structure plan in the form of local plans. These may be:

(1) *District plans*: if based on a comprehensive consideration of matters affecting the development and other use of the land;
(2) *Subject plans*: if based on consideration of a particular type or types of development and other use of land;
(3) *Action area plans*: covering areas selected for comprehensive treatment, dealing with major changes in small areas by development, redevelopment, and improvement.

Local plans must consist of a map and a written statement and must formulate in such detail as the authority thinks appropriate its proposals for the development or other land use of the area, ensuring that they conform generally to the structure plan. The subject content of local plans may be varied both in land-use scope and in precision. For example, a plan of a new housing area might show very detailed information about the design of local authority housing, but only an outline about private sector development, perhaps taking the form of a brief, covering use, density, materials, dwelling types and traffic circulation. Again for local plans, the Town and Country Planning (Structure and Local Plans) Regulations 1972 require the local planning authority to have regard to the resources likely to be available for carrying out the proposals formulated in the plan.

The most significant change between the 1947 development plan system and the 1968 structure plan system, lies in the distinction between strategic planning, which takes a form (structure plans) that has to be approved by the Minister, and tactical planning in the shape of local plans formulated and approved on a local level in the spirit of the structure (strategic) plan. It was intended that the post-1968 system should include ministerial control of the major policies and objectives of planning and their co-ordination nationally; while, on the other hand, local details of land-use – precisely those degrees of detail which proved so procedurally obstructive in the 1947–62 plans – were to be settled by local decision-making. A local plan for every action area must be prepared by the local planning authority as soon as is practicable after the approval of the structure plan by the Secretary of State. Local plans for other parts of the area covered by the structure plan may be prepared if and when the local planning authority considers this desirable, but there is no legal obligation to prepare any local plan, except for an action area, unless the Secretary of State specifically directs this to be done. If a local plan is prepared, it must be publicized and persons or agencies who wish to make representations given the right to do so. The local planning authority will have to hold a public local inquiry to consider objections made to a local plan, and submit the plan to the Secretary of State, who may direct that a local plan shall not be adopted by the local planning authority until he himself has approved it. The DoE is presently concerned that local planning authorities are tending to by-pass the approval process for local plans by drawing up informal plans, rather than facing the lengthy and costly process of inquiries. But whatever the form of the local plan, its purpose is to provide positive guidance both for developers and for planners engaged in day-to-day control of development.

Planning controls

No development by private persons, including industry and non-statutory organizations, may be carried out unless permission has been obtained from the local planning authority. Development includes the carrying out of building operations, engineering operations, or making any material change in the use of any building or land.

However, there are some types of development for which it is not necessary to apply for planning permission, either because permission is deemed to have been given under a general development order or because the operation in question does not legally constitute development within the meaning of the Town Planning Acts. Development by a government department does not need planning permission but it has been agreed that departments shall normally consult the local planning authority concerned so as to ensure, as far as possible, that no development runs contrary to the local planning policies. Of greater significance in the rural resource context, however, is the fact that the use of land for agriculture or forestry and the use of any existing buildings for that purpose does not constitute development for the purpose of the Acts (Town and Country Planning Act 1971, Section 22 (2) (e)), so no permission is required. Building or engineering operations carried out on agricultural land or land used for the purpose of forestry, and requisite for the use of that land for the purposes of agriculture and forestry are deemed to have planning permission under the General Development Order 1977 (SI 1977 No. 289), so that these activities can be pursued without the express consent of the planning authority. As far as agriculture is concerned, such development is permitted if carried out on land having an area of more than one acre; with the development of less than 465 square metres, less than 12 metres in height, and more than 25 metres from a classified road; with minor exceptions outlined in the Statutory Instrument, for example, near airports.

Many other small developments fall into the 'deemed planning permission', for example, small developments to dwelling houses, sewerage, drainage, and transport, so long as the specified conditions attached to the order are satisfied. In general, such items are relatively small in scale and the intention in declaring them 'permitted development' was to avoid clogging up the machinery of development control with minutiae. By the GDO dispensation, the farmer may undertake, on holdings greater than one acre, all the building and engineering operations likely to be carried out on a normal farm. However, dwelling houses, even if connected to a farm building, are not exempt, nor are buildings not specifically designed for agricultural purposes such as old railway wagons, carriages, or bus bodies. Similar considerations apply to development for the purposes of forestry.

The increasing intensification of agriculture has, however, resulted in more and more buildings specifically designed for agricultural purposes failing to meet GDO requirements and thus requiring planning permission. This situation has arisen because of the Department of the Environment's view that a building required for the use of livestock which do not depend at all upon that land for support, such as stables for horse breeding or an intensive pig or poultry unit, is not 'requisite for the use of the land' for such purposes. Thus, cases have been reported (*Country Landowner*, October 1974:47) of planning permission being refused for the development of three broiler houses on a farm since it was not proved that the broiler house was a building connected with farming operations other than those carried out in the building itself.

Another case reported in *Journal of Planning and Environmental Law* (1974) was of a pig unit which had been erected, with a 40 per cent grant from the Ministry of Agriculture, Fisheries and Food, on a 4.5 acre holding devoted to pig production. The pigs ran on the land during the summer months grazing on chicory sown in spring, but 99 per cent of the pig food was bought elsewhere and imported to the holding. It was upheld that, in the light of clear evidence, 99 per cent of the feeding stuff was bought in and in the absence of any other conclusive evidence that the building was requisite for the use of the land for agriculture, the owner failed to discharge the onus of proof that planning permission for the development was granted by the GDO. However, on general planning grounds the new building was not held to be detrimental to the rural scene and so planning permission was granted.

Nevertheless, apart from such elements of intensive agriculture, the general effect of the above provisions has been to allow the two primary rural industries a freedom from planning restrictions enjoyed by no other industrial activity. Elsewhere in the economy, except in the case of government departments, planning control may be exercised by assessing whether a proposed development conforms to the development plan and to any other material considerations. For example, planning control may be exercised over housing, industrial and commercial development where the latter results in a material change in appearance i.e. in the character of the street or skyline. This is not the case for development in rural areas associated with agriculture and forestry. As a result of this, two features in particular have excited comment. First, large scale farming methods requiring the use of substantial machinery have brought material changes in the appearance of the landscape by the uprooting of hedgerows. This is a matter entirely outside planning control, and although a gain in terms of efficiency to the farm, it is seen as an external diseconomy or amenity loss to society as a whole, and is openly regretted by voluntary amenity bodies. Second, there is often some criticism of the design of farm buildings since these have both grown in size, as in the case of large tower silos, and changed in type of construction from traditional brick or stone to concrete, metal sheeting, or asbestos. Such buildings are largely exempt from controls and are often erected with financial assistance from central government sources under agricultural support schemes.

Except for development associated with agriculture and forestry, planning controls operate in rural areas just as they do in urban areas. In considering whether to grant a planning application, the local planning authority must have regard to the development plan and to any other material considerations (Town and Country Planning Act 1971, Section 29). But the local authority can refuse permission for development, even if it is in accordance with the development plan, if there are material reasons for the refusal. Development control in rural areas is particularly likely to affect the siting and design of houses, coastal preservation and development near the coast, development near or of buildings of special architectural or historical interest, development near trunk roads and out of town shopping centres in the rural-urban fringe.

If planning permission is refused, or granted subject to conditions, the developer can appeal to the Secretary of State for the Environment against the decision. The Secretary of State may order an enquiry and either uphold the planning decision, vary its conditions, or dismiss it and allow the appeal. Moreover, if the planning decision involves the owner or occupier in loss through depreciation in the value of the land or buildings concerned, it may be possible for him to claim compensation. Compensation cannot be paid unless the refusal of permission or the imposing of conditions comes from the Secretary of State either on appeal or because the application has been called in. The types of development and land use to which compensation applies are set out in Part 2 of Schedule 8 to the Town and Country Planning Act 1971. The current rights to compensation in development and planning are summarized by authors such as Hamilton (1975). The amount of compensation payable is the difference between the actual value of the claimant's interest in the property, and the value it would have had if unconditional planning permission had been granted for the development. In addition, where his property has become unsaleable at a reasonable price because of a planning or highway proposal, the owner has the power to enforce its purchase by the appropriate authority with the help of a planning blight notice.

If development is carried out without the requisite planning permission, or if the conditions attached to permission are not observed, the local planning authority can serve an enforcement notice on the owner, the occupier, and any other person who appears to have an interest. This notice may require the demolition of a building erected without planning permission, the restoration of an altered building to its previous condition, and anything else necessary to restore the status quo. The local planning authority is not obliged to serve an enforcement notice: the law simply gives it the opportunity of doing so if it seems expedient with regard to the provisions of the development plan and to other material considerations. If a planning authority, having served an enforcement notice, wishes to bring building operations or other works to an immediate halt, without waiting until the enforcement notice takes effect, a stop notice can be served. Failure to comply with an enforcement or a stop notice is an offence and penalities are much the same in both cases: a fine of up to £400 on summary conviction, or an unlimited amount if convicted on indictment; and, after being convicted of non-compliance, failure to take all practical steps to comply with it can incur a further fine of £50 (or an unlimited amount if convicted on indictment) for each day on which the offence continues.

A local planning authority can, in the interests of proper planning and amenity, issue a removal order on any existing building or works specifying that they should be removed or altered. In deciding whether such an order is expedient, recourse must again be made to the development plan and any other material considerations. Orders may also be made, in similar circumstances, requiring the present use of any land to be discontinued or continued only subject to certain new conditions.

There are a number of controls other than those under the Town and Country Planning Acts which developers must take into consideration. These are: building regulations, developments near rivers and watercourses (Land Drainage Act 1961), smoke control (Clean Air Acts), development involving a building of architectural or historical interest (Ancient Monuments Acts), development

involving tree felling or planting (Forestry Acts), development near
pipelines and development affecting highways.

Special landscape areas

The Town and Country Planning (Landscape Areas Special
Development) Order 1950 named certain areas for the specific
purpose of restricting undesirable development. The regulations are
solely concerned with the restriction of agriculture and forestry
buildings normally exempt from planning permission. In these
areas, local planning authorities apply higher standards to all
proposed development than might be accepted elsewhere. These
regulations cover such areas as Keswick, Cockermouth, Ennerdale,
Millom, Penrith, Lakes, Windermere, North and South Westmorland, Bakewell, Chapel-en-le-Frith, Tintwhistle, North Lonsdale
and a small number of areas in Wales.

Conservation areas

Every local planning authority must, from time to time, determine
which parts of its area are areas of special architectural or
historical interest, the character or appearance of which it is
desirable to preserve or enhance, and designate them as conservation
areas (Town and Country Planning Act 1971, Section 277).
Conservation areas are special policy areas resulting from the Civic
Amenities Act 1967. Prior to this date, conservation policies were
designed to secure the protection of individual buildings. This policy
tended to overlook the setting or surroundings of the building and
the overall character of the village (i.e. externalities or neighbourhood effects). The 1967 Act was directed to securing the protection
of complete areas rather than buildings. Since 1967, more than 4000
areas have been designated as conservation areas in urban and rural
settlements.

Conservation areas have a number of general purposes. First, they
aim at safeguarding listed buildings of architectural or historical
interest and other buildings contributing to the character of the area,
both by statutory powers and by the use of grants or loans for
improvements to, or repair and maintenance of, important
buildings. Secondly, they aim for a closer control over new development by insisting on detailed designs or sketches before any decision

is given, with particular attention being given to material, colours, building lines and height. Thirdly, a more critical assessment of existing development is usually undertaken, including advertisements and 'permitted development'. Fourthly, greater attention is paid to details like street furniture, signs, poles, wires and lighting, which can all detract from the appearance of an area. Developers, whether private, local authority or statutory undertakers, are encouraged to give priority to minimizing clutter and unsightliness. Finally, local effort and initiative from individuals or local societies is encouraged. General references to conservation include Ward (1968), Worskett (1969) and *Built Environment* (January 1974), 3, No. 1, a special issue on conservation. Further documentation is provided by Reynolds (1975), on the aims and objectives of conservation, and by Chapman (1975) on financial problems.

   Most rural conservation areas cover the older core of a village, but as Woodruffe (1976) has pointed out, some have been drawn to include the whole of the village (Dorset County Council, 1970), while occasionally an area of open land may be included, particularly if it is an historic site or an integral feature of the settlement (East Lothian, 1974). Bloxsidge (1975, 1976) provides a list of conservation reports issued since 1970 by local planning authorities in England and Wales.

Green belts

The original London Green Belt was established by special Act of Parliament in 1938. Since then, the introduction of statutory development plans has made it unnecessary to have special Acts to establish green belts for other cities; this can be done under normal procedure. The method of maintaining green belts through the machinery of the Town and Country Planning Acts was laid down by a ministerial circular 42/55, in which the Minister asked local planning authorities to consider the establishment of green belts, several miles wide, wherever they were desirable in order to check the further growth of a large built-up area, to preserve the special character of a town or to prevent neighbouring towns from merging. Once a green belt had been designated by incorporating it in an amendment to the development plan, approval for the construction of new buildings, or for the change of use of existing buildings, was not to be given, except in very special circumstances, unless the buildings in question were required for agricultural purposes, sport, institutions standing in extensive grounds, cemeteries, or other purposes suitable to a rural area. Existing towns and villages within a green belt were not allowed to expand further, except for a strictly limited amount of infilling and rounding off. By 1970, green belt submissions covered 14,800 square kilometres, or about 9.7 per cent of the total land surface of England and Wales.

Protection of agricultural land

In dealing with applications for planning permission, a local planning authority is required to have regard to the provisions of the Development Plan, so far as material to the applications, and to any other material considerations (Town and Country Planning Act 1971 Section 29(1)). A material consideration in applications for planning permission is the safeguarding of all agricultural land.

In this respect, there have been many circulars published since 1950 giving advice to local planning authorities and these have formed the basis for dealing with applications affecting agricultural land. The most recent circulars, and the ones which are still operative, are 71/71, 24/73 and 75/76 and there is advice contained in Development Control Policy Note No. 4 – Development in Rural Areas. While all applications are dealt with on their individual merits, there is a general presumption against development of agricultural land, unless what is proposed is essential to the interests of agricultural or other rural activities. Government policy for the protection of agricultural land is to ensure that, as far as possible, land of a higher agricultural quality is not taken for development where land of a lower quality is available, and that the amount of land taken is no greater than is reasonably required for carrying out the development in accordance with standards. Thus, agricultural land is safe-guarded through the development plan, in siting areas of new development, as well as through development control. Planning authorities rely on the Ministry of Agriculture, Fisheries and Food's assessment of land quality, which classifies land by grade according to its physical characteristics in relation to food production.

However, the decision to develop one area for urban growth in preference to another cannot be based solely, as the planning system implies, on the relative quality of the agricultural land in the two areas. To state that this should be the determinant and criterion by which planning decisions are made, is to fall into a simple economic trap, since urban development imposes a capital cost upon society which may be lower if good quality land is utilized. Good land, perhaps because of its superiority in drainage or topography, may introduce a cost saving element because it is considerably cheaper to build upon since fewer and less elaborate site works are required. Moreover, the good land may be nearer to existing physical infrastructure of roads, electricity, water, sewerage and would thus require less infrastructure provision when developed. The relevant criterion, given effective demand for development, is the comparison between the discounted annual difference in the social revenue from agriculture between good and poor land, compared to the (any) extra capital cost of diverting development from good to poor land. If the discounted annual value of the difference in agricultural production is greater than the cost of diverting development, then the good agricultural land should be safeguarded and development diverted. However, if the discounted annual value of the difference in agricultural production between good and poor land is less than the cost of diverting development, then the urban development should be allowed on grounds of economic efficiency. Thus, land classification schemes based on agricultural considerations alone are less useful as a criterion and means of site choice than they might otherwise appear to be.

Minerals

Because of the national need for minerals, planning authorities have been strongly advised by DoE that a fundamental concern of planning policy must be to ensure a free flow of mineral products at economic cost. However, planning authorities try to balance economic and amenity aspects of mineral working. Thus, it is a general policy to ensure that mineral working is carried on with proper regard for the appearance and other amenities of the area, and that when the working is finished the land should, wherever practicable, not be left derelict, but restored or brought back to some beneficial use. Where mineral workings would, according to the planning authority, involve too great an injury to the comfort and living conditions of the people in the area or to the amenities generally, mineral working can be limited or even prevented. The major external diseconomies of mineral working are dust (e.g. from limestone quarries where crushing takes place), noise (e.g. from machinery which may work throughout the night), vibration (e.g. from blasting) and an increase in road traffic (e.g. heavy lorries transporting the mineral from the site). In striking a balance between the economic demand for minerals and the interests of amenity, consideration will be given to whether economic demand can be satisfactorily met from other sources with less damage to amenity. Planning authorities are also concerned with the equally important matter of ensuring that mineral deposits are not unnecessarily sterilized by surface development, but are kept available for future exploitation.

Mineral undertakers have long-standing powers to obtain rights over land containing mineral deposits. These were extended by regulations made under the Town and Country Planning Act 1947. With the range of rights available, mineral workings cannot, without good cause, be prevented by private land-owners. Mining operations are classified as development, so all mineral workings, ancillary buildings, depositing of waste and the construction of means of access to sites, require planning permission. The long term planning that is required for mineral exploitation means that planning permissions have generally been given for a working with a long life, commonly not less than fifteen years and, on occasion, up to sixty years. Before reaching a decision on a mineral application in rural areas, the planning authority may consult any interested parties such as the Ministry of Agriculture, the Forestry Commission, the River Authority, the Countryside Commission, Nature Conservancy and the Inspector of Ancient Monuments as appropriate. The views of these bodies may lead to conditions being imposed on the granting of the application. Conditions may specify, for example, a phased programme of work (i.e. so much extraction per year, landscaping of the site, screening of the site from a road or houses with baffle banks of topsoil taken off) and a planned programme of restoration (i.e. where practicable a developer can be required to return the land to a condition comparable to that in which he found it).

In 1972, the Stevens Committee was appointed to examine the operation of the statutory provisions (except the provisions of the Opencast Coal Act 1958) under which planning control is exercisable over mineral exploitation, working, waste disposal and reclamation. The Report on Planning Control over Mineral Workings (1976) contains a comprehensive statement on the effectiveness of existing legislation, with recommendations in regard to the use of this, and it proposes supplemental legislation. The proposals include a series of devices to prevent mineral dereliction to give consents more validity and permanency and to enable review to ensure proper restoration. Changes envisaged include, for example, new enforcement rights. In addition to the present procedures of 'enforcement notice' and 'stop notice', a 'contravention notice' is proposed which would prevent operators profiting from an un-authorized operation and deter them from using the legal process to prolong the period of profit making. For less serious matters, a 'compliance order' is suggested which would enable speedy action to determine whether a breach has occurred and to stop it. Stiffer maximum penalties are called for, severe enough to deter operators both from persistently breaching planning control and embarking on a course of profitable breach of conditions.

Planning control over the operations of the National Coal Board is subject to special provisions. The continued working of mines begun before 1 July 1948 is permitted development and, therefore, does not require specific planning approval. Any development carried out in the immediate vicinity of a pithead in connection with the coal industry constitutes permitted development under the GDO. However, certain restrictions can be imposed on the erection of buildings in the interests of amenity. Mining operations on new sites require planning permission in the ordinary way. Rural areas, however, are mainly affected by open cast mining, rather than deep mining, since urban settlements have tended to develop around the latter. Open cast mining by its very nature has a greater visual impact on the landscape than that of deep mining. The NCBs (1974) *Plan for Coal* envisaged output from open cast sites expanding from 10 million tons to 15 million tons per year in order to fill the gap between domestic supply and effective demand, which developed as a consequence of the rise in the price of oil. Open cast mines can be developed more quickly than deep mines and the NCB finds them particularly useful for coping with temporary or unforseen changes in demand. Although open cast mining constitutes only about 10 per cent of coal production, its impact is substantial in some rural areas, as in West Durham and the Northumberland coast, where open cast mining is being extended. Open cast mining often provokes opposition from local inhabitants and particularly from amenity societies.

The Opencast Coal Act 1958 laid down the procedure operated by the Secretary of State for Energy. The NCB must serve notices of its intention to work a particular site on the local authorities concerned and, if they raise objections, a public local inquiry must be held. The arguments for and against mining a particular site can best be appreciated by reading the inspector's report of an inquiry, for example, the inquiry into the Butterwell site near Morpeth (File No. CO/11/0180 and CO/12/091) in March 1975. The NCB case for mining at Butterwell was an economic one. Butterwell was a large site (about five times the average size) and would economize on capital expenditure, excavating machinery and coal disposal area. It also had easy access to the railway network and enought output to economically justify rail collection. The NCB, on the basis of a discounted cash flow model, expected to earn considerably more (on the capital employed) than the Test Discount Rate set by the Treasury for projects in nationalized industries. The demand for steam coal already existed at Blyth Power Station, which was being temporarily met by coking coal from Durham. The demand for coking coal was due to expand upon the opening of the new Redcar Iron and Steel Works. Objectors to the Butterwell project were concerned with the disamenities which would be created during the operation of the site. The inspector, a surveyor and planner, concluded that:

> the introduction of a very large quarry into the rural area with its attendant activities such as extra vehicular traffic, blasting and the operation of earth moving equipment, can have only a very disturbing effect on the residents of the area

and would

> be entirely foreign to the existing rural landscape and have an adverse effect on the appearance and character of the rural area

but felt that

> a decision on the desirability or otherwise of the opencast working of Butterwell must be dependent upon economic factors outside my knowledge and I do not, therefore, propose to make any recommendation.

The final decision in open cast mining cases rests with the Secretary of State for Energy who can direct that planning permission for the operations concerned be deemed to be granted. In this case, authorization was granted for Butterwell in December 1975. Authorization may include conditions of the sort commonly applied to planning permissions and must include conditions to secure the restoration of the site. Where the land is in agricultural use, it is usually returned to that use after restoration. The NCB has a good history of restoration and indeed there can be a resultant improvement in amenity.

5 The preservation and use of the countryside

The law relating to development and its control applies to rural areas as it does to towns. However, in view of what many regard as the particular need for preserving the natural beauty of the countryside, and for enabling the public to derive enjoyment and recreation from the externalities (see Chapter 2) associated with many resource stock and service flows in rural areas, additional legislation has been made to reinforce the general requirements of the Town and Country Planning Acts.

The Countryside Commission

The National Parks and Access to the Countryside Act 1949, set up the National Parks Commission. The latter was given a new title, the Countryside Commission, and a wider range of activities by the Countryside Act 1968. It now has powers and duties of:

(1) designation of appropriate tracts of countryside in England and Wales as National Parks;
(2) designation of appropriate tracts, other than National Parks, as areas of outstanding natural beauty (AONB);
(3) establishment of long-distance routes for the use of walkers and horseback riders;

(4) advising public agencies (e.g. local authorities), reviewing all matters relating to the enjoyment and conservation of the countryside, and promoting or encouraging the implementation of suitable proposals in this connection;

(5) publicizing the proper use of the countryside for purposes of recreation.

National parks

The Countryside Commission has so far designated ten national parks: the Brecon Beacons, Dartmoor, Exmoor, the Lake District, the North Yorkshire Moors, Northumberland, the Peak District, the Pembrokeshire Coast, Snowdonia, and the Yorkshire Dales. However, it may, in the future, designate other areas if it sees fit. In fact, an eleventh, the Cambrian Mountains National Park was designated in 1972, but the Secretary of State for Wales (1973) decided not to confirm the order because of the strong and widespread opposition to it. The ten national parks cover 13,620 square kilometres, or 9 per cent of the total area of England and Wales.

Land in national parks is not nationally owned, nor are they parks in the commonly accepted sense. Basically, they are areas where the cultural landscape is of prime value, showing a subtle blend of man made and natural features. The Dower Report (Ministry of Town and Country Planning, 1945) defined a national park as:

an extensive area of beautiful and relatively wild country, in which, for the nation's benefit and by appropriate national decision and action

(i) the characteristic landscape beauty is strictly preserved;

(ii) access and facilities for public open-air enjoyment are amply provided;

(iii) wild life and buildings and places of architectural and historic interest are suitably protected; and

(iv) established farming is effectively maintained.

However, national parks were not envisaged as rural museums but as areas where 'a progressive policy of management, designed to develop the latent resources of the national parks for open air recreation' would be embarked upon. It is now a statutory duty of the Countryside Commission to consider ways in which action is necessary to preserve and enhance the natural beauty of the national parks, and to make recommendations to the Secretary of State and the planning authorities. Consultations between the Countryside Commission and local authorities are a statutory obligation.

To give effect to proposals agreed between the Commission and the local planning authorities, the latter must exercise powers available to them under the Town and Country Planning Acts as well as under the National Parks Act and the Countryside Act. To answer the consideration of national park matters in isolation from planning matters affecting the rest of a county in which a park might be situated, the local planning authority is required to appoint a special committee for the park. In cases of parks lying in areas of more than one authority a joint board might be instituted, but in the event only two joint planning authorities have been set up: the Lake District Planning Board and the Peak District Planning Board. Apart from the provisions for consulting, or receiving recommendations from the Countryside Commission, the planning control procedure within a national park is the same as elsewhere. The fact that planning applications will be dealt with by a special joint board, committee, or sub-committee set up to administer the planning of the park, will ensure that special consideration will be given to any application which seems to threaten the amenities of the park. A local planning authority may arrange for the provision of camping sites, caravan sites, parking places, cafes and restaurants, hostels, chalets and other accommodation, subject to the limitations that arrangements to provide accommodation, meals or refreshments may not be made unless existing facilities are inadequate or unsatisfactory. The local planning authority may also undertake the provision of public sanitary conveniences, receptacles for refuse and litter, with attendant servicing.

Local planning authorities may also make by-laws and appoint wardens to ensure the observance of any by-laws for national parks, and may restrict certain types of traffic on roads within national parks. The Lake District Special Planning Board, for example, have proposed by-laws to restrict the navigation of power-driven vessels on Ullswater, Coniston and Derwent Water to a speed of ten miles per hour, with certain exceptions for vessels carrying out safety or statutory functions. If confirmed by the Home Secretary, one particular effect of these by-laws would be to terminate water skiing which is presently carried out on all three lakes. The Countryside Commission (1977) strongly supported the Lakes Planning Board over the supposed incompatibility of fast motorboating with the objectives of national park designation.

A problem which has concerned the National Parks Commission and its successor, the Countryside Commission, is that of development by government departments and statutory undertakings. The number of alien intrusions is a formidable one: Fylingdales Moor Defence Early Warning Station on the North Yorkshire Moors; masts for the GPO, for air transport in communications, navigation, defence, police and other services; the nuclear power station in Snowdonia; two oil refineries astride the eastern boundary of the Pembrokeshire Coast Park; and increasing demands from water undertakings in almost every national park. Effort has been expended to make 'inevitable' developments as inoffensive as possible.

Some national park committees (for example, the Pembrokeshire Coast Park Planning Committee) have pointed to the conflict between extending the use of beautiful pieces of countryside and the danger that if this opportunity is offered too widely, the result will be the destruction of the beautiful tract. The Lake District Planning Board has warned that tourism in the Lake District is, by its sheer weight of numbers, killing what it seeks to enjoy. The response to this problem created by open access to a resource, has been the adoption of standards and additional development, rather than pricing, as remedial policy instruments. Thus, for example, the Goyt Valley Traffic Experiment, set up jointly by the Peak Park Planning Board and the Countryside Commission, involved the closure of three roads through the Goyt Valley on Saturdays, Sundays and bank holidays May to September 1970 and 1971; the provision of four car parks at the valley approaches, two picnic areas, footpaths, and a nature trail; the provision of a free minibus service linking the valley with the car parks; and the provision of wardens to control traffic. Members of the sailing and fishing clubs were given 'exempted vehicle' status (Miles, 1972). The standards approach creates problems of economic efficiency. Before the restrictions were put into effect, 21 per cent of motorists had driven through the valley, without stopping, as part of a longer recreation drive. Moreover, fluctuations in visitor patterns due to the weather made it difficult to match the demand for transport with the available minibuses. Charges for the car parks only covered 35 per cent of the operating costs of the whole scheme.

With the issue of conflict very much in mind, the National Park Policies Review Committee was set up in 1971 'To review how far national parks have fulfilled the purpose for which they were established, to consider the implications of the changes that have occurred, and may be expected, in social and economic conditions and to make recommendations as regards future policies'. The resultant Sandford Report was published in April 1974 and saw the over-riding priority as one of conservation to maintain the beauty and ecological qualities of national parks, with the adoption of environmental quality as the primary criterion in all matters, including roads and traffic management and the provision and management of tourist facilities. Among other recommendations the report argued against development out of accord with national park purposes and, that in the most beautiful parts, development should only be permitted in the case of the most compelling national necessity. The systematic provision of alternative attractions around the main centres of population, and particularly between them and the national parks, was also advocated. The Government accepted many of the Committee's main recommendations and immediate policy is likely to follow the conclusions reached by the Secretaries of State on the Committee's findings. It accepts the Committee's conclusion that the twin purposes of preserving and enhancing the natural beauty of national parks, and of promoting their enjoyment by the public, may now be in conflict in some areas, and where this happens priority must be given to the conservation of natural beauty (DoE Circular 4/76). The Secretaries of State for the Environment and Wales agreed too that the scope of the Landscape Areas Special Development Order, which requires the agreement of the planning authority to be obtained to the design and external appearance of agricultural buildings which are within the GDO limits, should be extended to siting as well as design and materials, and that the Order should be applied to the whole of every national park. They also accept the recommendation that, in selected cases, farmers should be helped in meeting the extra costs incurred as a result of meeting the stringent design standards appropriate in the national parks. Compensation is already provided where a planning application must be submitted in respect of an agricultural or forestry building which would otherwise satisfy GDO requirements. Legislation is envisaged which will allow compensation payments to be made by national park authorities as discretionary grants and included in their annual estimates. The Sandford Committee pointed to the widespread view that national park purposes were in danger of being damaged, or had been damaged in some areas, by tree planting with minimal attention to landscape considerations. They recommended that in national parks, forestry be brought within the formal process of planning control, but the Government declined to act on this recommendation. It is now government policy that investment in trunk roads should be directed to developing routes for long distance traffic to avoid national parks, and that no new route for long distance traffic should be constructed through a national park, or existing road upgraded, unless the need is compelling and cannot be met by any reasonable alternative means. The Secretaries of State endorsed the recommendation that, in national parks, environmental quality should be the primary criterion in the planning of road systems, but they did not propose to act on the Committee's recommendation that road improvements in national parks which would alter the width or alignment of the highway, should be excluded from planning permission granted by the GDO. With increasing demand from road transport in the future, the question of roads in national parks is likely to reoccur.

Other more general conflicts in national parks concern services such as electricity or telephones for people living in national parks. It is unreasonable to expect that residents should shoulder all financial burdens involved as, for example, in placing electricity or telephone cables underground, or in using expensive building materials for the sake of a pleasant appearance. Such public goods should be paid for by all who enjoy them. For this reason, if national parks are provided for the nation, it has always been argued that their costs should be met from national funds. By convention, the government to rate-borne expenditure is a 3:1 ratio in national parks, i.e. the National Park Supplementary Grant is approximately 75 per cent of approved expenditure. The grant amounted to £1.9 million in 1974–5 and £2.7 million in 1975–6. Of course, other subsidies accrue to national parks through the operation of cross-subsidization by nationalized industries, for example: electricity, telephones, gas, etc. (costs for rural settlements in these cases are given in Chapter 11) and through the provision of other local government services, such as education and highways (costs of which are also given, for selected rural areas as examples, in Chapter 11).

Areas of outstanding natural beauty

Both the Dower and Hobhouse Report (MTCP, 1947) proposed that, in addition to national parks, certain areas of outstanding natural beauty should be subject to special protection. These were areas in which it was thought that the 'positive management' which, it was assumed, would characterize national parks, was not required, but that their contribution to the wider enjoyment of the countryside was so important, that special measures should be taken to preserve their natural beauty and interest.

Thirty three AONBs had been declared by 30 September 1976, covering 14,478 square kilometres (Countryside Commission, 1977), including such areas as Gower (189 square kilometres), the Quantock Hills (99 square kilometres), the Northumberland Coast from Warkworth to Berwick (129 square kilometres), the Shropshire Hills (777 square kilometres), the Malvern Hills (104 square kilometres), the Chilterns (800 square kilometres), the Cotswolds (1507 square kilometres), the Wye Valley (325 square kilometres), the Lincolnshire Wolds (560 square kilometres), the Sussex Downs (981 square kilometres), and the Scilly Isles (16 square kilometres). Generally AONB are smaller than national parks, and they are the responsibility of local planning authorities who have powers similar to those of park planning authorities. Exchequer grant aid for improvement schemes is provided on the same basis as for national parks, but local planning authorities have often been reluctant to make use of their powers. The annual reports of the National Parks Commission and Countryside Commission include examples of improvement schemes, but the Countryside Commission recognize that progress has been slow.

Long distance footpaths

Some progress has been made with long distance routes. By 30 September 1976, these hikers' highway routes were complete on the Pennine and Cleveland Ways, the Pembrokeshire Coast Path, Offa's Dyke, the South and North Downs Ways, the Ridgeway Path and the South-West Peninsular Coast Path in North and South Cornwall, South Devon, Somerset and North Devon and Dorset. These long distance footpaths extend in total to 2413 kilometres. Proposed new routes include Dartmoor Way, Wolds Way (North Yorkshire and Humberside), Peddars Way and Norfolk Coast Path and the Cambrian Way. Proposals for routes show the route with the existing rights of way, and may contain proposals for the improvement of paths, provision of accommodation, meals and refreshments. Although eligible for Exchequer grants, the implementation of approved proposals rests with district councils. The uncertain legal status of existing footpaths and occasional slow progress with the creation of new rights of way, have often held back the completion of approved long distance routes.

Access to open country

Under the National Parks and Access to the Countryside Act 1949, local planning authorities were given power to arrange, by agreement with landowners and occupiers or by the making of orders, that the public should have access to stretches of open country. For this purpose, the term 'open country' means any area which appears to the local planning authority to consist wholly or predominantly of mountain, moor, heath, down, cliff or foreshore, woodlands, and river or canal, other than those operated as commercial or cruising waterways by the British Waterways Board.

If approved by the Secretary of State, a local planning authority may make arrangements as to public access with the owners and occupiers of any land which is open country within the meaning of the Act. These arrangements may include provision for the local planning authority to make payments, in consideration of the making of the agreements and as a contribution towards any expenditure incurred in consequence of the agreements. If an agreement cannot be made, the local planning authority may, subject to the Secretary of State's confirmation, make an Access Order. Before making any kind of agreement or order which affects a national park or AONB, the local planning authority must consult the Countryside Commission. The public has a right of access for purposes of open air recreation to any land or waterway covered by an access agreement or Access Order. This right is subject to certain duties that persons entering upon the land do not break or damage walls, fences, gates, hedges, light fires, kill or molest wildlife or damage plants, shrubs and trees etc. Persons having an interest in any land or waterway covered by an access agreement or order must not do anything which reduces substantially the area to which the public have access, except in certain circumstances.

If the value of a person's interest in any land is depreciated in consequence of an Access Order, compensation will be payable by the local authority. Claims for compensation must be made within six months of the order, but to allow the effect of the order to be judged, compensation will not normally be calculated and paid until five years later, when interest at a rate prescribed by the Secretary of State will be added in respect of the five years.

Little information is available on the operation of the provisions under access agreements and orders; indeed, it was not until 1960 that all counties completed their surveys of rights of way and mapped them in their respective areas, which they were statutorily obliged to do under the 1949 Act and which were supposed to be completed by 1952. Many councils decided that no action was needed under the 1949 Act to secure increased facilities for access. The Countryside Commission's annual reports usually provide a table of access agreements concluded during the year, and an up-to-date account is provided by Gibbs and Whitby (1975) and referred to in Chapter 7.

Country parks

The Countryside Act 1968 permits country parks to be provided by local authorities so that the public, especially those living in urban areas, can enjoy open-air recreation in country surroundings. When establishing country parks, local authorities are expected to take into account their location in relation to urban or built-up areas, and the adequacy of existing facilities for the enjoyment of the countryside by the public. Country parks were envisaged by the 1966 White Paper, *Leisure in the Countryside*, as allowing town dwellers to enjoy open-air leisure without travelling too far, easing pressure on the more remote and solitary places, and reducing the risk of damage to the countryside from people simply settling down for an hour or two where it suits them. Country parks are not normally less than twenty-five acres in extent, readily accessible for motor vehicles and pedestrians, providing an adequate range of facilities, and operated as a single unit and managed by a private or statutory body. Up to September 1976, 132 country parks had been approved for grant aid, including twenty-two managed by private owners. During the financial year 1975–6, the Countryside Commission contributed about £525,000 in grants for country parks.

Picnic areas

The Countryside Act 1968 also provides new powers for local authorities in relation to picnic sites. Picnic sites are something better than lay-bys where families can stop for a few hours to picnic, sit and enjoy the view and fresh air, and perhaps explore footpaths. Local authorities are empowered to provide and manage picnic sites. By September 1976, 165 picnic sites had been approved by the Countryside Commission and grants for the year 1975–6 amounted to £176,000.

The coastline

A considerable part of the coastline of England and Wales is protected in some way. National parks and areas of outstanding natural beauty cover some 30 per cent of the coastline and, additionally, development plans indicate areas of high landscape value, nature reserves and sites of special scientific interest. Then there are coastal areas owned or protected by the National Trust. Demand for recreation areas for holidays and retirement on certain sections of coastline is growing, and there is demand, too, for industrial development in certain areas such as Milford Haven and Southampton Water. These are problems which must be resolved. One administrative answer was an argument for stringent protection of the finest coastal scenery. Heritage coasts were initiated in 1973 and the number of defined heritage coasts now (September 1976) stand at thirty-three, representing a total length of 1059 kilometres. These include North Northumberland (93 kilometres), Gower (55 kilometres), North Anglesey (29 kilometres), Great Orme (6 kilometres), Mevagissey/Amsterdam Point (22 kilometres) (Countryside Commission, 1977). Discussions are in progress with local authorities on a further nine heritage coasts, amounting to a further 199 kilometres of undeveloped coast. Each heritage coast has a conservation officer working within the county planning department. The work of the heritage coast officer is mainly the development of solutions for landscape conservation problems with the co-operation of landowners and farmers, and the organizing of improvement schemes.

Nature reserves

The Nature Conservancy was created by Royal Charter in 1949 to provide scientific advice on the conservation and control of the natural flora and fauna of Great Britain; to establish, maintain and manage nature reserves and to organize and develop the research and scientific services needed for these purposes. Nature reserves are areas of land managed for the purpose of preserving flora, fauna, and scientific services needed for these purposes. Nature reserves are areas of land managed for the purpose of preserving flora, fauna, ties for the study of, and research into, matters relating to the fauna and flora of Great Britain and the physical conditions in which they live. The functions as regards the creation of nature reserves are regulated by the National Parks and Access to the Countryside Act. The Conservancy has powers to acquire land or to enter into agreements with owners in order that nature reserves may be established. In agreement cases, the owner remains in full possession and has responsibility for management, but agrees to manage in accordance with the advice of the Conservancy, so as to preserve the scientific interest of the particular area. Agreements may provide for defrayment of costs and for compensation. Local planning authorities can also, in consultation with the Conservancy, set up Local Nature Reserves. The Nature Conservancy Council, or the local authority, as the case may be, may make by-laws for the protection of any reserve established by them. These by-laws may, among other matters, prohibit or restrict the movement by persons, vehicles, boats or animals within all or part of the reserve. The declaration of a reserve does not of itself, therefore, confer any public right of access whatsoever. Furthermore, the powers to make access agreements or orders are not applicable to reserves. However, as much access is allowed as is compatible with proper scientific management, and about half the land in national nature reserves is generally open to the public without any restriction, the remainder being subject to permits.

Areas of special scientific interest

Land which is not part of a nature reserve may be the subject of an agreement between the owners and occupiers and the Nature Conservancy Council, with the object of making it an area of special scientific interest. This applies to areas which are of special interest because of their flora, fauna, geological or physiographical features. The agreement may provide for the carrying out of any work considered necessary, payment of some or all of the costs involved and the imposition of restrictions. Opposition to the proposal in 1965 to build the Cow Green Reservoir in Upper Teesdale, centred on the fact that, although the site did not fall within a nature reserve, in 1950 Widdybank Fell, abutting Cow Green, had been notified to the Durham and Westmorland County Councils by the Nature Conservancy as a Site of Special Scientific Interest, a status it shared with a further 50,000 acres of Upper Teesdale. The importance of Widdybank Fell was well understood, though how far the rare flora on the fell impinged upon Cow Green was by no means clear and even botanists were in disagreement. (We return to the question of Cow Green Reservoir in Chapter 13.)

Caravan and camping sites

Caravan sites are subject to special provisions contained in the Caravan Sites and Control of Development Act 1960, and the Caravan Sites Act 1968. The authorities were concerned to avoid any extension of the rash of caravans which had sprung up in certain coastal areas before the 1939–45 war. The administrative reaction to the demand for caravan sites was to grant planning permission for short time limits. However, this could inhibit the good site operator from making long-term investment in his site and thus prevent the attainment of higher standards. The two 1960 Acts, reinforced by the 1968 Act, set up a dual procedure whereby a site would require, in addition to planning permission, a site licence from the public health authority. The objectives of this new form of control were to establish high and detailed standards of layout on a longer-term basis than hitherto in order to encourage a higher level of investment, and thus better provision of services and equipment, and greater security for caravanners. Planning authorities tended to allow concentration of investment in areas long lost to caravans – for example, the coast-line between Rhyl and Colwyn Bay – while keeping other areas as free of caravans as possible. In attractive rural areas, demand for caravan sites is easily understandable, and is often seen by farmers as a valuable supplementary income source to farming, where annual site rentals could handsomely exceed the freehold agricultural value of any unit area of land. Local authorities, including county councils and the planning boards of national parks, may provide sites for caravans, with attendent services and facilities. Camping sites for holiday and recreational purposes may also be provided.

Planning applications for holiday caravan sites are subject to high refusal rates. For example, in 1973, of 1770 planning applications for holiday caravan sites, 902 (51 per cent) were refused, 576 (33 per cent) granted for a limited period only, and 292 (16 per cent) granted without time limit, (DoE, 1974).

Part II

6 Land use
and conversion

The main focus of this chapter is the way in which land is transferred
from one use to another. We begin with a brief statement on the
current allocation of land amongst uses and the pattern of ownership. Questions of taxation and its effect upon land values are then
discussed and the processes of land transfer from agriculture to
urban use and from agriculture to forestry are considered in turn.
Finally, the issues arising from the recent Community Land Act and
the Development Land Tax Act are outlined.

Use and ownership

The pattern of land use in Britain is dominated by agriculture which,
according to Edwards (1974) accounts for more than four-fifths of
our land surface. Urban uses cover 8 per cent, and 7.5 per cent is
under forest. The land within agriculture is of variable productive
quality and the uses to which it is put are similarly diverse. Table 6.1
shows the distribution of land uses in the United Kingdom.

Another approach to land use is to assess its *potential* productivity
as opposed to its actual use. To this end, a system of classification
has been developed by the Ministry of Agriculture (1966). The broad
results of this physical classification are shown in Table 6.2.

Table 6.1   Distribution of agricultural land uses, UK 1976

	Thousand hectares	Per cent of total
Total tillage-crops and fallow	4,821	25.40
Temporary grasses and lucerne	2,153	11.30
Total arable land	**6,975**	**36.70**
Permanent grass (five years and older)	5,081	26.80
Total crops and grass	**12,055**	**63.50**
Rough grazings — sole rights	5,386	28.40
— commons	1,126	5.93
Total crops grass and rough grazings	**18,567**	**97.80**
Woodland and other land on holdings	419	2.20
Total agricultural area	**18,986**	**100.00**

Source: Ministry of Agriculture, Fisheries and Food (1976).

The general dominance of the medium to poor grades of land emerges clearly from the table. This dominance is particularly apparent in Scotland with its high proportion of rough hill grazings. The minute proportion of Grade 1 land raises questions as to the usefulness of the classification. Would more categories be useful? How should they be defined? — and so on.

The distribution of ownership of land is also important and features largely in debates regarding changes in the taxation system.

Table 6.2   Estimated distribution of agricultural land by grades, 1976

Grade	England and Wales	Scotland	Northern Ireland	UK
1	2.9	0.3	—	1.8
2	14.6	2.4	3.3	9.8
3	48.7	13.6	42.0	36.4
4	19.8	10.2	49.0	18.2
5	14.0	73.5	5.7	33.7
	100.0	100.0	100.0	100.0

Source: Economic Development Committee for Agriculture (1977).
Note: Due to rounding errors, percentages may not add up to 100 per cent.

The long term trend in the UK as a whole, has been for owner-occupation to increase as the traditional landlord-tenant system has declined. Important milestones in the history of land occupation in the UK were the introduction of estate duties, and the series of Agricultural Holding Acts at the end of the nineteenth century, which undermined the dominance of landlords. Comparable data are not easily available, but the gradual erosion of the landlord-tenant system can be seen in Table 6.3:

Table 6.3   Distribution of agricultural holdings by type of occupation, Great Britain 1891 and 1974

	Rented	Owned	Part owned Part rented	Total
1891 no. (thousands)	481.0	75.5	22.0	578.5
per cent of total	83.1	13.1	3.8	100.0
1974 no. (thousands)	97.3	146.1	–*	243.4
per cent of total	40.0	60.0	–	100.0

Source: Ministry of Agriculture, Fisheries and Food (1968) and (1975a).
* The omission is due to a change of presentation in recent censuses.

However, the above table includes land which is owned outright or which is rented on a secure agreement that usually runs for several years. There are other important categories of land occupation which complicate the picture. For example, a proportion of land is let in unsecured tenancies. The best known example of this is the system known as *connacre* in Northern Ireland. But similar short-term letting arrangements are to be found in the north of England, where grass-parks may be rented and in Scotland, where both arable and grassland may be let on such terms. The interest of such arrangements is that the short-term rents obtainable are often very high. The amounts paid in rent would be expected to approach the full marginal value product of the land to the tenant who pays it but, in particular seasons, it is likely that the rents offered may be influenced by the tenant's cash flow position. Thus bumper harvests are likely to be followed by highly competitive bidding for short lets which may even exceed any reasonable expectation of marginal value product.

Another complication which has recently been pointed out by Rose *et al.* (1977) arises from the existence of trusts. According to these authors, many farmers who are revealed as tenants by the agricultural census are in fact owner-occupiers. That is they farm land which is owned by family trusts and for which they pay rent to the trust. This land is therefore quite correctly recorded as rented in the agricultural census though, in the majority of cases, the trust arrangement is a tax avoidance device which has little or no impact on the farming system. Trusts are more prevalent amongst larger farms hence, in terms of total acreage, the degree of misrepresentation by official statistics is likely to be particularly severe.

Apart from the allocation of land between landlord and tenant, official statistics tell us little about the actual pattern of ownership of land. For this information we must turn to surveys by Gibbs and Harrison (1977). These authors have collated information from a wide range of sources and compiled an interesting picture of the importance of different agencies. Their findings for 1976 are summarized in Table 6.4:

Table 6.4   Landholding by public (and semi-public) bodies, 1976

	Thousand hectares
The Monarchy	181.0
Government departments	1,378.8
Nationalized industries and public services	375.8
Local authorities	251.5
Educational establishments	133.9
Conservation authorities	115.7
Church land	69.5
Financial institutions	78.9
	2,585.1

These estimates relate to farm and forest land of all kinds – they include the small amount of land held in leasehold as well as freehold. Less than half the total is agricultural. Because the estimates relate to ownership, they will understate the total area controlled by public and semi-public bodies because of the possibility of such agencies becoming tenants of private landowners. They also conceal a great deal of complexity which arises where only some of the property rights attached to land are transferred to other uses. For example, it is quite possible to have several different tenants on a piece of land each renting a different attribute such as cultivation rights, shooting rights and fishing rights. The position may be further complicated by legal devices such as access agreements (see Chapters 4 and 7), and ancient rights of way in the form of footpaths and bridleways may also affect productivity in its primary use.

Finally, the statistics on owned and rented land do not include common land. The relevant area was noted in Table 6.1, where it can be seen that an estimated one-sixth of rough grazings in the UK are grazed in common. Common land is an ancient form of definition of property rights. Most of the traditional common lands have been swept away by enclosure over the centuries. The remaining agricultural commons are found in hill areas where the potential rewards from enclosure, in terms of enhanced agricultural productivity, are trivial in relation to the major transactions cost of bringing it about.

Taxation and prices

For more than a century, questions of land values and taxation have been the subject of occasional political controversy. Estate Duty, payable on the death of an owner, was first levied on land in 1894. This tax has been one important factor in reducing the number of rented farms. Where an estate was inherited and the new owner survived for only a short term, the burdens of taxation on the estate might well be sufficient to break it up. However, landowners have always been well represented in Parliament and a number of tax concessions, designed to help them, have been made. An exhaustive list of these is beyond the scope of this text but the following are notable:

Estate Duty: Since 1949, the duty on agricultural land has been abated by 45 per cent. Because the tax is progressive, the effect of this concession in terms of the industry's aggregate tax liability cannot be assessed.

Rate Relief: Under the Local Government Act of 1929, agricultural land and buildings (other than the farmhouse) have been freed from rates. With the growing importance of 'factory farming' methods in the 1960s, some buildings were rated. Recently the Layfield Committee (1976) has recommended that this rate relief should be removed. The Committee estimate that this would produce annual revenue in excess of £100 million for England and Wales alone. The Government has decided not to implement this recommendation.

Capital Gains Tax: CGT was introduced in 1965, although it was applied at a lower rate on agricultural gains than on others (30 per cent against 40 per cent – 42 per cent for limited liability companies). An abatement of this tax has been possible under the so-called 'roll-over' provision, where the proceeds of the sale were re-invested in agricultural land. In fact, this provision, which had obvious inflationary implications for land values, was withdrawn in December 1973.

Capital Transfer Tax: CTT was introduced in the Finance Act of 1975. It replaced Estate Duty and was particularly intended to be less easily avoidable. It is levied on transfers of wealth between individuals whether alive or on death. Different rates of tax are levied on different types of transfer and there is a schedule of exemptions for different classes of recipient. As with estate duty, there are also exemptions from CTT for transfers of agricultural property up to a maximum of 1000 acres or £250,000 in value. These concessions have been enhanced from the farmer's point of view by adjustments to the valuation procedures involved in assessing tax liability.

It is widely believed that CTT is an anti-landlord tax. Support for this view comes from the ceiling on the size of properties eligible for relief, and from the abolition of the 45 per cent abatement of Estate Duty with the tax itself. However, one obvious consequence of taxing land might be a fall in its price, which will, in turn, reduce the owner's tax liability on transfer. Thus it remains to be seen whether this gloomy view of the impact of CTT on landownership is justified. It is notable that Peters and Eckford (1976) conclude, on the basis of a careful study, that: '. . . contrary to popular belief, the replacement of Estate Duty by Capital Transfer Tax is unlikely to have a dramatically, adverse effect upon agriculture'. However, it does seem likely that landlords, particularly large landlords, will be affected by the tax. Both the value of their estates is likely to decrease and their tax liability will probably be larger under the new tax. It is by no means so likely that the structure of farm sizes will change in response to the tax, partly because landlords who have to pay CCT are likely to raise the cash to do this by selling off whole farms, and partly because there are few farms greater than 1000 acres or valued at more than £250,000. For a recent assessment of the likely impact of CCT on farm structure see Ross (1976) and Harrison (1976).

Land values, as can be seen from the above discussion on taxation, are of interest for a number of reasons. They affect the ability of individuals to buy, or the incentive for owners to sell, and they will thus determine the rate of entry of new farmers into agriculture and, to some extent, the rate of loss of land from it. Their level determines the yield of various taxes but also reflects the incidence of taxes. Finally, land values have been highly volatile in recent years and this volatility has an obvious effect on the wealth of landowners. We therefore discuss briefly the factors affecting land values in the last few years.

In considering the land market, the simplest economic model would postulate a perfectly inelastic supply schedule for land as shown in Fig. 6.1(a). In such a situation, the effect of a tax on land (such as CTT) would be to cause a demand shift from D_o to D_1. The price falls from P_o to P_1, the difference between these two being equal to the rate of tax. However, if land was somewhat elastic in supply, only part of the tax would go to reduce its value. In Fig. 6.1(b), because the supply schedule is elastic, the effect of the demand shift is to reduce the price from P_o to P_2, which is less than the rate of tax (P_1-P_2). This might occur where the effect of the tax is to drive the least productive land out of cultivation (q_o-q_1), or to make it sufficiently cheap for it to be transferred to some other use.

The existence of such underlying market relationships would explain why land values fall when a tax is introduced and, conversely, why they rise when a tax is removed or a subsidy applied. This phenomenon is important in the context of subsidies, because

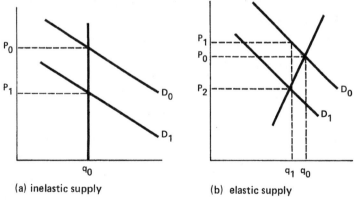

(a) inelastic supply   (b) elastic supply

Figure 6.1. (a and b)

once a subsidy is introduced, it cannot be withdrawn without reducing land values. Those who would expect their interests to be damaged by such an event would argue very strongly against the withdrawal of subsidies. The abatement of Estate Duties, which used to apply to agricultural land was, in effect, a subsidy to landowners (moreover, a subsidy which encouraged many non-agricultural interests to acquire agricultural land). Replacement of this tax with the less easily avoidable CTT would be expected to reduce land values. Hence, naturally, land-owning interests were strongly opposed to CTT. How much they overstated their case will not become clear until CTT has been in operation for a few years.

Taxation is, of course, only one of the factors affecting land values: others are non-agricultural competition for land, the amount of investment funds available for land purchase, the level of agricultural productivity and the expected level of farm output prices and input costs. No single study has succeeded in linking all of these effects together for the UK, but two recent articles are worth noting. Hyder and Maunder (1974) examined land prices during the 1960s and into the early 1970s. Further information for the early 1970s is then provided by Munton (1975). The difference in period covered by the two studies is important because there was a rapid rise in land values in 1972 and 1973. Munton covers this period, whereas Hyder and Maunder do not.

The main purpose of Hyder and Maunder's work is to explain the price of farms, that is the price paid for land purchased for agricultural use, in terms of average and marginal revenue, and several other variables. Only some of their detailed results can be quoted here, for example they find, for 1967, that:

$$Y = 85.0 + 11.66X$$

where Y = the price of land
and X = estimated average net revenue of land.

This, they suggest, underlines the importance of non-agricultural factors (such as sporting potential or possible development value) in determining the price of land. Thus, even if average net revenue (X) fell to zero, the land would still be worth £85 per acre because of these factors. They also examine the relationship between rents and land values by regions and conclude, in contrast with earlier work, that the relationship in 1967 was close. They then move on to a more complex multiple regression analysis of regional farm prices. In this analysis they incorporate many more variables, including farm prices in the preceding year, the current rate of interest, the annual return per acre from farming and the housing value of the farm.

Munton's (1975) study relates to a short period – 1971-3 – when there was a short lived but very steep increase in agricultural property prices. During the period 1969–71, average land prices were steady between £250 and £300 per acre. The steep rise, which began at the end of 1971, reached a peak in excess of £800 per acre. Thus values nearly trebled in less than two years. Munton found that this rise in price was accompanied by a five-fold increase in the amount of land bought by 'institutions', a doubling in the proportion of land sold with sitting tenants, and a significant rise in the number of sales in which there was some hope of a further sale, at enhanced prices, for development purposes. Munton's analysis is less formally analytical than that of Hyder and Maunder, but he does suggest a number of special factors which would have contributed to the price boom. These include the commodity price rise of 1972-3 (see Chapter 10 for a fuller discussion of this topic), the interest of institutions in buying land as a hedge against inflation, the availability of investment funds and landowners' unwillingness to sell land. Since 1973, the decline in land prices is attributed to factors such as the withdrawal of the 'roll over' concession on CGT and the introduction of CTT.

Conversion – issues

Apart from the existing problems of landownership and prices, perhaps the main policy questions and debates arise in the context of the conversion of land from one use to another. Most of this competition arises either in the context of withdrawal of land from agriculture for housing and other urban uses, or in the transfer of land to forestry. Largely because of the institutions and agencies involved, and perhaps because different quality land is at issue, these two problems are seen as quite separate. However, in economic terms, the two markets are closely similar. The controversy over conversion centres around two main types of question which are discussed in turn: *first*, the rate of transfer and whether this threatens future food production, and *second* the evaluation of particular conversions. Finally, we review recent developments in the attempts to administer the conversion process.

The rate of transfer is a remarkably complex question and even its historical size is not precisely established. It is thus difficult to settle the more important question as to whether the rate of transfer poses other problems. An early contributor to this debate was Wibberley (1959), whose book attempted to make economic sense of the process of land transfer to urban use. Wibberly points out that urban growth proceeded at a modest pace until the 1930s, when rapid suburban developments around major cities led to a sharp acceleration. Between 1900 and 1925, the area under urban development (in England and Wales) increased by 15 per cent (slightly slower than total population), whereas from 1925 to 1950, the increase was 57 per cent. Champion (1974) documents the more recent situation (for England and Wales), showing that the total rate of transfer has not yet exceeded the peak annual rate of 35.8 thousand hectares in 1936-9. During 1965-70, it averaged 24.3 thousand hectares. As we saw in Table 5.2, Scotland contains a large proportion of poor quality land and we thus find a much higher rate of transfer to forestry in Scotland. Adapting Champion's data for the UK, we may obtain an overall picture of the transfers of land to different uses as shown in Table 6.5:

Table 6.5   Annual rates of change of land in different uses, UK 1950—65

Use	Total 1965		Average annual gain (+) or loss (−) 1950−65	
	Thousands of hectares	*Per cent of total*	*Thousand hectares*	*Per cent of total stock*
Agriculture	19,624	81.5	−42.0	−0.21
Woodland	1,817	7.5	+19.0	+1.05
Urban development	1,912	7.9	+17.3	+0.90
Unaccounted for	739	3.1	+ 5.7	+0.77
Total	24,092	100.0		

Source: Champion (1974).

More recently Best (1976), has pointed out that, in Great Britain, forestry and urban development were taking land from agriculture at similar rates in 1961-71.

The more difficult question of whether the rate of loss of agricultural land is proceeding at a rate sufficient to cause a problem, has recently been raised again by the Centre for Agricultural Strategy (CAS, 1976). The CAS paper applies the basic methodology derived earlier from Wibberley (1959) and further refined through a number of papers ending in one by Wibberley and Edwards (1971). It develops forecasts of land requirements from assumptions about future rates of growth of population, income, agricultural productivity and the degree of self-sufficiency in food production. These variables combine to indicate the amount of agricultural land which will be needed in 1980 and 2000. This is then deducted from the present (1974) agricultural area and the result compared with projected losses of agricultural land to both forestry and urban development. As a wide range of assumptions is made, many possible results are available. Central conclusions are, first, that there is unlikely to be a serious problem of land shortage during the 1980s. Secondly, extending the time horizon to 2000, the report suggests that there is more cause for concern.

Taking a median population (61 million), a low growth of output per area (1.5 per cent against the historic 3 per cent), real growth incomes of 2–3 per cent, the CAS estimates that a 10 per cent 'loss' of agricultural land could just be sustained without increasing our dependence on imported food by the year 2000. From this the CAS concludes that the situation is 'not one in which there is much room for manoeuvre'. The report goes on to call for 'greater centralization of decision-making with regard to urban expansion ...'. The student who wishes to make up his own mind will have to read the report for himself. We disagree with these conclusions for the following reasons:

(1) Since the report was published the population forecasts to the end of the century have, again, been revised downwards.
(2) The assumptions it makes with regard to agricultural productivity are pessimistic; the income growth optimistic: see Dexter (1977) for an optimistic view. If either of these was adjusted only slightly, a much more favourable outcome would result.
(3) On the question of room for manoeuvre the report is un-realistic. If there was any reason to believe that national circumstances required a substantial increase in our degree of self-sufficiency in food over a twenty-five year period, then this length of time itself provides room for manoeuvre.

(4) Greater centralization of decision making in the allocation of land would have to be defended on the grounds that it did not cost more to introduce and operate, than the benefits it brought. The report does not discuss the cost of operating such a system, nor does it demonstrate that a workable administrative machine could be devised.

The study has received critical comment from a number of workers familiar with the issues it raises. The most serious criticisms arise from the lack of correspondence between the analysis and the prescriptions it contains. We might confirm this by considering what would happen if there was a drastic world food production problem arising from, say, widespread bad weather for several seasons running. The first consequence of this would be that food prices would rise steeply. In the UK our balance of payments would be adversely affected and food prices would rise. Farmers would have a substantial increase in income, much of which they would invest in expanding production. Land prices would also rise and the transfer from agriculture to forestry might be slowed down. Whether the transfer of land to urban uses also fell would depend upon whether the rest of the economy remained buoyant through the inflation triggered off by the rise in food prices. If it did not, and non-farm incomes fell relatively, there would be some reduction in land conversion. In some ways, such a set of circumstances is similar to the experience of the early 1970s (the agricultural aspects of this are discussed in Chapter 10). We have, in fact, survived such an experience without having to take emergency action. The extent to which we should plan for more extreme circumstances remains an open question. Perhaps a start in answering it would best be made by specifying, with some precision, the types of circumstances which might bring about a substantial change in our food supply situation. The student may find it useful to try to invent such 'disaster scenarios' and see what kind of mechanism could be used to overcome them. An important ingredient of such mechanisms will be the response of people to the incentives and opportunities they are offered, whether through a market or through a completely centralized control system.

Such studies can never be of greater value than the future estimates on which they are based. Since the Wibberley and Edwards (1971) study, Britain has joined the EEC, which means that policy objectives with regard to self-sufficiency are likely to be different. Actual rates of both population and income growth have also turned out to be less than seemed likely when the CAS study was completed. Clearly such resource budgeting studies need regular revision whenever basic market conditions change. They are also somewhat crude in allowing for only some of the relevant variables and we should not seek to draw over-strong policy reactions from them.

Such broad studies of conversion provide guidance for establishing land use policy at the national level. However, on a more local scale, particular problems of evaluation will arise in the context of urban developments and afforestation. A useful model of this process has been developed by McInerney (1976) who emphasizes the intertemporal aspect of such changes and, in the case of housing, the irreversibility of the change. The model is summarized in Fig. 6.2 which shows the 'before' allocation of the fixed stock. The optimum use of land, represented on the horizontal axis, in one single time period, would be where the marginal net social benefit of land in housing (MNB_H) is equal to the marginal net social benefit of land in

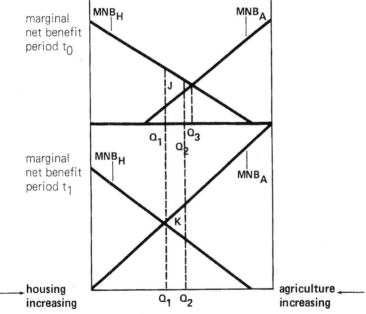

Figure 6.2

agriculture (MNB_A). This point, for period t_o is clearly where the two curves, MNB_H and MNB_A, intersect at Q_3. If the system started from some point to the left of Q_3, and the decision was to be taken for t_o alone, then a move in the direction of Q_3 would add to the net aggregate value of housing services and agricultural output taken together.

However, if we then recognize that future time periods, represented in this model by period t_1, are also important, the optimum may shift. In Fig. 6.2, period t_1 is shown as one in which MNB_A has shifted upwards: agricultural output is now more valuable than it was in period t_o, perhaps because of the onset of food shortages due to rapid population growth in t_o. The optimum allocation in t_1 alone would be at Q_1, but this would not be possible if society had moved to Q_2 in period t_o. Thus, from the beginning of t_o, we have to decide upon the optimal allocation of land between the two uses and in both periods simultaneously, and where the general tendency is to take land out of agriculture for building. Suppose we moved from Q_1 to Q_2 for both periods. This would yield net benefits represented by area J in t_o at the expense of losses of K in t_1. This suggests a criterion, for judging whether a move is desirable or not, of

$$J \gtrless \frac{K}{(1 + i)}$$

where i is the discount rate linking the two periods. The optimum, yielding maximum net social benefits for both periods together, would be where the equality held. This criterion can be extended to many time periods and the model provides a useful illustration of the processes at work in land conversion. To make the model fully functional, we need a great deal of further information on the position and shape of the MNB curves for agriculture and housing.

Another context in which the model may be applied is in conversion of land to forestry. This use is in fact the greatest single destination of conversions from agriculture (see Table 6.5), although the quality of the land converted to forestry is much poorer than that taken for urban development. It will also be recalled (from Table 6.4) that the Forestry Commission is the largest single landowner in the country. Since the Commission only came into existence in 1919, its *average* rate of acquisition of land can be seen to be more than 20,000 hectares per annum. Much of its present acreage was acquired in large blocks in its first few years, so that its recent rate of acquisition has been much less than this. Moreover, the land planted with trees is commonly of lower grades, so that the cost in terms of agricultural productivity has been much less than the area might imply. Nevertheless the extension of both state and private forest has been highly controversial in the last few years. Forestry policy has been subject to detailed examination from time to time and policy adjustments have been made.

The last major round of discussions of forestry policy took place in 1972 following the publication of a cost-benefit study (HM Treasury, 1972). This report was innovatory in that it contained estimates of the value of recreation in forests as well as the value of timber produced. It also presented calculations of the cost per job created in rural areas as a result of the conversion from agriculture. The report is of sufficient interest to be worth summarizing here: it provides a useful practical illustration of many of the issues raised in Chapter 2.

First, the report deals with a number of different decision options. In particular, these are the management of existing forest and new planting: allowing forest land to revert to agricultural use is only briefly discussed. Secondly, the analysis is applied in three different stages or modes. Stage O is a straightforward financial accounting in which only actual and expected cash expenditures are included in the calculations. In Stage 1 resource costs, which are essentially social opportunity costs, are substituted for market prices and the calculations are repeated: at this stage estimates of the value of recreation are included. In Stage 2, the possibility of responding to the results of Stage 1 in order to improve performance, is included.

The resource cost concept is important in that it involves estimation of the value of agricultural output on land converted. This requires estimation of the effect of various subsidies on the output of hill farms, and deducting it from market revenues (this problem has already been outlined in Chapter 2). The value of inputs used, including labour, is then deducted from this calculated 'revenue'. The stream of revenue is then discounted to the present at 10 per cent. This relatively high rate, compared with those previously used in evaluating forestry, was defended on the grounds that the rate was set by the Treasury for all public sector investments. The manpower used in both agriculture and forestry was valued at an estimated 'shadow price' which took account of the probability of unemployment and some other effects. This shadow wage, which amounted to

44 per cent of market wage, was applied for the first twenty-five years of the forest rotation, after which the full market wage was charged. This assumption implies that the structural unemployment will be cured after twenty-five years – an assumption which might lead to questions as to the effectiveness of our employment-creating policies! If that assumption proved to have been pessimistic then, because of the heavy effect of discounting during the first twenty-five years, it will have had relatively heavy impact on the costs of agriculture which would appear a less attractive option.

The basis of the calculation of the value of forest recreation is described in the next chapter. Here, taking the estimates at face value we may note the effect they have on the result. In Fig. 6.3 this effect is illustrated, for a single period, using marginal net benefit curves. If we were comparing only the marketable outputs from the two systems, then the two lower MNB curves would apply. MNB_F and MNB_A intersect at Q_1 and this represents the optimal allocation between the two uses. However, by introducing forest recreation benefits into the argument, a new set of marginal net benefits must be added in, which takes forestry onto MNB_{RF} and shifts the optimum allocation to Q_2. It would also be possible to take the argument a stage further and acknowledge the recreation potential of hill farming land. This would move farming on to a new, higher curve

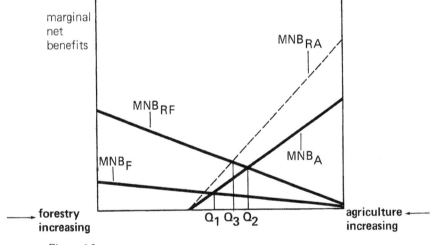

Figure 6.3

MNB_{RA} and, again, shift the optimum land use back towards Q_1. Clearly, the final optimum identified will depend upon the relative magnitude of the value of recreation associated with each land use, as well as the value of physical product involved.

In fact, the CBA study made no allowance for the recreational value of hill farming land. This would be defensible if it could be shown that the value of such benefits is likely to be trivial in relation to the value of forest recreation. However, a more serious attack on the CBA study came from the private forestry interests, whose activities were also compared with those of the Forestry Commission, although somewhat less directly. In an appendix to the CBA study, a number of case studies of the impact of tax concessions on private forestry is presented. The overall impression from these calculations is of the poor investment opportunity offered by forestry, whether private or public, and it is therefore not surprising that foresters were alarmed at the CBA study. Their response was to publish a lengthy critique of the CBA study (Wolfe and Caborn, 1973) which questions some of its findings and seeks to present forestry as a more attractive investment. Wolfe and Caborn test the sensitivity of the CBA study's conclusions to its assumptions and argue against some of them. In the context of recreation, they point out that, because private woodlands are more attractive, more mature (hence more accessible) and better located than state forests, their recreational potential is much the greater. They estimate the annual value of recreation in state forests to be £1.1 million, compared with £3.1 million for private forests. However this discussion of *potential* is somewhat hypothetical, in that realization of the recreational value under discussion would require that access to private woodland should be available. In practice, substantial areas of private woodland are not open to the public, so that this particular claim cannot be established in reality. Wolfe and Caborn would have been on surer ground if they could have based their estimates on the amount of land actually made available for recreation.

In addition to allowing for recreation, the CBA study also attempted to take account of import saving by multiplying the net value of imports saved (that is, output displacing imports, minus the cost of imported inputs) by an import saving factor (ISF). This ISF is in effect a shadow price for foreign exchange. It was applied by simply multiplying the appropriate items in the accounts by a factor of 1.20.

Average cost per job in

	hill farming (£ thousands)	forestry (£ thousands)	Cost per extra job in forestry (£ thousands)
Exchequer cost	10.2	18.9	25.7
Resource cost	0	9.9	15.3

Note: this table is derived from Tables 1 and 2 on pages 76 and 77 of the CBA study. In each case, the costs shown are the arithmetic mean for the three conservancies shown in the source tables.

Another important aspect of forestry studies of this kind is that the value of timber has to be forecast nearly sixty years ahead. The results are likely to be sensitive to the timber price assumptions made, because small rates of change compounded over such periods become very large indeed. (An increase of 1 per cent per annum would exceed 85 per cent over such a period.) The CBA study reviewed timber prices and reached the conclusion that there was no basis for assuming that real prices would increase. This conclusion was reached despite the past rising long-run trend of prices. The report argues that various factors, including the emergence of substitutes, favourable developments in harvesting and transport costs (as planted forests increasingly replace virgin forests) would combine to hold prices at their present level. Factors likely to enhance demand were not sufficiently strong to suggest an increase in real prices in the long term.

The CBA study argues its case well and it is notable that Wolfe and Caborn do not dissent from this view, although they subject the assumption to an approximate sensitivity analysis from which they conclude that a major change in real net revenues would be needed to yield a positive NPV from forestry discounted at 10 per cent. The conclusions as to prices were reached *ex ante*, probably towards the end of 1971 and the beginning of 1972. However the report had not long been published when a very substantial rise in timber prices occurred. Some of the relevant price series are documented in Table 6.6.

At first sight, these price changes at least suggest the desirability of further thought about the CBA study price assumptions. However, if we examine the prices in real terms, deflating (dividing) by either of the general price indices given, it is evident that, although there was a substantial increase in money prices in 1973 and 1974, *in real terms* the prices of imported softwood have since then fallen. The cost of land as an input into the forestry enterprise is a major component of the cost of new planting. This, in turn, reflects the relative enthusiasm of other potential buyers, including farmers and institutional investors. Earlier in the chapter, we saw that land prices rose markedly at about the same time as timber prices. Thus, we may conclude, real price movements since the CBA study was published have not yet seriously challenged its main assumptions. Whether further changes in prices may be expected after the effect of the oil price increase in 1972 and 1973 have worked through the economic system, remains to be seen.

The overall conclusions of the CBA study were thus somewhat unfavourable to forestry expansion at rates experienced up to then. However, some changes in policy were introduced following publication of a White Paper in 1972. These included small reductions in the Commission's annual planting programme and the introduction of new arrangements, whereby local authorities and the Ministry of Agriculture would be consulted when new planting was under consideration on a particular site. A new dedication scheme setting out the conditions under which private forests would receive government support was also produced. This scheme differed from its predecessors in making slightly better provision for amenity and recreational aspects of conversion to be taken into account.

The final component of the argument about forestry relates to the cost of job creation. It has become traditional to defend forestry as a land use on the grounds that it creates employment, hence helping to retain people in rural areas. This argument introduces another objective into the Social Welfare Function which is applied here: the efficiency benefits flowing from forestry cannot be added directly to the job creation benefits. In practice, the cost per job is calculated for forestry and agriculture in the CBA report and the two may be compared. The results of these calculations are noted in Table 6.7 where it is apparent that both average financial and average resource cost per job created in forestry are much greater than those for agriculture. Moreover the costs per extra job in forestry are higher still. However, the methodology used to produce the forestry estimates is not beyond question. In the case of a forest, the labour requirement varies throughout the production period. Peak labour requirements are at planting, thinning and felling stages. How many 'jobs' are then created on a given area of land over the whole forest rotation? The CBA study's answer to this is to discount the labour requirements to the beginning of the cycle at 10 per cent. The resulting estimate is a 'cost per present number of jobs created over the forest rotation'. This approach greatly reduces the importance of jobs in the thinning and harvesting operations and gives most emphasis to those created in the first few years.

However there is a strong case, against these arguments, for treating job creation costs quite differently. Obviously some kind of discounting of jobs created is appropriate in that, as with efficiency benefits, we are concerned to have them available sooner rather than later. However there is some inconsistency in the CBA study discounting employment over the whole rotation yet, at the same time, only applying its shadow wage rate to labour for the first twenty-five years. The latter implies that structural unemployment will become unimportant after that period, thus, to be consistent, it should be ignored (discounted at an infinite rate) after twenty-five years. Perhaps there is a good case for recognizing the importance of the time profile of benefits of job creation, just as there is with efficiency benefits. Whether this should be incorporated through appropriate shadow pricing techniques, or whether discounting over a particular period is appropriate, is open for discussion. This would seem to be one of the analytical issues which is not yet resolved, but which could become important if we are serious in our attempt to produce policies which will reduce rural unemployment.

This information on the forestry policy debate is presented here in some detail as an example of the contribution of economic analysis. It is acknowledged that there are assumptions in the CBA study which are questionable and some of the criticisms raised by Wolfe and Caborn have substance. Thus the CBA study conclusion, that forestry is not a socially profitable activity, should not be taken as an ineluctable truth which has been established for all time. It perhaps does represent a reasonable assessment of the desirability of extending our forests based on knowledge available in 1972. But more importantly, it has provoked a very healthy debate about forestry policy and, by trying to cast it in a CBA framework, it has focused attention on the relevant variables for discussion. Its contribution has been in making explicit the assumptions and issues which enter into such a complex policy question.

Conversion – institutions

The Community Land Act 1975 and the Development Land Tax Act 1976 have implications for the conversion of land from one use to another. These Acts give effect to the Government's proposals for the community ownership of development land as set out in the White Paper (1974):

(1) to enable the community to control the development of land in accordance with its needs and priorities; and

(2) to restore to the community the increase in value of land arising from its efforts.

Development land is defined in the Community Land Act as land which 'in the opinion of the authority concerned is needed for development within 10 years ...'. Planners have always been conscious of the dissatisfaction with the way in which land owner-ship, planning and development are regulated. Perceived dissatis-factions are numerous and range from insufficient land becoming available for development, excessive capital gains from urban fringe land, excessive capital costs in developing urban fringe lands, arbitrariness and inequity, backlog in major public works, rocketing property values, inability to provide social facilities, fast-rising agri-cultural land values, land as an over-attractive medium for invest-ment, conflict between local authorities and developers, compulsory acquisition procedures and market value as a basis for compensation (Royal Town Planning Institute, 1974). Ironically, the whole problem arose from the planning process itself. When the Town and Country Planning Act 1947 came into force, all development required official or deemed consent. The requirement of obtaining planning permission to develop land had the effect of shifting the supply schedule for certain types of land, notably for housing, to the left, with the effect of raising the price and reducing the quantity available, thereby creating an artificial scarcity. Thus the decision of the local planning authority, or an appeal to the Minister, would enrich the landowner by allowing him to sell at an artificially high price. To avoid such capital gains being made by landowners who received planning permission, the Act provided that the State would, in effect, sell the right to develop when planning permission was granted, in return for a development charge levied by the Central Land Board. The Act also provided for landowners to make claims on a £300 million fund for loss of the development value of their land. Implementation soon revealed one defect: there was no financial incentive to a landowner to develop or to sell his property, and the result was to further shift the supply curve to the left, resulting in a lesser quantity of land being available and even higher prices. Consequently, the Town and Country Planning Act 1953 abolished development charges. The Town and Country Planning Act 1954 limited compensation payments (to existing use plus 1947 development value) when a landowner was prevented from reaping development value in his land, either by planning restrictions, or by compulsory acquisition at existing use value. The Town and Country Planning Act 1959 abolished the 1947 and 1954 compensation codes and provided that all land compulsorily acquired should be paid for at full market value. The Land Commission Act 1967 again attempted to collect a levy on the development value of land when land was sold or compulsorily acquired, but this was abolished in 1970. The Land Compensation Act 1973 reaffirmed the principle of market value compensation for land compulsorily acquired, and also included additional payments for occupier's disturbance, injurious affection and so on.

The Community Land Scheme (1975) can perhaps be best explained by quoting from DoE Circular 121/75 which set out the phases for implementation:

Phase 1. From the first appointed day authorities will have a general duty to have regard to the desirability of bringing development land into public ownership. They will need to pay special attention to meeting the planning needs of their areas, particularly in relation to housing and industrial development. To help them carry out this role they will have powers to buy land to make it available for development. When the development land tax provisions come into force, authorities' purchase will be made net of land tax otherwise payable by vendors.

Phase 2. As authorities build resources and expertise .. the Secretary of State will make orders ('duty orders') providing that land for the kind of development and in areas specified by the order must have passed through public ownership before development takes place. Authorities will continue to buy net of development land tax during the whole of this phase.

Phase 3. When duty orders for all relevant development cover the whole of Great Britain the second appointed day can be brought in. This will have the effect of changing the basis of compensation for land publicly acquired for new development from a market value (net of tax) basis to a current use value basis i.e. broadly its value in its existing use taking no account of any increase in value conferred by the grant or hope of a fresh planning permission.

Since the Community Land Act 1975 and the Development Land Tax Act 1976 have only been on the statute books for a short time, their effect has not been substantial. Moreover, implementation of the Community Land Act has not been pursued with vigour, primarily because the Opposition have pledged to repeal the Act when they are returned to power. Implementation has also been impeded by financial difficulties on the part of local authorities. The Development Land Tax Act 1976 could still operate if the Community Land Act was abolished, but the long-term effect of taxing development value is to shift the supply curve of land for conversion to other uses to the left.

7 Recreation and amenity

This chapter deals with two related subjects, both of which arise mainly from the class of economic phenomena known as *externalities*, which were mentioned briefly in Chapter 2. Our interest in recreation arises essentially from the management or regulatory problems it poses. Amenity, by contrast, relates to the group of problems which arise when changes in land use are proposed. Our concern with amenity questions arises, then, mainly in the context of evaluation.

Rural recreation

Studies of the economics of rural recreation differs from the mainstream of recreational economics, in that their primary focus is on questions of land use. Recreational economics, in the wider sense, is concerned with people's recreational behaviour – their response to the whole range of opportunities available – as an indicator of the satisfaction they derive from it. Studies of rural recreation, by contrast, mainly originate from the pressure on rural land resources and from attempts to cope with such problems. Recreation is seen as one of several possible ways of using rural land and the problems and policies arising are often inextricable from questions of land use. Those seeking a broader coverage of recreational economics should consult Vickerman (1975). More specifically rural studies will be reviewed here.

The questions to be addressed are: first, how much recreation will there be in the future, that is how much *recreational pressure* on the land base should be expected. Second, what facilities are or should be provided not only in the more rigorous context of the *demand* for particular facilities, but also in the more difficult setting of the institutional options open to society. Then, drawing on the experience of attempts to deal with the recreational problems, we briefly discuss the related question of amenity.

The level of recreational pressure on land resources will depend upon variables such as the number and age distribution of the population seeking recreation, accessibility of the land to people in terms of both distance (or cost) and legal rights. The importance of distance will depend, in turn, upon more detailed questions such as the level of incomes, the cost of travel and the value of time. Pressure will also depend upon what moves are made to increase the supply of recreational facilities.

In the context of rural recreation, we might start from the assumption that the population seeking recreation is predominantly urban. This is doubtless true in areas such as the Peak District National Park, but there will be many other situations where enjoyment of rural recreation facilities is by no means an urban monopoly. Moving to a more predictive approach, we might expect recreational pressure to rise with incomes, to fall as travel costs rise but to increase as the amount of leisure time available for recreation increases.

Qualitative evidence on the growth of recreational pressure may be inferred from the membership of clubs, from attendance at specific functions and from expenditure data. For example, Thomson and Whitby (1976) quote data relating to membership of the National Trust, showing that the total increased threefold between 1967 and 1974 and that it had more than doubled in the previous ten years. Similarly, Burton (1970) quotes statistics showing the growth of television and radio licences, and Vickerman (1975) presents time series of expenditure on leisure-related items as published in the Family Expenditure Surveys (DEP, 1957 *et seq.*). The growing interest in many outdoor pursuits could similarly be documented by reference to the membership of appropriate clubs.

However, this is at best an imprecise way of measuring overall recreational demand because, as incomes rise, people will increasingly join a number of clubs. To the extent that multiple membership increases without a corresponding increase in participation, the trend of total membership will overstate the growth of demand. Because of such sources of imprecision, there is very little hope of precisely measuring the growth of recreational demand.

Interest in recreation, particularly from planners, has resulted in some general household surveys of recreational participation. For example, in a survey in the North-east, National Opinion Polls Ltd (1969) obtained a large volume of data from 4000 respondents on recreational participation over two weekends. The results of this survey are of very limited value, however, because the sample is not large enough to allow significant estimates of the less popular activities. Thus the report points out that where estimated participation falls below ten thousand, differences between estimates cannot be taken as significant. The survey does indicate the relative importance of rural leisure activities to a predominantly urban population and this aspect of its results is summarized in Table 7.1.

The table shows the importance of rural activities relative to others (which include a much wider range of more highly organized

Table 7.1   Estimated leisure participation* by certain activities

Activity	Saturday		Sunday	
	Number (millions)	*Per cent of total*	*Number (millions)*	*Per cent of total*
Fishing	0.011	0.7	0.019	1.0
Sailing	0.003	0.2	0.003	0.2
Other boating	0.004	0.3	0.012	0.6
Rambling/nature study	0.003	0.2	0.002	0.1
Riding/trekking	0.006	0.4	0.004	0.2
Trips to coast	0.092	5.9	0.187	9.8
Trips to country	0.043	2.8	0.129	6.7
Sub-total Outdoor recreation	0.162	10.5	0.356	18.6
All activities	1.550	100.0	1.915	100.0

Source: North Regional Planning Committee (1969).

*The estimates here relate to the population aged 12 and over; the total was estimated at 2.6 million at the time of the survey in 1967.

forms of recreation). It appears that trips to coast or countryside are the majority outdoor activities and most of the others listed attract only small numbers. It is also notable that trips to the coast out-number those to the country – perhaps because the coast is particularly accessible, by public and private transport, to the population in this region. For many types of outdoor recreation transport is the main item of cost and distances are therefore an important determinant of recreational participation at a particular site.

Surveys of recreation have been carried out in a number of regions in the UK, but because of the small samples used, the detail they contain is of little use. Indeed much larger and more comprehensive surveys in the USA (for example Adams *et al.*, 1973) have run into similar difficulties, where cross-classification produces sub-samples which are too small to produce statistically significant measures of participation.

Given these problems in measuring participation directly, we might attempt a more basic approach, starting from the amount of leisure time available. Thus the importance of work patterns in determining leisure behaviour may seem self-evident, yet it is notable that there has been little change in the length of week worked by men in manufacturing industry since the end of World War II. There has, however, been a reduction of the average weekly hours of women and youths. The stability of mens' hours indicates that they have used reductions in the 'basic' week, to which the standard wage applies, as a means of increasing their income from overtime. Hence the working week has not decreased. However there has, at the same time, been an increase in the amount of leisure time available, arising from the lengthening of holiday entitlements. These are documented in Table 7.2, where the contrast between 1961, when most of the population had less than two weeks holiday, and 1976 where over 80 per cent were entitled to more than three weeks, is notable.

Other factors involved in the growth of leisure time available are the increase in the number of old-age pensioners, and of children staying on at school to later ages and entering full-time higher educa-tion. Old-age pensioners constitute a potentially highly mobile group. They are often affluent (many have more than one pension) and have few commitments which would prevent them from participating in recreation. Improvements in medical care may also have enhanced their capacity to participate in and enjoy outdoor

Table 7.2   Distribution of paid holiday entitlement of full-time workers by duration, 1961–75, manual workers

	Percentage			
Duration	1961	1966	1971	1975
Up to 2 weeks	97	63	28	1
2–3 weeks	1	33	5	1
3 weeks	2	4	63	17
3–4 weeks	0	0	4	51
4 weeks and over	0	0	0	30
Total	100	100	100	100

Source: Central Statistical Office (1976b).

recreation. Furthermore, concessionary travel arrangements for old-age pensioners, whose numbers are now approaching 10 million in the UK as a whole, have made rural recreation more cheaply available to them. By extending their education, children and youths also extend their formal leisure time. Thus students may be able to allocate up to six months in the year to recreation. The rarity of such single-minded pursuit of leisure undoubtedly arises partly from academic constraints and from financial stringency. However, students are comparatively fortunate in being able to choose when to take their leisure over a large part of the year. They are also able to benefit from concessionary travel schemes and from group booking arrangements, and the recreational facilities of academic institutions are often well developed. Thus the growing number of pensioners and the extension of formal education are both likely to increase the amount of leisure available and hence the level of recreational participation.

In practice, the extent to which growing recreational pressure will be felt depends upon the rate at which recreational opportunities are supplied. There are obvious difficulties in measuring the physical supply of such opportunities. Clearly, a national park can only provide recreational experiences, of the kind it is expected to offer, for a limited number of people, unless the quality of experience is to deteriorate. Obviously its recreational capacity is a great deal less than its capacity to accommodate more gregarious activities. Country parks, by contrast are not expected to provide solitude and would therefore be able to accommodate many more people per hectare before a qualitative change would occur. However, we may measure changes in the supply of facilities by reference to change in spatial supply prices. This concept, which is used by Vickerman (1975) embraces changes in the cost to the individual of participating in a recreational activity. Such changes could arise from movements in transport costs, or from more widespread provision of facilities. The consumer will perceive them as supply shifts and will thus move up or down the demand curve in response to them. The vertical magnitude of such shifts may be inferred from the measurable changes in supply price.

At a more practical level, some of the changes in provision of rural recreation may be inferred from official data. Thus the area under National Parks, Areas of Outstanding Natural Beauty, Country Parks and similar arrangements may be stated, and these are recorded in Chapter 5. However, apart from noting that such increases in provision will have tended to reduce recreational pressures, there is not much formal analytical use to be made of them.

Models of recreational demand

The best known model which has been used in establishing demand relationships for particular recreational sites was developed by Marion Clawson (1959). A number of modifications of the technique have been proposed and the model has been used in several studies in this country (see, for example, Smith, 1971; Lewis and Whitby, 1972 and HM Treasury, 1972).

Clawson distinguishes five steps or stages in the outdoor recreation process which add up to the 'whole recreational experience'. They are: anticipation and planning; travel to the site; on-site recreation; travel home; recollection.

He then postulates that a demand function for the 'whole experience' offered by a recreational facility may be obtained from data on the rate (per thousand population) at which people visit the site from population zones and the cost they incur in gaining access to it. The first variable (v_i) corresponds with the quantity variable of conventional demand theory and the second (p_i) with price. Having estimated this whole experience demand function, he then uses it to *predict* what would be the volume of participation (V) at the specific site, from the population data. This stage requires the basic

Table 7.3   Basic data for estimating 'whole experience'
demand function for a hypothetical recreation type

Zone	Population (N_i)	Total visits ($N_i \cdot v_i$)	Visit rate/ thousand (v_i)	Cost per visit per person ($£p_i$)
A	2,000	8	4	0
B	1,000	3	3	1
C	1,000	2	2	2
D	2,000	2	1	3
Total	6,000	15	—	—

assumption that the residents of all zones will react to a change in
price of the facility in precisely the same way as they would to an
increase in the distance they have to travel to reach it. An example
may help to explain the steps in the estimation process.

In Table 7.3 the data needed to establish the 'whole-experience'
function are recorded and the relationship is presented graphically in
Fig. 7.1.

The equation here is:

$$v_i = 4 - p_i \tag{1}$$

Now, in order to calculate the site-specific function, we substitute a
set of prices in (1), and calculate the number of visits from each zone
corresponding with each price. This provides a set of price/quantity
data for the site specific function as tabulated in Table 7.4 and
plotted in Fig. 7.1.

Table 7.4   Data for site-specific demand of
function for a hypothetical site

Zone	Price	Visits $\left(V = \sum_{i=0}^{I} v_i \cdot N_i \right)$
A	0	$(8 + 3 + 2 + 2) = 15$
B	1	$(3 + 2 + 2) = 7$
C	2	$(2 + 2) = 4$
D	3	$2 = 2$
Total	—	28

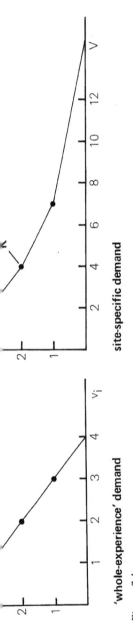

'whole-experience' demand

site-specific demand

Figure 7.1

These functions may now be used for estimating the 'value' of the facility, or predicting participation rates under given price assumptions. Published studies have concentrated most on the evaluation problem, not least because they have related to facilities which are not priced. Another, less controversial, use is in predicting participation at similar facilities. The value of a facility is usually estimated in terms of the consumers surplus generated by a site, that is, it is approximated by the area beneath the site-specific demand curve to the left of the equilibrium level of participation. In the example here, it is the whole of the area under the site-specific demand curve, amounting to £52.33. An alternative method of evaluation has been developed by Brown, Singh and Castle (1964). This mode of evaluation relies on the assumption that the facility is owned by a revenue maximizing, non-discriminating monopolist. Such a monopolist would seek to charge the one admission price which would give him the largest possible revenue. Where the demand curve for the site is known, this is identified as the point at which the elasticity of the demand curve takes the value 1.0. This point may be identified by multiplying together a series of co-ordinates of V by p_i. In this particular example, the point is labelled K in Fig. 7.1 and at that point the revenue obtained from the facility would be roughly £8.3.

The substantial difference between this value and the consumers' surplus calculated (£8.3 against £52.3), should be noted because both methods have been used in different contexts. Theoretically, the consumer-surplus concept is more defensible as a general measure of recreational benefit. However, when recreational benefits are to be added to other sums calculated as simple market revenues, there may be merit in using a consistent measure, which might in this case be monopolist's revenue. The latter also has some operational advantages in that it is based on the location of a point towards the centre of the site-specific demand curve. Those parts of the curve are estimated with greater certainty than the price intercept, which is a critical variable in determining the size of the consumer-surplus measure. The price intercept in fact tells us the price (or distance) which is just great enough to reduce visiting to zero, a point which may be difficult to establish from the data.

Another use to which the Clawson-type models may be put is that of forecasting participation at and estimating the recreational value of new facilities. Mansfield (1971) used a Clawson-type model in this way and Lewis and Whitby (1972) used whole experience functions estimated for one reservoir to predict participation at another. Such a use of the model requires that the two facilities in question shall be similar qualitatively in the experience they offer and, further, that they shall be broadly of the same size. This latter condition did not hold in the Lewis–Whitby example, with the result that recreational potential at the new site was almost certainly understated.

The way in which this use of the Clawson model might work may be seen by extending the example above. Suppose that an identical facility were to be constructed at a new location, so that the effective 'price' charged to the residents of the four zones became quite different. Suppose, further, that travel costs to the new site were as shown in Table 7.5:

Table 7.5 Data for site-specific demand function for a hypothetical new site

Zone	Cost per visit ($£p_i$)	Population	Predicted number of visits
D	1	2,000	6
A	2	2,000	4
B + C	3	2,000	2
Total	–	6,000	12

The difference in location of the facility reduces the number of visits and, correspondingly, the recreational benefit. On a consumer surplus basis, recreational benefit would now be £32 and the monopoly revenue would be £8.

Since it was first proposed, the Clawson model has been used in a number of studies and many modifications have been proposed and tested. These include the incorporation of a measure of income in the population zones (see, for example, Lewis and Whitby, though Vickerman finds socio-economic groups to be a better means of explaining participation). Other workers have taken account of time, in addition to travel cost, in the whole experience function (for example, Smith, 1971). Also Brown and Nawas (1973) proposed that individual observations should be used in estimating functions, rather than grouped data, as is usual. Other problems which remain to be adequately dealt with are those of accounting for 'intervening opportunities' – where there is more than one purpose to a recreational journey – and the related problem of measuring the quality of recreational opportunities.

A rigorous critique of the Clawson model has been published by Vickerman (1975). He sets out a much more elaborate model which incorporates supply as well as demand and which includes the 'trip generating' effect of new recreational facilities. Whether this approach succeeds in replacing the simpler Clawson model and its derivatives, will depend partly on the research resources available to recreation administrators. Another alternative to the Clawson model has been proposed and tested recently by Sinden (1974). His model starts from individual consumers of recreation and attempts to establish their preferences on a cardinal scale. This information is then put together in the form of a demand schedule and consumers' surplus is measured from it.

Clearly the last word on the measurement of recreational demand has not yet been written. Given that rural recreation is income elastic, the pressures on facilities may be expected to grow over time. Hence there will be continued interest in the provision of new facilities and choices to be made with regard to their location. Until a perfect tool for evaluation is found, the Clawson-type models will provide some basis at least for ranking alternatives. Until the Sinden model has been more widely tested, its contribution to the problems of evaluation cannot be judged.

Recreational institutions

Some of the legal and administrative means which have been developed in the recreational context have already been described in Chapter 4. In this section, we attempt to relate them to empirical studies of rural recreation and discuss their effectiveness. The section draws partly from a paper by Thomson and Whitby (1976) which focused on the slightly narrower, but closely related question of rights of *access* to rural land for recreational purposes. Three types of access were distinguished: inherited access; by-product access; purposive access.

A major type of inherited access consists of common land. Although there were 610 thousand hectares of common land in England and Wales in 1956–8, the general public had rights of access to only 130 thousand hectares of it. However, there undoubtedly was (and is) *de facto* access to a much larger area of unfenced common rough grazings than the *de jure* situation would suggest. This category also includes footpaths and bridleways which provide a huge mileage of walking potential. Pedestrians' traditional rights to use footpaths and bridleways are contingent on their regular use.

Recreation is provided as a by-product by a number of agencies. These range from agencies such as the Ministry of Defence, through the Forestry Commission and the Water Authorities to the National Trust. During the past decade and more, there has been an increasing tendency for such organizations to provide recreation. Thus water authorities are required, under the 1973 Water Act, to produce recreational proposals at the design stage of a project. The Forestry Commission now explicitly incorporates the provision of recreation among its objectives. The National Trust for England and Wales includes the provision of access to its properties in its terms of reference. Indeed, most organizations owning land for public purposes have an interest in providing recreation and many of them are explicitly charged with a duty to do so.

The implications of this for resource allocation are far-reaching. Thus an organization whose land-using activities appear unprofitable, or are unpopular politically, may seek wider public support by offering recreational facilities. This might seem to be a somewhat cynical abuse of public funds and there is indeed such a danger. Perhaps the best safeguard against such abuse would be the development of adequate measures of recreational benefit and their rigorous application in analysing policies. The Treasury (1972) study of forestry costs and benefits was a case in point. In that study, future recreation benefits were estimated for the state forest using the Clawson technique and they comprised a substantial proportion of the estimated net benefit from forestry. Unfortunately, the study overlooked the possible recreational benefits from hill farming and from private forest.

This criticism brings us back to the starting point of cost-benefit analysis, namely defining the project. The Treasury study was explicitly intended to compare the economics of private hill farming and public forestry. Rather more implicitly, it also presented an analysis of the private economics of private forestry. Recreational benefits were calculated for state forests, thus implying that the recreational value of the same land under hill farming or private forest would be zero. The latter contention has been challenged by

Wolfe and Caborn (1973), who have pointed out that the *potential* recreational benefits from private forest exclude those possible from Commission forests. This is partly because of the greater maturity of private forest and partly because a greater proportion of it is found in the south of England, nearer to the centres of population. However, it is also true that land under hill farming now has recreational potential and that such benefits, although difficult to estimate on a national scale, are by no means negligible.

Recreation is purposively catered for at the national level by national parks, areas of outstanding natural beauty, nature reserves, long-distance footpaths and access and management agreements. In contrast with other countries (e.g. the USA), the ownership of land in national parks in Britain is not altered by the existence of the park. However, the tighter planning controls introduced with a park do amount to a change in the allocation of property rights between existing owners and the state. The operation of national parks was subject to a wide-ranging review (National Park Policies Review, the Sandford Committee, 1974) recently, and a number of suggestions made for improving their performance. Among these was a suggestion that particular areas within the parks should be set aside as Heritage Areas, where particularly tight conservation could be practiced. (It is, however, notable that this suggestion was not unanimously supported.) At the time of writing, there has been no action on this particular proposal.

Another means of promoting, or regulating the recreational use of the countryside is through *Access* Agreements. The legal basis of these arrangements has already been discussed (see Chapter 4); here we merely record the facts. There are about 50 access agreements in England and Wales covering some 30,000 hectares (Gibbs and Whitby, 1975). The majority of the area is found in national parks and much of it is hill land. The picture of access agreements which emerged from this study is of a useful device for regulating rural recreation, especially where recreational pressure is growing. The annual cost of agreements is modest at some £3 per hectare. Within that total, payments to landowners and tenants was a small item of cost (less than 5 per cent), whereas wardening amounted to some two-thirds of total costs as measured.

The closest alternative to access agreements is for local authorities to obtain access by purchase, which they are enabled to do under the same legislation. Naturally, this is much more costly (£17 per hectare per annum) – they are buying all of the rights to the land rather than the access rights alone. A major disadvantage of access agreements is the legal cost of negotiating them. The Countryside Commission has attempted to reduce such legal costs by introducing model agreements. Nevertheless such costs, together with the relative lack of control that local authorities can obtain through access agreements, appear to have made purchase an attractive means of gaining access.

Devices similar to access agreements are used in a number of other contexts. For example, access agreements have been negotiated between fishing clubs and canoeing groups. The Nature Conservancy Council uses similar instruments for managing nature reserves. Also landscape and management agreements, which would allow farmers and landowners to be compensated for managing their land in particular ways thought to be environmentally desirable, though leading to lower agricultural productivity, have been suggested. Subject to the problems of transactions cost mentioned above, such devices appear to offer an attractive (efficient) means of internalizing some of the externalities which result from recreational land use.

Country parks represent a more thoroughgoing and specialized approach to recreational provision. Country parks are mainly established on land which is owned outright by local authorities and they are managed solely and intensively for recreation. They are comparatively small areas and can be strategically placed to provide alternative attractions to natural areas of attraction. Country parks thus offer a means of trying to direct recreational pressure from the most popular sites. Because country parks are smaller and more intensively managed than other recreational sites, data on their use can more easily be collected. Some of the available data on the used parks and picnic sites are recorded in Table 7.6. The median for all sites is given, rather than the mean, because of wide variation from

Table 7.6   Country parks and picnic sites
median Sunday summer visitors per site

	Country parks	Picnic sites
1974	1,223	299
1975	1,425	431
1976	1,043	426

Source: Countryside Commission (1977).

site to site. There is no obvious reason why participation should have fallen in 1976, which was an exceptionally warm dry summer, unless such unusual weather conditions encouraged visitors to travel further in search of new experiences. This data series has not yet become long enough to draw serious inferences.

Long-distance footpaths and bridleways, of which the Pennine Way is the longest (402 km), the first opened (1965) and probably the best known, are an important means of providing recreation. There are now some 2,400 km of such paths (Countryside Commission, 1977) on thirteen distinct routes and a further four routes are under discussion.

Another response, on the part of farmers and landowners, to recreational pressure (often combined with other economic pressures) has been to fail to keep up maintenance expenditures. In the case of some hill areas, this has led to derelict or semi-derelict landscapes, with stone walls collapsing, broken fences and gates and it has also reduced agricultural productivity. An ingenious response to this problem which has been tried in the last few years has been the Upland Management Experiment (Countryside Commission, 1976). Under this scheme, 'experiments' have been carried out in Snowdonia and the Lake District. The essence of the procedure is to appoint a project officer who stimulates all kinds of work contributing to landscape improvement. Some of the work is done voluntarily, some of it is paid part-time and some full-time. In essence, this may be seen as making good past under-investment in fences and walls. It has several virtues in that it represents a positive response to recreational pressure, it encourages a sense of participation amongst the local people and it achieves results at modest cost.

Amenity

The amenity value of land is another example of an externality (see Chapter 2, page 50, and Chapter 6, page 140) which must be taken into account when conversion is under consideration. In this concluding section, we discuss the nature of this good and the problems which arise in assessing its value. Amenity value is a somewhat elusive concept. It is widely used in the land use context to include all benefits other than those arising from primary production. This definition would include recreational benefits as well as the satisfactions people absorb, more passively, from living in or driving through beautiful landscapes. Enough has been said about recreational benefits and the way in which they may affect public decisions. In this section we shall concentrate on the non-recreational aspects of amenity.

Attempts to quantify the amenity conferred by particular landscapes have not, so far, risen above the essentially subjective. Inevitably such techniques begin by compiling estimates of the quantity of various attributes which would, together, add up to 'amenity'. These are then added together in some more or less arbitrary way.

An example of such a study, relating to Lanarkshire, was published by Duffield and Owen (1970). These workers classified the recreation environment of each grid square of the county on the basis of four criteria: its ability to support land-based recreation; its ability to support water-based recreation; the scenic quality of the area; the ecological quality of the environment.

These four attributes are broken down into sub-criteria which are used to locate the grid on a point scale. Most of the relevant information can be obtained from maps and official data sources. When the square has been evaluated on each criterion, the four scores are then expressed as percentages which are then aggregated. The maximum possible score is 400, though most squares scored less than 200. The main weakness of this technique is in the arbitrariness of the conventions it includes. For example, should each of the four criteria be afforded equal weight? Manifestly from some points of view they should not. Clearly the list of criteria is not exhaustive and, to this extent, the data from such a study must be interpreted with great caution.

At another extreme of numeracy is Nan Fairbrother's (1972) highly readable account of our landscape. This is, in essence, a descriptive study and an intensely subjective one, in which the preferences of the observer are allowed full play in evaluation. Somewhere between those two studies is the widely acclaimed *New Agricultural Landscapes* (Westmacott and Worthington, 1974) study produced for the Countryside Commission. The report is too detailed to summarize fully, but its main approach is to record the known descriptive information about rural landscapes and to record the ways in which they are changing. The report is based on case studies of seven farming areas in which the existing landscape was studied, and important sections deal with surveys of farmers' attitudes towards landscape conservation. Following that report, the Countryside Commission has been putting together policy objectives on landscape conservation. As a move towards implementing these objectives and providing motivation for landowners and farmers to conform with policies, the Commission (1977) has been seeking to obtain exemption from Capital Transfer Tax (see Chapter 6, page 130) on land of outstanding 'scenic, scientific or historic interest where certain undertakings are obtained for the conservation of those interests, and where provision is made for public access'.

The Treasury (1977) has produced a memorandum setting out the approach which is being adopted where decisions are made on such exemptions. It now remains to be seen whether the incentives offered to landowners will exceed or fall short of those required to motivate them as desired. The policy choice here between tax exemption arrangements, which negate the redistributing intentions of a particular tax (but appear to cost less because a tax which is not collected is not recorded as a cost), and the payment of direct transfers to individuals in payment for a particular act (as in the case of access agreements described above), is an interesting one. From the point of view of society as a whole, we might argue that the choice should be based on a rational assessment of the relevant costs (including transactions cost) but administrators may prefer the course which seems easier to them, which, in this case, is probably the introduction of exemption from CTT. This has some weakness as a policy instrument in that the response of individuals to it will obviously be determined by their liability for CTT. As we saw in the previous chapter, this means that only those with large areas of land and who have no other means of reducing their tax liability will be interested in the concessions. These arguments would suggest that, if landscape amenity is to be preserved across a wide front, a strong case could be made for a more positive set of incentives to promote landscape maintenance on the part of small and medium-sized landowners (such as access agreements and the upland management experiment). It must also be borne in mind that the many institutional landowners, whose importance was documented in the previous chapter, will be unlikely to respond to small financial incentives and, because they are taxed differently, will not be motivated by concessions on CTT. The need for effective policy instruments in this context thus remains.

What can we say about the value of amenity? There has been little empirical economic work on this topic, though its importance has been recognized for some time. Some quantitative work has been directed to negative amenities – disamenities – an example being the studies of noise in connection with the Third London Airport (Roskill, 1970). Following the arguments developed in Chapter 2, relating to shadow pricing, we might begin an attempt at evaluation by looking at levels of expenditure on amenity. Thus direct payments to farmers to compensate them for the extra cost of building environmentally acceptable structures in the national parks, indicate what society is 'prepared to pay' for such an amenity. The social cost of access agreements might also be taken as an indication of the value placed on access by society. The fact that such decisions are not validated by a market and, all too often, are not adequately scrutinized by the political process either, greatly detracts from their usefulness as implicit prices. The only other approach which is feasible would be to examine how people respond to an amenity by modelling their behaviour with the use of techniques such as Clawson's. This suffers the severe drawback of heavy cost. It is more costly than with recreational studies because people 'consume' amenity in many different ways, often in very small quantities, and often jointly with other goods. Thus, for many situations, the quality of information produced, and the resulting resource savings, are unlikely to be sufficient to justify the expenditure needed to evaluate amenity in cash terms. Under such conditions, the best information obtainable at reasonable cost would come from the careful examination of other decisions.

8   Conservation

Conservation is used in at least two related but distinct senses and in this chapter we shall be dealing with both. First, it is used in the context of *natural resource conservation*, in which we are particularly concerned to identify and move towards optimal rates of resource utilization. Secondly, there is the context of *environmental conservation* in which a collection of attributes – 'the environment' – is to be conserved. These different approaches may be unified if we redefine 'the environment' as a natural resource: it does, nevertheless, have some particular characteristics which justify considering it separately. In this chapter, we review conservation problems in that order, seeking to identify theoretical optima, then move on to describe and apply the 'materials balance' approach to the environment, finally we review some of the policy problems arising in connection with agriculture and the environment.

Natural resources

We should note first of all that the very concept of natural resources is highly ambiguous. Ricardo (1817) referred, in his classic exposition on economic rents, to the 'original and indestructible powers of the soil'. Such a concept may indeed be meaningful where new land is being opened up. However, once the land has been brought into cultivation and capital has been invested in improving it, its 'original and indestructible powers' become more elusive. It is therefore important to remember that the 'natural' component of any resource is unlikely to account for all of its value: indeed, it is likely to account for different shares of its value over time. Schultz (1953) points out that the share of land as an input into American agriculture fell from 19 per cent in 1910 to 17 per cent in 1950. Moreover, within this declining share, the proportion due to investment (in drainage, fences, fertilizer) has increased and therefore the residual share, attributable to the initial endowment, has declined more rapidly.

McInerney (1976) has attempted a comprehensive theoretical statement of the optimal rates of consumption of various types of natural resource. He sees the essential ingredients of the problem in that the important natural resource choices are societal ones, that intertemporal aspects of the choice are central and that the constraints within which society must choose are outside human control. The last attribute sets natural resources apart from others, in that it emphasizes the biological and geological processes at work in determining the fixed initial stock of resources from which we start and/or the predetermined flow charateristics of resources.

McInerney then divides natural resources into four polar types, which he characterizes as: non-renewable (oil); recyclable (steel); biological (fish); flow resources (land).

It is emphasized that these are stereotypes. There will, of course, be many composite resources exhibiting characteristics of more than one group. The variables which determine optimal depletion rates will have different typical magnitudes for each of these classes of resource: they are the size of initial stock, the planning horizon, present and future demand schedules and the magnitude of extraction costs. From these, he defines a further variable – user cost – which embodies future consumption forgone as a result of current consumption. The general model he proposes identifies the social optimum rate of depletion as indicated in Fig. 8.1. Here the marginal social benefits (MSB) are indicated by the familar downwards sloping curve. The total stock of the resource is represented by OS. Marginal social costs (MSC), at low levels of consumption, consist solely of extraction costs (MEC): that is, up to OQ_1 may be consumed in the current period without interfering with future consumption. To put this another way, maximum possible total future demand for the resource must be less than $Q_1 S$. Further additions to current consumption, after Q_1, impose increasing user costs on future generations, represented by the vertical distance between

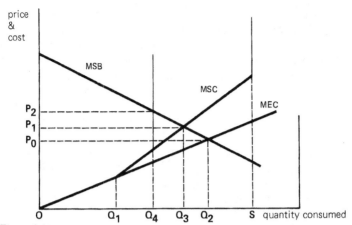

Figure 8.1

MEC and *MSC*. The optimal rate of extraction would be Q_3 – a
level of consumption which reflects both present and future
preferences. However, if the resource extractor considered only the
current period, his supply schedule would be MEC and he would aim
to produce Q_2. If the resource extractor behaved in this way, then
resource depletion would result. Society might seek to drive
consumption back to optimal levels by a tax on production or
consumption, or perhaps by tightening up the definition of property
rights so that the extractor had some incentive to move back to Q_3.
This last option might be achieved, for example, by adjusting the
valuation procedures so that reserves of unexploited resource were
more easily saleable. It is also possible, perhaps where monopoly in
the ownership of a resource exists, that private owners *overprice* so
that under-utilization results. Thus a monopolist could price at P_2 so
that consumption fell to Q_4.

McInerney then extends his model to apply to the four polar
resource types, already noted. These have different characteristics
with regard to natural rates of regeneration and recycling possibilities. The model relating to land has already been described in
Chapter 6.

Materials balance
Another fruitful analytical approach to conservation which has been
developed in the past decade is the so-called *materials balance*

approach. This approach is spelt out in detail for the US economy by Kneese, Ayres and D'Arge (1970). It emphasizes the pervasive nature of externalities, underlining the fact that virtually every productive activity releases waste materials to the environment. The importance of the materials balance idea is in emphasizing the role of all parts of the economic system as producers of unwanted residuals. This emphasis contrasts with the traditional economic view of pollution as a (local) external effect. The approach can usefully be extended from physical materials to energy. It begins from the physical laws governing matter and energy, and uses these and known physical magnitudes to build up an inter-related accounting system of stocks and flows.

The residuals produced by economic systems may be (as with fossil fuels) carbon dioxide and water (with foods), heavy metals which become toxic if they accumulate, or they may have a more ephemeral impact such as a loud noise or a bad smell. Particular substances may go through several transformations in the sequence from resource to production and to consumption, but the end point of these processes is the return of waste to the environment. These wastes may be individually trivial in magnitude but those that are not biologically degraded ('absorbed') by the environment will accumulate. Such accumulations may occur at low annual rates, but they may ultimately cause serious dislocations in the economic system. This problem is well recognized in the context of atomic sources of energy, where a great deal of research and development effort has been applied to the safe 'disposal' of the waste produced. Disposal in this context is in fact achieved by storage.

A contrast with the atomic energy case is traditional agricultural production. The farming systems of two hundred years ago were balanced and self-contained in that their main source of energy was the sun and substantial recycling of residuals occurred. In Fig. 8.2 the main exogeneous input to the agricultural system is solar energy. The crop plant 'fixes' this, through photosynthesis, as carbohydrate, which forms the basis of most substances in the plant, and part of this is harvested for animal feed or for direct consumption as feed. The resultant waste is returned to, or left in, the soil where it breaks down and eventually is recycled through further plant growth. Two important constraints existed in the system. First, the amount of energy that could be applied to enhance or control the rate of growth was limited to the rate of work that could be achieved by men or

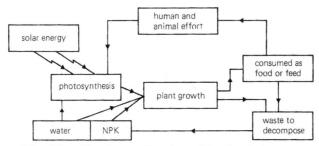

Figure 8.2.   Material and energy flows in traditional agriculture

draught animals. This constraint was reduced to insignificance by
the development of engines based on fossil fuels. Secondly, the rates
of plant growth that could be achieved were frequently limited by the
availability in the soil of nitrogen, phosphate and potash (N, P, K,
respectively). The amount of N available could be increased by the
activities of nitrogen-fixing micro-organisms in the soil, particularly
those associated with clovers and legumes. P and K, under traditional agricultural systems came direct from the soil and their availability could only be affected by different cultural practices such as
growing deeper rooting plants. The development of artificial
fertilizers in the nineteenth century removed this constraint. The first
fertilizers were all mined – that is they were depletable resources –
and, indeed, P and K still come from such sources. N, on the other
hand, can be obtained from the atmosphere and fixed chemically.
Since N comprises 80 per cent of the atmosphere, this might suggest
that we have unlimited supplies. However, as with many technological changes, what had really happened was that one constraint,
soil N availability, had replaced another, energy availability.
However, the likelihood of the energy constraint binding is remote
as coal may be used in N fixation.

We may thus redraw the modern agricultural system, as in
Fig. 8.3, which brings out the importance of fossil fuels, though it
does not give it quantitative significance. For this we may turn to
related work on British agriculture which seeks to establish the
'energy balance' of the industry. A recent report (Joint Working
Party, 1974) contains a number of estimates of the energy used in
and produced by UK agriculture. These estimates are extremely
crude, but they provide an interesting basis for further work. The
energy budget is summarized in Table 8.1 in terms of terakilo joules.

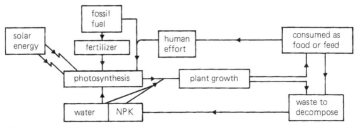

Figure 8.3   Material and energy flows in modern agriculture

On the input side, the overwhelming importance of direct fuels is notable. In addition to the energy consumed in manufacturing, this energy is mostly used to displace the draught animals and human drudgery of traditional agriculture. Fertilizers constitute a major energy demand, at least part of which could be displaced by nitrogen-fixing crops. This option is less attractive than it might seem because cashing in on naturally fixed N would require substantial changes in rotational practices. The energy content of imported feed is notable, so too, is the residual plant nutrient content of the feed which may supplement artificial fertilizer. The outstanding fact on the output side is the contrast between the energy content of the different components of output and their market value. Thus crops contain

Table 8.1   Approximate annual energy budget for UK agriculture

Energy input	TkJ	Energy output	TkJ
Fuels	121	Arable crops	88
Fertilizers	71	Horticultural crops	4
Agrochemicals	1	Livestock	94
Machinery	152		
Imported feed	73		
(Solar energy)	not accounted		
Total	418		186

Note: *TkJ* are terakilo joules, equivalent to 10^{15} joules. The measurements are made at the farmgate. The energy content of inputs is measured in terms of primary energy, that is, allowing for losses in conversion to the required input. Outputs are measured in terms of energy available to man.

nearly half the energy output of UK agriculture, but in value terms they amount to less than one third of output.

In Table 8.2, the relative importance of the components of gross output of UK agriculture are compared on the two separate bases. Comparison shows that the energy content of crops (apart from horticulture) is much less valuable than that of animals. Thus, *if* agricultural output was only used as a source of energy, these estimates would be puzzling: because food is consumed for a number of different reasons, which vary in importance from one item to another, it is not surprising that the two distributions do not coincide. The last column, obtained by dividing the second by the first, indicates the relative 'price' of energy in each item of output. Generally, the higher the apparent price, the more important are non-energy factors in determining demand. Most obvious here is horticultural output, which is very valuable in relation to its energy content, because it is consumed as a fresh source of vitamins and as a luxury garnish to less exciting staple foods. All the meats have a high unit value, although the differences between them are not immediately explicable.

Table 8.2   Distribution of output by energy content and by value: UK agriculture

	Percentage distribution* of output in terms of		
	(1) *energy*	*(2)* *money value*	*(3)* *'unit price'† of energy*
Cereals	29.6	11.6	0.39
Potatoes	8.1	4.0	0.49
Sugarbeet	9.7	1.7	0.18
Horticulture	2.1	12.8	6.10
Beef	10.7	18.0	1.68
Sheep	2.7	5.0	1.85
Pigs	9.1	12.1	1.33
Poultry	6.5	12.6	1.94
Milk	21.5	22.2	1.03

Sources: Joint Working Party (1974) and Annual Review of Agriculture (1977).

*   Both distributions relate to the early 1970s.

†   The 'unit price' of energy is calculated by dividing column (2) by column (1).

This comparison has been presented at length to underline a very basic point about materials balance approaches: namely, that they cannot yield policy conclusions unless they have money values built into them. The source of money values may be subsidized prices, as in the above comparison, or it may be imputed shadow prices (see Chapter 2) obtained from some other source. But without evaluation of some kind, such models lack prescriptive power. Ways in which the materials balance approach has been incorporated in input-output models (described here in general terms in Chapter 3), are reviewed by Pearce (1976).

The main limitation of the application of such principles to the problems of rural development in Britain, would be lack of knowledge as to the quantitative importance of residuals accumulating in the environment. Whether or not some of the residuals produced are retained on farms and recycled, depends upon fortuitous factors such as rainfall immediately after manure is spread on land. The level of rainfall where heavy fertilizer applications are used will also determine the amount of plant nutrients flushed through into water courses. Very detailed knowledge of soil types and rates of application of fertilizers and manures would be needed before it could be shown that a 'problem' worthy of a policy-maker's attention was in existence. Meanwhile, it is likely that the more local and relatively temporary environmental problems generated by British agriculture will cause headlines in the papers. Because most of our rivers are short and fairly fast, flowing residuals deposited in them are quickly carried out to sea. Bio-degradable substances can usually be broken down fairly quickly under such circumstances, and if the other residuals are removed by rivers, the 'problem' ceases to be 'rural' or even national, but becomes international in its ramifications. Before sensible locally operating policies can be put into effect, the scale of nuisance will have to be carefully estimated and evaluated. The ways in which such an evaluation might be undertaken have been reviewed by Hodge (1976). He indicates four types of approach: through the direct cost of abatement policies; from the effect on property values, that is, from individuals' 'implicit valuations', as revealed, for example, by their behaviour in the property market; the legal controls in use may yield evaluation data and, finally, evaluation might be pursued by direct questionnaire surveys of those sustaining the environmental impact. In the agricultural context, he favours the survey approach –

a conclusion which is supported by the general lack of data from other sources.

Once the environmental implications have been assessed, there remains the very intricate problem of translating them into some general form in which they can be evaluated alongside estimates of costs and benefits in money terms. This problem was briefly mentioned at the end of Chapter 2, in the context of intangibles. The presentation may be taken a step further by incorporating the information in an 'environmental impact statement'. These statements, which were first introduced in the USA, present as much information as possible about a project in a standardized format. The format provides for information on variables, such as the scale and duration of impact, the alternatives which could be considered and the commitment of resources. Clearly, such a statement could incorporate much of the material already prepared in an economic appraisal. Its particular appeal would seem to be in providing for further data on intangibles to be added. In Britain, the possibility of incorporating environmental impact statements into the planning system has been considered by Catlow and Thirlwall (1975) but, so far, policy action has not been taken.

A related environmental conservation issue is to be found in the interaction between farming and wild-life. There has been public agitation during the last few years over the degeneration of the countryside, and the amenity aspects of this were discussed in the last chapter. Another strand of the argument has also been raised recently by the Nature Conservancy Council (1977). Their report on the interaction between modern farming and wild-life represents a useful attempt to analyse a familiar problem and produce some policy proposals. The report is summarized here and we then attempt to present its arguments in economic form.

The report begins by asserting the importance of wild-life conservation. The strength of this 'demand' rests upon two main arguments. First, it is important to keep as much genetic material as we can in the wild-life population, because this is the source of new characteristics in cultivated crops: 'Generally speaking, therefore, it is wise to ensure the survival of as many species as possible'. The report argues for '... maintaining biological diversity and so keeping the options as wide open as possible for our own and future generations'. Secondly, the report stresses the 'cultural value' of a diverse flora and fauna because of man's interest in it. The problem arises because farmers, in pursuit of profit are, quite rationally sweeping away natural habitat at an alarming rate. The report presents some detailed information on the rate at which some forms of habitat are disappearing and compares the numbers of species present under modernized and unmodernized farming systems.

From this information, the report concludes that there is a quite inevitable conflict between the farming community and the rest of the population. Farmers should be offered incentives to farm consistently with the maintenance of more wild-life. These incentives should be designed to follow a national land use strategy which should be developed as a matter of urgency. The arguments in this report are consistent with the externality models presented in Chapters 2 and 6. The situation implied by the report is illustrated in Fig. 8.4. Left to themselves, farmers would choose to operate at A, whereas conservationists would prefer them to be at C. As we have seen earlier, aggregate not social benefits would be maximized at N, which would imply a substantial cut in agricultural activity.

The problem, however, is that we really do not know where the MNSB curve for conservation lies. As far as the evidence available goes, we could easily assert that it cuts the axis at K, rather than N, and hence that only a minor adjustment to agricultural activity is called for. The conservation case is strengthened by the argument (put forward by Krutilla (1967), that as natural habitats become

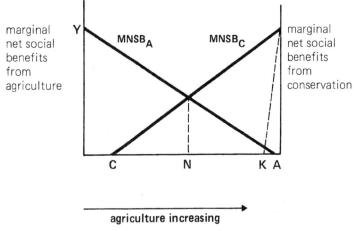

Figure 8.4

rarer, they become more valuable. Thus an increase in the demand for food might cause the $MNSB_A$ to shift upwards, but this could well be offset by a similar shift of $MNSB_C$. Furthermore, the conservationists can assert that, at some point in the decline of a species or habitat, its disappearance is inevitable. The dilemma remains, though, what exactly is being lost. If it is simply genetic variability, this can be preserved artificially with very small amounts of land; if it is the cultural value of wild-life, we should ask how many people are concerned and what is their 'willingness-to-pay' for its conservation. In order to calibrate the model above, we would also need information on the cost of conservation. The NSB curves are obtained by deducing social costs from willingness-to-pay. The main items of cost would be the loss of agricultural production and possibly other benefits, such as recreation. Until some of these magnitudes can be established, there seems little chance of a rational conservation policy. Meanwhile, perhaps we must accept as satisfactory that the land at present controlled by the Nature Conservancy Council, and managed with conservation in mind, is enough for present purposes. However, this argument rests heavily on present food and timber price levels.

If the commodity price levels maintained in Europe lead to continuing agricultural surplus problems, it is likely that there will be a renewed interest in land retirement (from agriculture) as a means of controlling supply. The existence of such policies would offer scope to conservation bodies, and other public land users, to take over more land for their own purposes.

9　Population

Rapid technological progress in agriculture, industry and tertiary sectors, continues to have substantial impacts on population and labour in rural areas. Agricultural productivity has been improved and continues to improve in two ways. First, by technological improvements, including higher-yielding varieties of crops, greater use of fertilizer and new chemical methods of weed, pest and disease control. Comparable technological improvements have taken place in animal husbandry. Secondly, structural and organizational improvement contribute to improved productivity. Structurally, farm size has been modified by a decline in the smallest categories, with a slight increase being recorded in the number of large holdings. Proportionately, large holdings now account for a much larger number of all units. Organizational change has occurred through specialization and concentration of production.

These changes continue to lead to an increased intensity of farming systems and a substantial increase in the volume of capital invested in agriculture, with a considerable substitution of capital for labour. The effects on the agricultural labour force have been documented by Heath and Whitby (1970), who noted the rapid decline in the number of hired workers, so that the average number of regular male hired workers per full-time holding fell from 2.1 to 1.8 between 1963 and 1968. Similarly, in the secondary and tertiary sectors of the economy, technological, structural and organizational improvements have led to increased productivity, and to increases in the operational size of units which, in rural areas, has often resulted in labour shedding and to a concentration of activities in larger villages and towns. The regrouping of population in rural areas (e.g. by Lindsey County Council, 1973, and Nottinghamshire County Council, 1969) is a response to these market trends. It is recognized that an economic and efficient provision of services, including social and community facilities, requires that population should be concentrated rather than dispersed throughout a particular area.

In Great Britain, spatial 'population planning' has long formed one of the goals of national economic, regional, and local physical planning. The Barlow Report (1940), apart from declaring in favour of well planned satellite towns as a means of relieving congestion in the existing badly planned, perhaps too large and, in most cases, unhealthy conurbations, stated firmly that growth in London and its immediate surroundings was excessive and ought to be diverted elsewhere. One of the reasons advanced for this was the undesirable extent to which London acted 'as a continual drain on the rest of the country both for industry and population'. Regional planning organizations have also set population targets. The Northern Economic Planning Council (1966) stated:

> The aim must be rather to strive for the kind of economy and environment which will attract enterprising people from elsewhere, and in sufficient numbers to outweigh the normal outward movement. It may be thought optimistic to postulate a reduction of new outflow by 1971 to about one-half of the average experienced over the period of 1959-64 . . . and the achievement of a state of balance by 1981. But these are figures which should and can be achieved, provided that continued support is given through government policies.

This theme is echoed by the Highlands and Islands Development Board which noted in its first annual report that:

> most opinions, as we have studied and listened to them, accept that depopulation of the area is the central problem . . . (and that) . . . we will do our utmost to generate major growth points, involving substantial increases in population, wherever the natural advantages of the area seem to warrant it. (Grieve, 1972)

At a local physical planning level, the concern over population levels appears as in Northumberland County Council's (1969) development plan for rural areas:

> The over-riding matter for concern of a rural policy for Northumberland, however, is to devise a plan that will enable the run down of the rural community to be halted . . . (and) . . . In some circumstances one can take the view that basic economic changes must result in a redistribution of population, and that as farming appears still to be in a strong economic state in Northumberland then there is no cause for alarm. The population trends in Northumberland, however, have been on a dramatic scale and go beyond the point where one could regard the process in a tolerant way.

Thus the usual politically induced population constraints in rural areas are: first, the maintenance – right or wrong – of a minimum population in these areas (this means that a labour force which leaves agriculture in response to socio-economic stimulae, as opposed to demographic increase, has to be absorbed by growth in the rural industry and service sectors); and second, the prevention of a relative decline in area *per capita* income (this is a difficult objective for remote rural areas, since they often grow at the slowest rate).

Little research has been undertaken on the inter-relationships of population levels to other socio-economic goals. Population targets in rural areas may be inconsistent with maximum efficiency of resource use, although population levels in rural areas are usually based on equity as well as on efficiency criteria. However, equity and efficiency objectives themselves may be in conflict. To consider population levels in rural areas as a problem by reference either to efficiency or equity criteria, is inadequate. The establishment of a case for rural policy requires that both be considered.

Rural population 'problems' only exist to the extent that some social objective has been stated and shown to be desirable in some way. If the actual situation differs from this objective, or will differ in time, a problem may be said to exist. But it is only in terms of some derived social welfare function that allocates factors of production (efficiency), income level, distribution (equity), general satisfaction and distribution of wants, that population 'problems' can be identified. The 'problems' associated with population and labour decline are not new on the rural scene; indeed, they are more than a century old (Saville, 1957) and their most dramatic manifestations occurred in the last thirty years of the nineteenth century. Analysis of the processes of change reveals their continuing presence and emphasizes the need for periodic reassessments of population and employment in rural areas.

Fertility

Rural populations have a number of characteristics which are distinct from those of urban populations. Population change is basically a function of fertility, migration and mortality. Sophisticated demographic models would resolve these into component parts to further approach reality. For example, fertility, which is obtained by expressing live births as a rate per 1000 women of child-bearing age, may be influenced by the age of the mother and the duration of marriage. In general, fertility rates decline with advancing age of mother and with lengthening duration of marriage. Thus, age-marriage-duration specific fertility rates are often calculated. Fertility varies not only with age and duration of marriage, but also with occupation, social class, area of residence (rural or urban), religion and many other factors. In India, consummation of marriage may not take place until one or two years after the original ceremony; the length of a period of low fecundity after a birth may depend upon the extent of psychological and biological changes reducing sexual drive; infertility may result also from social or religious 'taboos' concerning intercourse following a birth; or from the use of methods of birth control, which themselves vary in efficiency and therefore in their practical effect; or from divorce, abortion, remarriage, or widowhood. Such questions are of importance in considering the difference that exists, even in primitive peoples, between a woman's actual fertility and the maximum number of children that it is physiologically possible for her to bear. For an introduction to demography and demographic terminology, the reader is referred to Benjamin (1968) and Cox (1970).

Fertility has, generally, always been higher among women in rural than urban areas (Table 9.1), but the difference has narrowed considerably since the 1940s. In the past, this difference exacerbated the pressure on resources, especially where rapid technological progress or structural change and organizational improvements occurred simultaneously in agriculture, and alternative employment

Table 9.1 Ratio of local adjusted birth rate to national rate,* by type of settlement aggregate, England and Wales

	1950	1953	1956	1959	1962	1965	1968	1971
Conurbations	0.94	0.94	0.95	0.95	0.98	0.98	0.98	0.97
Urban areas >100,000 population	1.03	1.02	1.00	1.00	0.98	1.00	1.01	1.01
Urban areas 50,000– 100,000 population	1.01	1.02	0.99	0.99	0.98	0.99	0.99	1.00
Urban areas <50,000 population	1.02	1.04	1.02	1.01	0.96	1.02	1.03	1.05
Rural areas	1.09	1.09	1.06	1.04	1.01	1.02	1.01	1.04

Source: Registrar General (1968).

*Obtained by multiplying crude birth rate per thousand by Area Comparability Factor, and expressing the result as a ratio of the rate for England and Wales as a whole.

Crude birth rates for local areas may not be comparable one with another because populations on which they are based may contain different proportions of women of child bearing age. In order to eliminate differences between local birth rates due to this cause, a standardizing factor, termed an Area Comparability Factor, is calculated by the Registrar General.

opportunities were not being created. Demographic increase or an excess of births over deaths can thus lead to out-migration. Although fertility is still higher in rural than urban areas, crude rates of population increase (births per 1000 resident population) are often not. Population change in many rural areas since the nine-

Table 9.2 Components of population change in selected rural areas

Area	Per cent population change 1961–71		
	Natural	Net migration	Total
Great Britain	6.0	·–0.7	5.2
England	6.0	–0.1	5.8
Rural Northumberland	1.0	–5.0	–4.0
Wales	3.6	–0.3	3.0
Merioneth and Montgomery	0.9	–5.0	–5.2
Rural Carmarthen	–0.3	–3.2	–3.4
Scotland	6.6	–6.3	0.7
Sutherland	0.9	–4.4	–3.4
Roxburgh	1.3	–4.2	–2.9
Wigton	4.7	–10.9	–6.1

Sources: 1961 and 1971 Census and HM Treasury (1976).

teenth century has resulted in a loss of working age groups, and an increase proportionately, if not absolutely, in retired persons. The resulting age structure differs from the national position with a lower percentage of both children and of persons in the normal reproductive age groups. Thus many rural areas have a significantly lower rate of natural increase (births over deaths) than elsewhere and in some areas the local population is not even reproducing itself (i.e. deaths exceed births, for example, in rural Carmarthen, resulting, irrespective of out-migration, in a natural decrease – see Table 9.2).

Mortality

Mortality rates have generally decreased steadily since the nineteenth century, but considerable rural-urban differences exist (see Table 9.3).

Death rates are higher in industrial and urban areas than in rural areas. Agricultural workers have one of the lowest ratios of actual to expected deaths among occupational groups in Britain. In 1934, the Registrar General undertook some investigations into differential mortality and suggested that, in rural areas, it appeared as though men's relatively healthy occupational surroundings were sufficient to offset any adverse effects of their lower average incomes and poorer housing conditions – though there was less likely to be a balance between the two forces in the case of wives (see Table 9.3). In some areas, such as the crofting counties of Scotland, analysis of census data shows a rate of mortality higher than average for young

Table 9.3   Ratios of actual deaths by type of settlement aggregate, 1950–2 and 1968 to expected deaths, based on the national experience, England and Wales

	1950–2		*1968*
Type of area	*Men*	*Women*	*Total population*
Conurbations	1.065	1.026	1.05
Urban areas >100,000 population	1.065	1.037	1.06
Urban areas 50,000–100,000 population	0.989	0.966	0.99
Urban areas <50,000 population	0.981	0.998	0.98
Rural areas	0.876	0.941	0.91

Sources: Cox (1970) and Registrar General (1968).

Type of area	M	F	M	F	M	F	M	F	M	F
Conurbations	114	110	111	114	120	121	94	98	92	108
Urban areas >100,000 population	97	99	103	106	100	101	96	104	92	101
Urban areas 50,000—100,000 population	102	97	101	113	99	93	100	103	98	96
Urban areas <50,000 population	98	94	95	92	88	82	99	99	94	88
Rural areas	81	90	84	70	79	81	113	100	126	99
Per cent of total male and female deaths respectively	1.1	0.6	1.1	0.8	0.2	0.1	3.7	2.8	1.6	0.7

Source: Registrar General (1967).

* Standard Mortality Ratios (SMRs) express the actual number of deaths at all ages in each geographical area as a percentage of the expected number of deaths, i.e. the number that would have occurred in the area, if the death rate for each sex/age group had been the same as that of England and Wales. The SMR therefore provides a more meaningful comparison of the mortality in each area with that of the country as a whole, because it removes the effects of local variations in the proportionate sex/age structure of the population by a process of indirect standardization.

men, perhaps due to the selective out-migration of more healthy people to other areas.

Considerable variations exist between urban and rural areas in the causes of death. Mortality ratios are extremely low in rural areas for diseases of the bronchus and lung, and correspondingly very high in conurbations (see Table 9.4). Rural areas also have low SMRs for heart disease and for illness which may be attributable to mental stress (ulcers and suicides), but deaths from accidents are higher than expected.

Generally, rural regions have lower mortality rates than urban areas. The lower mortality rates results in an older population age structure, with consequent need for social and public services in rural areas.

Rural life

The idyllic portrayal of the English countryside has been a strong cultural theme. England's green and pleasant land has been epitomized by painters (Constable), poets (Wordsworth) and writers (Cobbett). Later writers consolidated the idealism of rural life into a tradition of its own out of a critique of urban industrialism, and conjured up a rural arcadia peopled by merry rustics and sturdy beef-eating yeomanry. The core of this tradition is that life in the country-side is viewed as one of harmony and virtue. The town is dis-organized; the countryside is settled. The town is bad; the country-side is good. Social relationships in the town are superficial and alienating; relationships in the countryside are deep and fulfilling. The English village has come to be regarded as the ideal community, and rural life as cultivating social values and continuing a cultural heritage (Country Landowners' Association, 1970). It is a tradition that has penetrated large areas of our culture, including literature, aesthetics, ideas about community, architecture, town and country planning philosophy and practice, and social science in general.

Town planning has always assumed some causality between the aesthetic and the social: an environment that meets society's aesthetic approval must support a socially beneficial way of life, just as the aesthetic inferiority of inner urban areas must accompany social deprivation. Many people feel that conurbations support lonely, alienated existences (higher suicide rates) which supposedly reflect the inhuman scale of city buildings; suburbia supposedly supports a life of dreary self-containment and conformity; but in the rural areas, the social structure is thought of as complementing the admired aesthetic qualities of the English countryside.

This view has been reflected in the main categories of sociological thought inherited from the nineteenth cenutry, which continue in varying degrees to influence our thinking in the twentieth century. Tönnies (1877) analysed the nature of society with the twin concepts of Gemeinschaft and Gesellschaft, usually roughly translated as 'community' and 'association'. In Tönnies' view, the European society of his time was in the throes of a relentless progression from Gemeinschaft to Gesellschaft. Urbanization was only one aspect of a whole set of interrelated social changes which affected the whole of society, as it became ever less dependent on agriculture and ever more commercial and industrial. He conceived of Gemeinschaft as characterized by an unity based on intimate personal living together and believed that such contacts satisfied fundamental wants and sentiments, and were built into deep-rooted and rich personal relationships. Gesellschaft, on the other hand, was characterized by impersonal and limited contractual relations established as a result of calculation and reflection. Gemeinschaft and Gesellschaft were thus two quite opposed ways in which men were bound together, and Tönnies considered there were elements of both Gemeinschaft and Gesellschaft in all social relationships and societies. Similarly, Durkheim (1893) sought to show that societies in which the social division of labour was not very marked (in which there were few specialized roles), exhibited a particular kind of social solidarity which he referred to as 'mechanical', whereas societies with a marked division of labour and a high degree of occupational specialization, were characterized by another type of solidarity which he referred to as 'organic'. The major features of 'mechanical' solidarity were the relative homogeneity of population and the uniformity of beliefs, opinions and conduct. In contrast, 'organic' solidarity obtained when a population was 'mentally and morally' heterogeneous, when there is a diversity of beliefs, opinions and conduct. Durkheim suggested that in societies with 'mechanical' solidarity, social cohesion derives from a certain conformity of the behaviour of individuals to a common standard. He thus saw 'mechanical' solidarity as based on the similarity of individuals, whereas he considered 'organic' solidarity to be based on interdependence arising out of diversity and complementarity.

Just as town planning has its roots in rural-urban contrast, so many sociological theories of social change derive their conceptual inspiration from this same contrast, which continues to inform town planning and sociology. Thus, for Redfield (1955), urban society constitutes a disorganized social milieu, whereas folk society is, like the little community, more orderly and harmonious.

Such a high regard for country life if often held by urban dwellers, but they rarely participate in it (and then only adventitiously as tourists, or from second homes and weekend cottages).

If the models of rural society and the rural community are retained as reference points, we are likely to see city life as 'disorganized', since it appears so much more fluid and less integrated. However, the modern conception of community is very far removed from older conceptions based on the model of the village. It suggests that in some ways, though the city does contain the 'unattached' and 'lonely crowds', not only do primary groups – families, neighbourhood groups, church congregations, pub clienteles, etc. – retain their importance, but new kinds of secondary associations are generated, since in large populations any minority interest, however small, may well bring together scattered individuals who would be completely isolated in a village, but who become part of a community in a big city.

The tradition of rural respect is far from dead today, although this idea has been disputed. It has been alleged that the characteristic village shows strife, feuds and mistrust among its inhabitants. From the point of view of morals, it has also been suggested that premarital sexual relations are common in some rural areas, that certain sexual aberrations, such as sodomy and incest, occur mainly in rural areas, and that the overriding trait of most rural dwellers is cruelty (Hirsh, 1969). Some statistical evidence to support such controversial statements come from Kinsey *et al.* (1948), who provided some evidence regarding one sexual deviation, that of bestiality. In America, the incidence of animal human contact for the whole population was estimated at 8 per cent, although among boys reared on farms, Kinsey reported that the incidence was much higher, around 17 per cent.

That rural life is interspersed by many difficulties on an individual level, has been made evident by two sociological surveys in northern England (Williams, 1956; Nalson, 1968). Williams, in studying Gosforth, a parish on the western fringe of the Lakeland fells in

Cumberland, thought that the economically induced shortage of farm workers there had probably greatly increased the functional importance of the family as an economic unit, creating cohesiveness and solidarity within it. The late age at which farmers' sons married was attributed to filial loyalty and to the subservient role of the sons in the family economic unit. This, with the fact that farm tenancies have become increasingly difficult to obtain in recent years, has, if anything, raised the age of marriage even higher than it was a generation ago – some farmers' sons do not marry until they are over thirty-five or even forty-five.

The average age at which farmers' sons in Gosforth married was, however, lower than that reported in parts of rural Wales and Eire; the latter, in particular, being characterized by a very high percentage of unmarried adult males. Farmers' daughters, like their brothers, tend to marry later than villagers, or than is usual in England and Wales as a whole. This delay is less than that of farmers' sons, probably because they have a much less important role in the economic unit. The son may have a choice between early marriage, with a risk of losing his parents' farm, and late marriage (when nuptial prospects are poor), with a chance of inheriting the farm. Other farming occupations face similar problems. In many hill sheep areas of Britain, the shepherd's skill is restricted in application to more remote areas, and his cottage, part payment for the job, is likely to be isolated, and consequently his financial and social position is not attractive to the limited number of females in the same class.

Williams found that the size of the farm families in Gosforth had halved over the last 150 years. He attributes this mainly to economic causes, and his investigations suggest that family size was un-connected with the introduction of modern methods of contra-ception. Pre-marital intercourse was high, judging by the amount of time that lapsed between marriage and the birth of the first child, particularly among farmers. Nalson (1968) cites the planning of pre-nuptial conception in an upland area of Staffordshire as a means of forcing the acceptance of a marriage by otherwise reluctant parents, who must then provide a home (and maybe a farm) for a son or a son-in-law.

Frankenberg (1966), in an account of social life, postulates the changing nature of society on a continuum between town and country, without passing any value judgement upon which is better.

The difference between the two ends of the continuum are striking in terms of type of community, social fields, role relationships of individuals, role conflict, status, networks of relationships, class divisions, organization, integration and alienation and other themes.

However, rural life tends to be viewed from within through gentleman's eyes – those possessing high status in rural life. From urban society, rural life is viewed through middle class eyes, especially those concerned with conservation who have proved to be fierce protectors of the visual aspects of the English countryside. Newby (1977) points to this marked contrast between the prevailing English attitude towards the plight of the agricultural worker, and the attention and esteem lavished on the English countryside and 'the rural way of life'. The agricultural worker remains relatively ignored and caricatured – 'yokel', 'country bumpkin', 'clodhopper' – in public consciousness. Yet Newby suggests that only a small proportion of agricultural workers (about 15 per cent) can be considered as deferential workers in the sense that they adhere to a reasonably consistent, deferential image of society. The deference which is often attributed to the agricultural worker can be seen to rest largely upon a fallacious inference made from his largely quiescent social and political behaviour. This quiescence, argues Newby, must be seen to result from the agricultural worker's dependence – upon the farmer for employment and in many cases housing – rather than from his deference. For the most part, the agricultural worker has acknowledged his powerlessness and decided to make the best of an inferior situation, contriving to take it somewhat for granted, while not necessarily endorsing it in terms of social justice.

The lack of any open rebelliousness helps to account for the agricultural worker's deferential image and the idyllic view of the countryside among outside observers. The servile appearance of the agricultural worker has often hid a covert form of opposition to those in power over him: most serious histories of the agricultural worker recognize that the placid exterior sometimes obscured bitter antagonisms which seem to be ignored in the conventional wisdom about English rural life. The dissatisfaction with the rural life – in terms of living standards and expectations – has been manifest in a continuing drift from the land, rather than strikes and other forms of militant action: the deferential worker has voted on the Gemeinschaft – Gesellschaft issue with his feet!

Migration

Many studies have sought to explain the reasons for migration from rural areas (Cowie and Giles, 1957; Saville, 1957; Bracey, 1958; Redford, 1964; House, 1965; House and Knight, 1966; McIntosh, 1969; Gasson, 1974; Mackel, 1975). This migration process is interpreted as a movement away from rural-agricultural economic activity and dispersed rural-agricultural community living due to (1) the higher income elasticities of demand for non-agricultural goods and services; (2) changes in agricultural productivity: the substitution of capital for labour, resulting in a left-shift in the demand curve for labour and (3) low income and adverse social conditions, all of which are forces tending to 'push' migrants out of rural areas. The converse of these conditions, factors 'pulling' migrants to urban areas are (1) the growth of the non-agricultural sectors of the economy; (2) centralization of populations in and around a network of non-agricultural occupational, industrial, and amenity-related facilities and (3) higher non-agricultural incomes, social amenities and better transport in urban areas.

The actual rate of migration depends upon urban pulls and rural-agricultural pushes, and the result of both forces is the emergence of a supply of rural-agricultural labour in excess of labour demand. This is reinforced, in some areas, by the higher rate of demographic increase due to the higher fertility rates and lower mortality rates than occur nationally, or in urban areas. The implication then, is that as numerous urban areas begin to emerge, and as rates of occupational and industrial expansion vary, urban wage rates exceed those in rural places, due to a shortage of labour in general or labour of specific skills. Consequently, urban places begin to compete for labour at rural places, with migrants selecting destinations of best economic advantage. A great many studies of migration relate to one or another aspect of this framework. However, there has been disagreement between the conclusions of individual studies. This is partly because there is no unanimity over the meaning or definition of the term 'migration'. Essentially, migration involves a person who moves from an origin, over an intervening distance, to a destination. There is considerable controversy over what this distance should be, and what time span is involved (Willis, 1974). Time is important, and various criteria have been proposed to restrict migration to those moves over some minimum duration (to exclude tourists and even journey to work!). It is often difficult, in practice, to distinguish between temporary moves and permanent moves for work purposes. The disadvantage of a minimum duration of residence (such as one year – used, for example, by the British census: 'what was your address one year ago?') is that it emphasizes the more permanent parts of the community: the shorter the duration of residence, the higher will be the migration rate within a given time period. All demographic statistics refer to some sort of territorial schema. Sociologists prefer to define migration as a move which involves a change in the 'community' of residence. Thus Thomas (1938) said: 'The accepted definition of internal migration is a change of residence from one community, or other clearly defined geographic unit, to another within national boundaries'. Unfortunately, among sociologists, there is no general agreement on what a 'community' is, let alone its areal extent. Lee (1966) defined migration 'broadly as a permanent or semi-permanent change of residence', and placed 'no restriction . . . upon the distance of the move'. Even with this definition, there still remains the problem of area: migration must be measured in relation to some spatial definition. In analysing statistics of internal migration, the choice of territorial unit is equivalent to selecting the kinds of migrants to be studied (Willis, 1974). Migration resulting from job changes tends to involve greater distances than changes in family status. In relation to the following comments, migration has been defined as a change of usual residence from that of one year ago, according to the population census definition. Thus internal migration is a change of usual residence within a local authority area. In-migrants are recorded as persons taking up usual residence within the local authority area, and out-migrants as persons leaving their usual residence and moving across the boundary of the local authority area and taking up residence in another area.

In industrial areas, internal migration is substantial, compared with gross in- and out-migration rates. With some exceptions, the pattern for the more remote rural areas is completely reversed, typified by low internal and in-migration rates per 1000 population, coupled with higher out-migration rates. The vast majority of local authority areas have high rates of short-term residential duration, but more typical of rural areas suffering from depopulation are quite high long-term residence periods and low rates of short-term residential duration (House and Willis, 1967). However, some parishes in rural areas have very high rates of population turnover. House and Knight (1966), using electoral roll data 1960–4, found population turnover in the parishes of Bardon Mill, Greenhead and Plenmellar, in the South Tyne, to be in excess of 50 per cent of the 1960 population of the respective areas. However, there is no reason to suppose in theory, or in fact, that large turnover figures are indicative of unstable areas likely to lose substantial population by net out-migration (Willis, 1974).

Out-migrants from rural areas are concentrated in the younger age groups: House (1965) found that between 1951 and 1961, in rural North-East England, 41 per cent of all out-migrants were under twenty years of age. But migration involves a two-way flow of people and in-migration still occurs to areas suffering from population decline. Net-migration (the difference between gross in-and-out-migration) exhibits distinctive patterns for rural areas. Generally, rural areas exhibit loss across all age-groups, with the level of net-migration diminishing slowly until middle-age cohorts, with more salient male loss concentrated before twenty-four years of age. Market centres in rural areas exhibit either prominent loss groups below twenty-four years, with general stability or very slight but even age-spectrum outflow for all older age-groups; or a net inflow of school leavers, followed by a very sharp reversal and outflow in the young adult age-groups (House, 1965). Net in-migration, however, is often characteristic of rural settlements on the urban fringe and large settlements within commuting distance.

Population estimation and projection

The population is counted only at census years (decennially, with a quinquennial exception in 1966), and if it is desired to estimate the population appropriate to an intercensal year, some assumptions must be made as to the population changes during the intercensal period.

Intercensal estimates of local population on 30 June each year have been made for some time by the Office of Population Censuses and Surveys (formerly the General Register Office) for the Department of the Environment (Housing and Planning). They serve a number of functions, assisting central and local planning authorities with the preparation of, and later their reviews of, statutory development plans. They also form an input into regional plans, and into *ad hoc* studies, such as local land-use transportation plans. But one of their main uses is a financial one: to calculate the needs element of the Rate Support Grant. The needs element forms the largest single element in the RSG and amounted to £1758 million out of a total RSG of £2173 million paid to local authorities in England and Wales in 1972. The needs element payment is based annually on the total population of the local authority area (multiplied by a prescribed sum) and also on the number of persons under fifteen years of age (multiplied by a prescribed sum); with a supplementary financial payment calculated by aggregating a variety of sums of money allocated in accordance with other population and spatial character-istics of the area (Hepworth, 1976).

Estimates of population in sex and age groups require:

(1) an estimate (derived from the census in April) of population at 30 June;
(2) births for each sex mid-year to mid-year;
(3) deaths for each sex, and at individual ages last birthday at mid-year;
(4) emigrants and immigrants from mid-year to mid-year for each sex by age groups.

Births and deaths can be estimated by applying national fertility and mortality rates to local populations, corrected by an area comparability factor to allow for variations between national and local age structures. Alternatively, returns of births and deaths to local Registrar's of Births, Marriages, and Deaths can be used. Births and deaths recorded in this way are reallocated to place of residence. Migration is the most difficult variable to estimate because data on migration are lacking. Other sources of information are typically drawn upon to indicate the direction and pace of popula-tion change, such as returns by local authorities on house building and demolition, school enrolments, changes in numbers registered in institutions for the mentally ill or disabled and lists of Parliamentary electors (rated up by their proportion to the entire population at the last census). Estimates of migration are thus often subjective judge-ments likely to represent average conditions. Schneider (1956) gives an early account of the work which went into preparing local popula-tion estimates.

The need for accurate forecasts of future population levels and distributions is equally acute. Population projections were first used for long-term financial estimates under the Contributory Pensions

Acts and other schemes of National Insurance, but today, projections have become increasingly important in many other areas of government planning. Area health authorities (whose boundaries are co-terminous with counties and metropolitan districts) produce plans for the provision of services to the population they serve. Some view of the likely future size and structure of the population of each area is an essential requirement of these plans. Similarly, town and country development plans are essentially long-term and decisions need to be related to expected requirements, often fifteen or more years ahead, in relation to the development and other use of land in the area, such as housing, social service provision, roads etc.

There are a number of major methods for projecting population (Isard, 1960). Principal among traditional direct methods are demographic component models (or cohort-survival models). This involves taking the number of people at each single age and estimating how many will survive to be one year older next year. The age structure of people entering and leaving the area is also taken into account, and those aged under one are estimated from the number of births each year. It is, therefore, necessary to make assumptions on the future number of births, deaths and migrants. Once this is done, the process described above can be repeated as far into the future as required. Projections can also be made with five or ten year age groups, with appropriate survival rates, for five or ten years block projections in time.

The basic method is thus the same as that used for intercensal estimates, except that the components of the calculation are not actual but future events. In the following formulae, the prefix relates to the calendar year and the suffix relates to age last birthday. The calculation moves forward from year to year separately for each sex and for each single year of age by the formula:

$$^{n}p_{x} = {}^{n-1}p_{x-1}(1 - {}^{n-1}q_{x-\frac{1}{2}}) + {}^{n}M_{x}$$

where $^{n}p_{x}$ = number of persons at mid-year n aged x last birthday
$^{n}M_{x}$ = net migrants inward (if outward, it becomes a negative quantity) in the period mid-year $n - 1$ to mid-year n, aged x last birthday at mid-year n
$^{n-1}q_{x-\frac{1}{2}}$ = probability of death within a year for a person aged $(x - 1)$ last birthday at mid-year $n - 1$.

At age 0 the formula is:

$$^{n}p_{0} = {}^{n}B(1 - {}^{n-1}{}_{\frac{1}{2}}q_{0}) + {}^{n}M_{0}$$

where ^nB = number of live births in period mid-year $n - 1$ to
    mid-year n

$n-\frac{1}{2}q_0$ = probability that a baby born in the period mid-year
    $n - 1$ to mid-year n will die before the end of that
    period.

The base population usually presents no problem. For mortality, a forecast has to be made of ^nq_x applicable to some year in the future. Age specific rates of mortality tend, despite the apparently dramatic nature of medical advances, to move slowly and steadily, and their extrapolation either by graphic representation or the assumption of a mathematical law of decrease (e.g. logarithmic) is generally reasonably accurate. Fertility and migration present greater problems, and assumptions continually change. Assumptions relating to the future are based on past events, updated in the light of recent experience and trends of variables affecting fertility and migration, such as duration of marriage, family size and factors affecting family size, illegitimate births, economic circumstances and government policy on migration (Economic Trends, May 1975; Office of Population Censuses and Surveys, 1975).

The demographic component method has also provided the conceptual framework for a number of population studies in rural areas, such as that of Jackson (1968) on population change in the Cotswolds and Willis (1971) on population trends in the Northern Pennines. Whereas projections are for single years of age in official national forecasts, such a detailed age breakdown of the base population is frequently not available for local projections, and so five year, or less frequently, ten year age groups are used. Local population projections face a number of problems in addition to those faced by national projections. Published data for local, particularly rural, areas is scarce. Annual births and deaths are not available by age or sex, being indicated in terms of crude rates for the whole population. Since the difference between local survival/mortality rates and the national rate may be considerable, especially in rural areas where, as we have already seen, SMRs are lower for many diseases and for many occupation groups, some adjustment of rates is necessary to allow for variations if accurate forecasts are to be made. Craig (1970) has considered several possible indicators of the variation of local to national mortality rates, in terms of frequency of collection and publication, areas covered and age-sex breakdown. Standardized mortality ratios are produced decennially, covering counties sub-

divided into county boroughs, urban areas and rural areas
(aggregates). (Registrar General, 1967). The age-sex breakdown is
not arrived at by quinary groups in all cases. Where the quinary
breakdown is not given, the rates must be averaged and smoothed
before being used to adjust the national mortality rates to
comparable local rates (Craig, 1970). Adjustment for spatial variations in birth rates is more difficult. An allowance can be made for
spatial differences in birth rates by applying total population (age
corrected) differentials to all fertility data for female birth-
producing cohorts 15-45, from the relevant Registrar General's
(annual) Statistical Review, Population Tables (Willis, 1971).
However, due to stochastic variations between individual years, it is
very difficult to project local area differential birth rates. This is a
very great problem in population projection in small, especially
rural, areas. Where total population is small, any demographic rate
is subject to stochastic fluctuation. Even with complete statistical
information, calculation of, say, a birth rate in an area is subject to
stochastic fluctuations through time and has a 95 per cent chance of
being in between

$$p \pm 2 \sqrt{\frac{p(1-p)}{n}}$$

where n is the population and p is the mean rate of birth. Thus n has
to be great if sufficient approximation is required. Random fluctuations can, therefore, become important in small area rural forecasts.
Migration is not only subject to considerable fluctuation from one
year to another, but is also the most critical demographic factor in
small area population forecasts. This can be shown by a sensitivity
analysis (Table 9.5) in which assumed birth, death, and migration
rates are each altered by a constant proportion, holding the other
two rates constant, so that the effect of each variable on the system
can be assessed (Willis, 1971). A 10 per cent change in migration
rates can result in radically different population projections,
compared with a similar proportional change in birth and death
rates in local areas.

Table 9.5 shows that any error in projecting mortality is not
serious in its effect on population projections, since it only advances
or delays by a few years the time at which the deaths will occur. An
error in fertility is more serious and persists for a long time. Migration, the most crucial variable in local future population projections,

Table 9.5 Sensitivity analysis: population projection 1971–91 with changes in demographic rates

	Population projection assuming current birth death and migration rates 1961–71		Assuming 10 per cent decrease in births		Assuming 10 per cent increase in deaths		Assuming 10 per cent increase in net out-migration	
	M	*F*	*M*	*F*	*M*	*F*	*M*	*F*
Bellingham	2,577	2,657	2,391	2,508	2,552	2,635	1,321	1,373
Glendale	2,648	2,634	2,501	2,498	2,614	2,602	1,369	1,364
South Westmorland	10,544	10,015	9,931	9,504	10,421	9,885	5,442	5,187

Source: Willis (1971).

is the most difficult to project because migration is partly an economic and partly a behavioural phenomenon. The problem arises of not only projecting basic economic variables determining migration and projecting the relationship of migration to these economic variables, but also of allowing for behavioural considerations. Behaviour is a function of the interaction of personality and the environment. In this way, different individuals behave differently in what appears objectively the same environment. Wolpert (1966) has used this behavioural approach to propose a model of migration as an adjustment to environmental stress. In his model amenities and disamenities effect the individual in terms of tolerance or flexibility along a slack-strain axis in his personality. Such a model, however, has never been evaluated and important gaps still exist in measurement and knowledge of the coefficients of susceptibility of the individual to the environment. Migration is also related to social mobility, social and locality participation and integration, and kin and friendship groups (Willis, 1974).

Attempts have been made to build economic models of migration (some incorporating behavioural characteristics) in order to assess in more detail the influence of variables affecting migration, with the hope of being able to predict future migration more accurately on the basis of expected changes in other endogenous or in exogenous variables. Such models have covered individual migration, inter-area migration, and occupational systems and associated migration (Willis, 1974). The important factors explaining migration are those associated with the area of origin, those associated with the area of destination, intervening opportunities and the personal characteristics of the individual.

Sjaastad (1962) was perhaps the first to propose a private cost-return model of migration, in which migration is treated as an investment from which the migrant expects to receive returns at least sufficient to offset the costs of moving. Expressed algebraically, migration will be economic according to a private cost-return model if the following inequality holds:

$$\sum_{n=1}^{N} \frac{(E_{dn} - E_{on})}{(1 + i)^n} - C > 0$$

where E_{dn} = earnings in the nth year at destination
E_{on} = earnings in the nth year at origin

i = rate of interest used to discount future earnings

N = total number of years over which future earnings are expected

C = cost of moving.

This can be reduced to:

$$h(E_d - E_o) - C > 0$$

where $h = \left[1 - \dfrac{1}{(1 + i)^N} \right] \Big/ i$

if it is assumed that the difference in income at the two places is constant in the future. This is not an unreasonable assumption, since agricultural earnings have averaged 80 per cent of industrial earnings in the post-war period. The difference in earnings, the discount rate, and the time horizon over which the earnings are to be discounted, need to be determined empirically. Potential migrants probably do not use such a decision rule in a formal way. However, most migrants, and non-migrants, have some idea of (any) differences in earnings between areas, have some preference for present consumption and earnings over future consumption and earnings, and have some time horizon over which they expect to work.

The model could be made more realistic by introducing other variables on *a priori* grounds, for example:

$$KWLh(E_d - E_o) - C + h \, \Sigma P_i > 0$$

where K = extent of information on job opportunities

        W = probability of obtaining employment at destination

        L = ratio of cost of living at origin to that at destination

        P_i = difference in annual monetary value of the ith non-monetary factor between destination and origin.

Non-monetary factors might include the value placed on proximity to relatives and friends (Nelson, 1959), type of environment, psychological costs of moving, etc. The above equation is a private cost-return model: all factors included are either private costs or benefits to migration. These factors alone are assumed to explain migration so that variables such as age and education (which affect migration rates) act entirely through the variables in the model.

Such a model has never been applied to rural-urban migration in Britain, but a transformed cost-return equation in a form which was tested by multiple regression has been applied to rural-urban migration in Taiwan, and the weights for the various costs and benefits estimated empirically (Speare, 1971):

$$\text{Migration} = f(E, U, K, C, H, F, F_{WP})$$

where U = unemployment
H = owner occupier
F = location of parents
F_{WP} = location of wife's parents.

The private costs and benefits of migration were not actually calculated by Speare, but 76 per cent of migrants and 84 per cent of non-migrants were correctly identified by the model, indicating that it provided a reasonable representation of the decision process followed by people deciding whether or not to move. The analysis indicated that variables which affect monetary costs and benefits, but which cannot be measured easily in monetary terms such as unemployment, home ownership and job information, are at least as important in the decision to move as those variables which can be measured in monetary terms. The location of parents and location of wife's parents also had significant effects on migration.

An earlier study in the USA (Diehl, 1964) related migration rate (farm-non-farm) to net farm income *per capita*. An equation was obtained of the form

$$Y_i = 18.536 - 0.047 \ (IF_i)^{**} - 0.079 \ (G_i)^* + 1.321 \ (S_i)^{**}$$
$$+0.094 \ (R_i)^* + 1.242 \ (A_i)^{**} \quad R^2 = 0.667$$

where Y_i = rate of farm/non-farm migration
IF_i = net farm income per capita 1950–60
G_i = capital gains during decade
S_i = skill variable – per cent of rural farm males with employment experience in occupations most frequently entered by migrants
R_i = per cent of rural farm population which is Negro
A_i = per cent of farm population in 10–24 year age group
** = significant at .01 probability level
* = significant at .05 probability level.

Elasticities of migration were also calculated by Diehl. A farm income 10 per cent larger than the regional average in area i was expected to result in an out-migration rate of about one less migrant per hundred expected total end of decade farm population. The large elasticities obtained in this study for age, income and skill variables support the hypothesis that these factors are of considerable importance in the mobility of rural manpower. Viewed in another way, two-thirds of the failure to migrate is explained by differences in age, skills, and race of the population and by costs of migration.

These types of private cost-returns model probably provide a reasonable representation of the decision process followed by people deciding whether or not to move, and it does not mean that precise implications are calculated: people have only vague concepts of costs and returns. There is a difference, however, between the choice of place of residence in view of maximizing individual utilities, as against that chosen in view of maximizing social utilities. Social utility depends largely on the marginal contribution to the social product while individual utilities depend mainly on average income and certain variables, such as attachment to birth place, closeness to friends and relatives. That is, marginal utility of migration factors to a person may not be the same as social utility to a community – marginal utility of type of environment (rural) may be in an area which does not provide maximal *social* utility. Government policies designed to affect the distribution of population will be considered in a later section.

Simultaneous models

Little research has been undertaken in the development of models of rural areas to assess the interaction of demographic structure, labour force characeristics, income, agricultural and urban structure. A linear   programming   model   of   southern   rural   Kentucky (Spiegelman, Baum and Talbert, 1965) is an admirable attempt given adequate data, but for local areas in Britain input-output data are not available, nor are they easily collected, although a national demographic input-output model has been constructed (Stone, 1971). A more modest type of model is therefore required. Such a cursory model, a simultaneous equation model,[1] has been employed

---

[1] The advantages of using simultaneous equation systems is given in Walters (1970), Chapter 8.

to investigate labour participation and income in rural areas in the Northern Pennines (Willis, 1971). The model had the structural form:

$$Y_1 = f(Y_3 + X_2 + X_4 + X_6 + X_7)$$
$$Y_2 = f(Y_3 + X_2 + X_4 + X_5 + X_6)$$
$$Y_3 = f(Y_2 + X_2 + X_3 + X_5 + X_6)$$

where endogenous variables were

Y_1 = income per capita from agriculture

Y_2 = income per capita from all non-agricultural economic activities

Y_3 = labour participation rate (total labour with jobs/total population eligible to work, i.e. males and females 15-64)

and exogenous variables were

X_2 = percentage of labour force in agriculture

X_3 = percentage of labour force unemployed

X_4 = median age of population

X_5 = percentage of population in each period in higher socio-economic groups (1, 2, 3, 4, 13)

X_6 = 1 if parish is service centre; 0 otherwise

X_7 = percentage standard man days[1] devoted to sheep.

The model was evaluated by a two-stage least-squares method since the equations are over-identified.[2] The purpose of such a model embodying *a priori* information is to attain an ideal situation in which, after appealing both to facts and to the model, only the hypothesis remains acceptable and is consistent with both. The structural equations are a set of autonomous relationships sufficient to determine the numerical values of the endogenous variables, given the values of the exogenous variables. Results presented below in Table 9.6 specify numerical values of the reduced-form equations. These are not autonomous and allow for the simultaneous effect of the other variables in the model on each endogenous variable.

The reduced forms record the change in income and labour rates

[1] SMDs (Standard Man Days) are the estimated labour requirements of different agricultural enterprises.

[2] Over-identification occurs where two or more ways exist of estimating one of the parameters of the model.

or a result of a change (perhaps policy change) in the predetermined variables. For example, a decrease of one unit in SMDs devoted to sheep production would raise agricultural income per head by 0.016 units; a rise of one unit in percentage of labour force in agriculture would increase agricultural income per 0.168. A generalized correlation coefficient[1] of 0.961 was obtained, measuring the extent to which the systematic relationships explain the fluctuations in the set of all jointly dependent variables. Thus approximately all the generalized variance of the set of jointly dependent variables has been accounted for by the regression relationship and approximately 5 per cent remains unexplained. Agricultural income *per capita* is positively related to the labour activity rate; but while the percentage of the labour force in agriculture is positively related to income, median age and percentage SMDs devoted to sheep are negatively related to income and, though highly significant, their coefficients are small. A unit increase in the percentage of the labour force in agriculture would only raise agricultural income by a small amount, as would any decrease in median age of population and SMDs devoted to sheep. The service centre variables indicate that agricultural *per capita* income is higher nearer or at service centres and lower in the rural hinterland, as would be expected. This latter variable, together with labour activity rates for the total working population (Y_3), are highly significant determinants of agricultural income; and any change in these variables (Y_3 and X_6) will result in radical changes in agricultural income *per capita*, compared with results from any other changes in the remaining variables in the model.

This analysis suggests that the direct effects of increasing activity rates would more than offset the downward pressure on agricultural income resulting from the older age structure in rural areas and the greater concentration on sheep production. In seeking higher agricultural income levels in rural areas, more attention should probably be given to increasing labour force participation by stimulating additional employment and facilitating movement from rural areas. The provision of more labour market information in these areas

---

[1] R^2 cannot be used in TSLS to estimate goodness of fit of each equation. The generalized correlation coefficient measures the extent to which the systematic relationships explain the fluctuations in the set of all jointly dependent variables. See Christ (1966). This measure is itself open to criticism.

might serve the same goal as well as promoting greater participation in the local labour force.

If depopulation is to be influenced and money incomes improved, relative to existing higher urban incomes, positive rural policies are needed. It may be questioned whether incomes can be effectively raised by transferring resources out of sheep and restructuring agriculture in remoter areas. The analysis suggests that the overriding need is to increase labour activity rates by providing more employment outside agriculture. There is at present a general lack of variety of rural employment. The largest coefficient influencing farm income, non-farm income and labour participation in Table 9.6 was that associated with the urban hierarchy: whether a settlement was classified as a service centre or not. Farm income could be raised by concentrating on agricultural areas near to service centres, and labour participation and non-farm income could be raised in a similar way. The apparently paradoxical lesson has to be learned: to develop rural areas, policies must aim at urbanization.

The model indicates the effect of demographic change, such as age-structure, socio-economic and employment structure on the *per capita* income in rural areas. Similar models could be constructed for other socio-economic sectors in rural areas, and these could be evaluated from available census data.

A study of the impact of industrialization in mid-Wales (Development Commission, 1972) estimated that Development Commission factories had slowed the decline in employment between 1961 and 1968 from 9.1 per cent, which would have taken place in their absence, to 7.4 per cent. Altogether the factories are estimated to have retained 2973 people who would otherwise have left the area. This reduced the decline of population in mid-Wales between 1961 and 1969 from a total of 4.3 per cent to 2.7 per cent. Half of these 2973 'prevented migrants' were in the child-bearing age-group and they have, therefore, had an impact on the natural change of the mid-Wales population out of all proportion to their number. If the Development Commission factories had not been set up, the excess of deaths over births (78 during 1968) would probably have been 36 per cent greater. Moreover, the Development Commission calculated that the expenditure incurred in financing the eighteen occupied Development Commission factories was £876 per job. At present levels of taxes unemployment benefits and supplementary allowances the annual returns to the Exchequer were estimated to be

Table 9.6 Reduced form coefficients of predetermined variables in income-labour model

Dependent variable to be explained	Predetermined variables – subject to policy influence	Percentage of labour force in agriculture	Percentage of labour force unemployed	Median age of population	Percentage of population in each parish in higher socio-economic groups	Parish 1 service centre 0 not service centre	Percentage SMDs devoted to sheep
		X_2	X_3	X_4	X_5	X_6	X_7
Y_1 Agricultural income per head		+0.168	+0.096	−0.048	+0.021	+0.209	−0.016
Y_2 Non-farm income per head		−0.133	+0.019	+0.024	+0.005	+0.626	—
Y_3 Labour participation rate		+0.278	+0.171	+0.007	+0.0376	+2.445	—

Source: Willis (1971).

running at the rate of 23 per cent per annum. A more sophisticated analysis, using Discounted Cash Flow techniques of investment appraisal, produced estimates of the annual returns to the Exchequer ranging from 27.6 to 30.9 per cent depending on the precise assumptions made. It was pointed out that in comparison with these rates of return, a minimum of 10 per cent per annum is required on low-risk projects undertaken for commercial reasons in nationalized industries.

However, the problem of what to measure and the nature of the results are determined by the terms of reference of the problem in question. If the terms of reference were broadened in mid-Wales, to take account of the extra costs of the provision of services in a rural area compared to many urban areas, then the return on capital would be very much lower. Factory development has benefited mid-Wales, but has the nation gained?

10   The labour market
and farm policy

In the previous chapter the demographic processes affecting rural
areas were analysed and the components of the so-called 'rural
population problem' were isolated. A limitation of demographic
analysis is that it has failed to develop causal models which can
be used for forecasting purposes. However, a component of
demographic change – migration – has been the subject of causal
analysis which is made possible by the fact that the majority of
migration decisions are conditioned by the labour market. Hence the
present chapter begins with an outline of the main rural labour
market – that for farm labour. The well-recognized 'farm income
problem' is explained in terms of this general economic model. This
explanation gives an indication of the likely success of policy
alternatives available to deal with the problem. Farm policies are
not, however, merely a matter of resource allocation; they are also
designed explicitly to influence the distribution of income. The
success of farm policies, judged by this criterion, is most doubtful
and there have been attempts to offset the maldistribution effects of
earlier farm policies through structural policies. The failure of these
policies is briefly documented and the chapter concludes with a short
review of the effect of the Common Agricultural Policy on British
agriculture.

Labour market theory

Classical labour market theory seeks to explain the allocation of labour as a resource and the market-determined distribution of factor income which results. This is a branch of economic theory which has generated a great deal of controversy because of early attempts to give it normative content; thus it was claimed that not only did the theory explain the distribution of income but it also justified it in some sense. The present interest of this theory is that it can explain part of the transfer of labour resources from the agricultural sector which has occurred during the past century.

The most developed part of the theory relates to the demand side of the market. It is postulated that the employer's hiring behaviour can be explained in terms of derived demand. That is, he will be prepared to pay the last worker he hires what that work will earn for him, and no more.

This marginal amount is determined by a number of variables:

(1) the technical possibilities of substituting labour for other inputs (e.g. capital);
(2) the price of other factors;
(3) the price of the product produced.

These three variables between them determine the shape of the marginal revenue product curve for labour which indicates the amount that each successive equal increment of labour will produce for a given firm or industry. The position is further complicated for a multi-product industry such as agriculture, in that producers can and do respond to changing product prices by adjusting the mixture of commodities they produce.

The supply side of labour market theory is much less developed. It postulates that individual workers will move from job to job in search of greater 'net advantage' – a concept which may incorporate wages as well as non-pecuniary items such as job satisfaction. Hence the construction of a supply function for labour would include measures indicating the relative strength of the financial pull of agriculture and some attempt to allow for these other items. A list might include:

(1) non-agricultural wages;
(2) the current rate of unemployment;

(3) the relative length of the working week in agriculture;
(4) the relative education status of farm workers;
(5) the relative importance of older workers in agriculture.

The first two of these would stand respectively for the pecuniary attractions of non-farm work and the probability of finding such employment. The relative working week would be a proxy for non-pecuniary factors, other measures of such factors being difficult to find. The last two of these would be justified as a proxy variable to indicate the importance of 'non-competing groups' in agriculture. This concept is one which may be important in the present context, because agriculture may attract those with less formal education, and commitment to it for a number of years may make it increasingly difficult for a worker to transfer to other employment. He may thus be 'boxed in' in agriculture as part of a non-competing group. During a period when the industry is rapidly reducing its use of labour, the proportionate size of this group would become large.

Empirical work relating this theory to the farm labour market has been extensive; two sets of studies are of interest. The first, published by Bellerby (1956), related to the whole farm workforce. The investigation covers several countries over a long period; for Britain the data relates to the period 1867 to 1938. This work focuses on a variable labelled 'the incentive income ratio', which measures the relative earning power of labour in agriculture and seeks to explain why it is nearly always found to be less than 100 per cent. For Britain, the ratio ranges from a minimum of 35 per cent in the late nineteenth century to a maximum of 81 per cent in the mid-1930s.

The work is essentially descriptive in its method and lacks the apparent precision of more recent econometric studies. The major reasons advanced to explain low farm incomes are:

(1) the low income elasticity of demand for food, which implies that agricultural incomes do not grow as fast as aggregate national income;
(2) flexibility in expansion of output, primarily due to the availability and adoption of new techniques;
(3) the low price elasticity of demand for food which causes wide fluctuations in price in response to moderate changes in output;
(4) the low *supply price* of agricultural manpower.

Bellerby (1956) lays considerable emphasis on this last attribute.[1]
The supply price of manpower is in effect the earnings it will accept
without changing occupation. Bellerby lists several factors which
might explain the low supply price: urban/rural differences in the
cost of living and in the structure of expenditure; lack of out-
mobility combined with high in-mobility to farm employment; lack
of social mobility; poor market organization. These aspects of rural
life are still often cited in support of policies to help rural people. It is
interesting that the difference in cost of living has probably been
reversed since Bellerby's work was published – typical items of
expenditure required for domestic purposes now cost more in many
rural areas than in urban ones. The evidence for this contention is
not hard to find: because of greater personal mobility in rural areas it
has become increasingly difficult for small shopkeepers to stay in
existence and they have only been able to do so by charging a substantial premium in excess of the urban price level.

The main criticism of Bellerby's work is that it lacks prescriptive
power. This is a comment which is quite commonly made on work
involving marginal productivity theory and in essence it follows
from the tautological aspects of the model. If we are to explain low
incomes in terms of low expectations, it becomes difficult to use this
as an argument for raising incomes. If people are prepared to put up
with being poor, should we concern ourselves? Nevertheless,
Bellerby's work is of interest as a very detailed and strongly
documented statement of what has since become known as 'the farm
income problem'.

More recent econometric work has been undertaken by Cowling
and Metcalf.[2] These researchers have tested a variety of labour
market models, one of which conforms to the classical model above.
They estimate the parameters of two separate functions, one to
explain the supply of and the other the demand for agricultural
labour. The functions are:

$$S1 = G(W_a; W_i; V_i) \qquad D1 = f(W_a; P_a; P_m; T)$$

Where $S1 = D1 = $ the levels of total labour use in agriculture measured in
thousand man equivalents.

[1] Chapter 3. He has been criticized for this emphasis by Ann Martin (1959);
his reply was published in 1960.
[2] The work appeared first as a series of articles which were then summarized
in a book: see Cowling, Metcalf and Rayner (1970).

W_a = farm wages
W_i = non-farm wages
V_i = non-farm unemployment
P_a = price of farm output
P_m = price of farm machinery
T = time trend.

In order to test these models they obtained data over twenty years, adjusting some of the variables to take account of inflation and changes in technology. Several statistical estimates of the parameters of these functions are presented and they might be useful for forecasting the effect of changes in explanatory or 'policy' variables on employment in agriculture.

The estimation technique and model specification used here may be criticized on the grounds that numbers employed in agriculture and the wages offered are simultaneously determined in response to the pre-determined variables.[1] In a subsequent study relating to the same period Tyler (1972) has adopted such an approach. Tyler postulates a much more elaborate model, including a production function and functions to account for capital and other inputs. The difficulties encountered with such a model arise from the shortage of adequate time series data to test them. Thus although Tyler's more sophisticated model has more theoretical appeal, the coefficients he estimates are often weakly significant and the results are correspondingly difficult to interpret.

Economic models such as these are useful in providing a quantitative description of past relationships. However, even if their coefficients can be unambiguously estimated, their usefulness for forecasting purposes will be constrained by the problems of obtaining realistic forward estimates of the explanatory variables they contain. The other main limitation in using econometric models for forecasting arises where the economic structures they portray are unstable. Thus a model calibrated in one period can only be used for forecasting in another if we may assume that the same relationships persist from one period to another.

---

[1] See Christ (1966), Chapter VI for a full explanation of the concept of identification in econometric models.

Agricultural policies[1]

It is useful, though by no means simple, to separate policies into their constituent goals and instruments. Often goals are framed in the most general language; for example, the general objective underlying British agricultural policy during most of the post-war period has been to *promote and maintain a stable and efficient agricultural industry capable of producing such part of the nation's food and other agricultural produce as in the national interest it is desirable to produce in the UK, and of producing at minimum prices consistently with proper remuneration and living conditions for farmers and workers in agriculture and an adequate return on capital invested in the industry*, which comes from the 1947 Agriculture Act.

In economic terminology, this general objective resolves into three components:

(1) a resource allocation objective embracing efficiency subject to a stability constraint;
(2) a production objective relating to a share of home produce in total consumption;
(3) a distribution objective reflecting concern for the income of those in agriculture *and* for the cost of food to those not in agriculture. The wording indicates minimal food costs as a goal and the level of incomes in agriculture as a constraint on the pursuit of this goal.

In practice, the production objective may be indicated as contributing to both of the others. Policy pronouncements have always called for production of commodities in short supply – in other words, those commodities which could be made available to the consumer without extra cost to the taxpayer.

The instruments used in pursuit of these general objectives have been extremely diverse. Immediately after World War II, the main concern was with efficiency, in particular with improving the balance of payments and production irrespective of cost was urged. In the early 1950s, production had expanded and world commodity

---

[1] A more extensive treatment of policy issues will be found in Ashton and Rogers (1967) or in Self and Storing (1962). A political scientist's appraisal has been prepared by Pennock (1962), a formal economic analysis was published by Josling (1969), who has also surveyed the economic analysis of agricultural policies (1974).

prices were beginning to decline, and by the mid-1950s, the Government had ceased to call for expansion. In 1954, the last of the war-time controls over production were dismantled and replaced by 'free' markets for food, with the return to the farmer being made up by deficiency payments, designed to bridge the gap between market prices and guaranteed prices. During this era, the level of internal market prices was determined on the world market. Since there was a tendency to oversupply international markets, not least because of other developed countries having over-estimated the demand for agricultural produce, internal domestic market prices fell. Since guaranteed prices had to be maintained out of taxation the Exchequer cost of agricultural support began to increase and governments attempted to check this increase. There were two main methods available to them – raising internal market prices by controlling supplies and reducing guaranteed prices – both of which were employed. During most of the 1960s, the agricultural policy debate had centred on the desirability or otherwise of further agricultural expansion, with the farmers demanding an increasing share of the home market, while the Government stressed the need for efficient production and the desirability of containing the cost to the taxpayer.

The desirability of agricultural expansion during the 1960s was advocated on efficiency grounds by agricultural interests. Agricultural interests here include official representatives of farmers, farm workers, landowners and their agents within the Government, namely the Ministry of Agriculture, Fisheries and Food. It is notable that these interests are all represented on the EDC for Agriculture.

Expansion received its fullest support in a report by the EDC for Agriculture (1968), which contained an unprecedented amount of evidence in support of an agricultural policy proposal. Briefly, the recommendation was that agricultural net output should be allowed to expand by 22 per cent over five years. This would increase net output by £185 million and the estimated 'net import saving' would be of the order of £220 million per annum by the end of the expansion period. The report, although detailed in its arguments, was vague as to implementation – perhaps sensibly, because discussions on the details of farm policy were the established prerogative of annual price reviews. Despite this reticence, the implied message is clear enough, namely that agricultural expansion needs some form of official support. This might mean relaxing some of the constraints on the expansion of farm output, in effect raising guaranteed prices; it would also mean taking steps to stem the outflow of labour from agriculture.

This latter point is interesting in relation to the work by Cowling and Metcalf cited earlier. These researchers prepared forecasts for the EDC, based on a single equation model, in which the main predictor variables were unemployment, the rate of change of unemployment and time. The precision of the forecasts was thus conditional on the reliability with which unemployment could be estimated in the future. Since the forecasts were semi-official, it is not surprising that the estimates of unemployment used were optimistic and consequently the forecasts were not fulfilled. Unemployment was relatively high during the forecast period and the manpower shortage suggested by this work did not materialize. It may also be that the basic relationships between wages and unemployment, which underlie the Cowling–Metcalf model, also changed at the beginning of the forecast period. According to more recently published work, by Bowers, Cheshire and Webb (1970), the relationships changed quite suddenly at the end of 1966 or the beginning of 1967. Moreover, the Government did not adopt the whole range of these policy proposals, although in the 1970s a somewhat more expansionist policy mood is apparent as Britain implements the Common Agricultural Policy.

The 1960s also saw the introduction of policies designed to improve farm structure. Such policies have been advocated for many years on the general grounds that it is illogical to attempt to solve the farm income problem by maintaining farm prices, unless parallel attempts are also made to reduce the number of farmers. Since the farm input suppliers have been making new and ever more productive techniques available to farmers, they have been able to increase their output without a comparable rise in prices. In theoretical terms, the supply schedule of agriculture has been shifting to the right under the influence of new technology. Maintaining the prices farmers receive encourages further production and surpluses accumulate.[1] The rationale of structural policies was thus

---

[1] Note that the surplus referred to here is not a physical surplus. Britain is a net importer of most temperate foodstuffs and does not, therefore, have physical surplus problems as a general rule. This, however, is no justification for arguing that economic surpluses are impossible under British conditions.

that agricultural production might grow less rapidly if there were fewer producers and that the importance of the farm income problem might be reduced by sharing out the same aggregate income amongst a smaller number of producers. The evidence for the first of these postulates is difficult to find. Do larger producers exhibit greater or less flexibility in the face of price movements than small producers? The traditional argument was that small producers were committed to agricultural production and would, therefore, actually increase output if prices fell. However, it can also be argued that very large producers must also increase output in order to service their large debts. There is perhaps more support for the idea that aggregate farm income could be shared amongst fewer individuals. This has some logical appeal and is certainly consistent with the facts that the number of farmers has declined relatively slowly and that aggregate net farm income has not grown very rapidly. The explicit objective of structural policy is thus to reduce the number of farmers, hence easing the transfer of resources out of agriculture.

This policy objective was justified, when it was first put forward, in terms of the failure of farmers to achieve a satisfactory level of income (White Paper, 1965). The intention was to encourage those farmers who were too small to leave the industry, thus releasing land to be amalgamated with the farms of those remaining. Such policies have been used in many other European countries and Britain was one of the last to try them. This is, at least in part, because the structure of UK farms is not as adverse as that of other countries, where many decades of protection of small farms has discouraged amalgamation. Tracey (1964) argues that when Britain repealed the Corn Laws in 1846 a period of free trade in food and raw materials was started. This contrasted with most European countries who opted for protectionist agricultural policies based partly on a philosophical belief as to the desirability of a healthy peasantry. Another institution in Britain which has facilitated structural change has been the well-developed landlord/tenant system which was swept aside in European revolutionary 'land reform' movements in the eighteenth and nineteenth centuries. The result has been that structural change has proceeded comparatively unhindered in Britain and that British farms are on average much larger than those in Europe.

Structural policies in Britain have apparently not been very successful and it is worth considering why this should be. It is useful to analyse this policy in the context of the different parties involved, that is: the outgoer, the new occupier, the owner and, lastly, the government representing the interests of tax payers and consumers, as well as other interested parties. The problem for the government in setting up structural policies was to design instruments to facilitate amalgamations, involving transactions between at least the first two parties, and possibly the third, within the overall constraint of its obligations as custodian of the national interest. Such a policy could be judged by the criterion of whether it did, in fact, increase the rate of amalgamation of farms at a 'reasonable' cost.

The structural measures introduced in the 1960s[1] included most of the components used in such policies in other countries. They offered incentives designed to speed up the rate of exodus of small farmers to persuade those leaving agriculture to allow amalgamation of their holdings and to assist those undertaking amalgamation. The incentives were offered to those contributing to the creation of holdings of at least 'commercial' size. The minimum size conditions may be relaxed in certain circumstances, the payments to outgoers are available to those freeing holdings requiring between 100 and 599 smds. The payments may be in the form of a lump sum or an annuity, depending on the age of the outgoer, and the amounts paid are related to the acreage released for amalgamation. The policy also embodies safeguards against refragmentation, in the form of a covenant, and re-entry of some outgoers receiving payments, in the form of a requirement that if they receive an annuity, they will not farm full-time elsewhere.

The response to these incentives has been modest, although the schemes have been modified to improve the rates of payment. In the ten years from 1967, the total number of amalgamations approved was less than 7000 (for the UK as a whole) and about 5000 payments to outgoers were approved. Roughly two thirds of the £50 million spent on those policies has been devoted to the amalgamations scheme, and most of this has been taken up with the cost of remodelling works.

Why did these policies fail? When they were first introduced, the amounts of cash offered were widely regarded as being too small – the payments to outgoers were derisively labelled 'the copper hand shake'. It is tempting to conclude that the levels of incentives were set

---

[1] For a review of the measures see Agricultural Adjustment Unit (1968); a critical appraisal has been published by Gasson (1970).

too low, but this leaves open the possibility that other institutional proposals might have achieved the desired result. For example, it may be that farmers are extremely loath to relinquish control of their land if it has development potential. Those who are tenants may be in the position that, even if their landlords were prepared to amalgamate, they might be unable to retire because they have not accumulated sufficient assets to provide for their old age; they may also have incurred liabilities to the landlord in the form of dilapidations. These arise where the tenant fails to maintain the farm fixed equipment at the level required under his tenancy agreement. It has also been suggested that the safeguards against refragmentation may have deterred amalgamators from using the statutory schemes. These arguments might all have been overcome by offering greater incentives, but it seems that they would have to have been very substantial, and perhaps far greater than the prospective efficiency and distribution gains following from these policies.

At present, it seems that interest in structural policies is on the wane. However, this policy state undoubtedly arises at least partly from tight commodity markets. Sensibly enough, there is no enthusiasm for assisting resource transfer out of agriculture when food prices are high. Five years ago, before the commodity price boom, there was much more interest in structural policies, partly as a means of reducing the pressure of supplies on agricultural markets. If, as is very likely excess supply conditions re-appear, structural policies, and more drastic means of supply control, such as land retirement, may well be put back on to the agricultural policy menu.

The impact of policy benefits

The main instruments of agricultural policy have been directed at raising farm prices or lowering input costs, and it is therefore not surprising that agricultural output has grown. But how do we know that farmers have in fact received any benefit from these subsidies, rather than having to pass it on to the suppliers of farm inputs? For example, the post-war period has seen a very rapid rate of increase in land values, part (many would argue a small part) of which must be attributed to capitalization of the expected future value of farm support. Similarly, the cost of farm inputs has risen steadily throughout the period, and this has been encouraged by the use of a formula for adjusting farm guaranteed prices which automatically takes cost increases into account. If, therefore, we take some account of these dynamic effects of agricultural policy, it becomes very difficult indeed to demonstrate their effectiveness. To the extent that they are successful, the classical labour market model would suggest that they will result in the retention of resources in agriculture which would otherwise have been transferred to other employment. It seems very likely that these policies will have had some effect on farm incomes and, proceeding on this assumption, we may now turn to the more difficult question of their effect on the distribution of incomes within agriculture.

Such a distribution is of interest from two points of view. First, the geographical spread of farm support is important in the context of regional policy and, indeed, of local settlement policy. Does the distribution of agricultural support tend to encourage types of farming found more commonly in some regions rather than others? Does it selectively impinge more on arable farming than on livestock farming, on uplands than on lowlands? Generally speaking, it seems that policy-makers have tried to achieve an even spread of support from these points of view. They have an obvious political motivation here in that it is very easy to accuse governments of gerrymandering if they introduce policies which are particularly favourable to a limited geographical area. However, it would be truly remarkable, given the efficiency of government support instruments, and the differential rates of technical progress in different sectors of agriculture, if support had been equally available to all types of farmer at all times.

Second, and perhaps more important, is the notion that the government should support small farms because they are in danger of falling below some predetermined level of income. Most policies have not been specific with reference either to particular sizes or types of farm, but one or two policies have been introduced which are restricted to small farms. The structural policy discussed above was one of these, and it was preceded by another type of policy – the Small Farmers' Scheme – which was designed to make it possible for small farmers to increase their size of business in order to make it viable. However, these exceptions apart, agricultural policies have been almost exclusively tied either to the level of output or to the volume of inputs used on the farm; and it is worth enquiring how effective they have been, therefore, in making the small farmer better off.

The study by Josling and Hammway (1972) cited earlier calculated Gini ratios for various types of agricultural support and for farm incomes in 1969. The main result was a confirmation of the general expectation that larger farmers derive more benefit from support payments than small farmers. Two points can be made about this study. First, the data used were measured *before* tax rather than after it. Since the taxation system is a major instrument of redistribution, it cannot be reasonably assumed that it is ignored in choosing other policy instruments, such as farm price support, to redistribute income. If income tax rates are taken into account (either explicitly or implicitly) in establishing support levels, then the success of farm policies in redistributing income can only be gauged from income after tax. A second objection, which the authors do recognize, arises from the static nature of the inequality measurements.

It may be argued that farmers base their decisions as to whether or not to enter agriculture, and whether to stay or leave, on their expected relative income over a number of years. Perhaps this *time stream* of income is what determines how 'well-off' they are in relation to their aspirations, and measurements of time streams should therefore be the dependent variable in analysing redistributive policies. One recent study (Stoakes, 1972), which analysed inequality co-efficients of the net present value of a ten-year stream of income, found that the degree of inequality detected was much reduced. Thus the range in the distribution of income is reduced by taking a longer view. The same study also found that the tax system had a substantial impact in moderating the inequality introduced by tying support payments to output in any one year.

British agriculture and the EEC

The negotiation of British entry into the EEC took more than a decade to complete and a recurring topic in the discussions was the problem of reconciling the differences in agricultural policy. The British system, relying on deficiency payments (DP) as the main instrument of price policy, was well adapted to a country relying upon imports for a large proportion of its food supplies. By contrast, the Common Agricultural Policy (CAP) of the Six, based upon protection at the frontier, maintained farm incomes by taxing imports to raise internal prices. Policies based on frontier protection

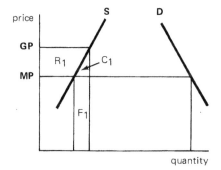

Figure 10.1

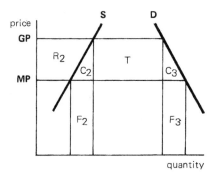

Figure 10.2

are advantageous to the countries pursuing them, when they are more nearly self-sufficient in food production.

The effect on the internal British food market can best be shown diagrammatically. Fig. 10.1 illustrates the DP situation with the domestic market shared between home and overseas producers. It shows the domestic supply schedule (S) and the total demand curve (D): the horizontal distance between these two schedules represents the potential import market. Under such a regime, consumers buy food at the market price (MP) and the government makes up the price to the guaranteed level (GP) out of taxation. This expenditure will amount to $R_1 + C_1$ in the diagram, which is in effect the Exchequer cost of DPs. By raising the price offered to home producers, the system encourages them to produce more (moving along the supply schedule) and encroach on the import share of the home market. The total value of imports saved in this way is F_1 but the total cost of resources used by domestic producers is $(C_1 + F_1)$; thus the net resource cost due to the inefficiency of the DP system is C_1.

Comparing this with Fig. 10.2, we can see the implications of changing to the CAP more fully. For the UK, this means raising both the price of imports and of home production. This is achieved by raising prices at the common external frontier of the Community and the revenue raised (T) is paid into central EEC funds and may thus constitute a net loss to the UK consumer. Also, consumers will respond to higher prices by reducing consumption; this affects further import savings of F_3 and consumption (efficiency) losses of C_3 in addition to C_2 and F_2 which compare with the previous diagram.

This analysis has been adapted from Josling's (1970) treatment of the problem. The full cost of the change in policy can be estimated using this type of model and assumptions as to the relevant market and guaranteed price levels and the position and shape of the supply and demand schedules. The conclusion from Josling's analysis (which is more detailed than that presented here) is that Britain incurs a substantial net cost by adopting the CAP, because of both the change in support system and the higher food price level. Whether or not this cost was a price worth paying in order to obtain entry to the EEC had to be judged in the light of expected benefits from entry.

Shortly after the conditions for British entry, which were influenced by these gloomy expectations, were negotiated, a massive increase in world commodity prices occurred. This had the effect of closing the gap (for a period) between MP and GP in Fig. 10.2, thus drastically reducing the cost to Britain of joining the EEC. Since then, the Common Agricultural Policy has become much more complex. The introduction of 'Green' exchange rates, which attempt to insulate farmers from the effect of fluctuating exchange rates, together with Monetary Compensatory Amounts, has produced a situation too complex to represent on a two dimensional diagram. The relevant institutional arrangements, governing the determination of prices, have been described by Irving and Fearn (1975). More recently McFarquhar et al. (1977) have presented some further estimates of the cost to Britain of being a member of the EEC. These estimates assume that Britain could buy food more cheaply on world markets: the net cost of membership is then estimated as the cost of food imports as EEC members minus the cost as non-members plus the UK contribution to the EEC agricultural budget (known as FEOGA). This cost is estimated for butter and the resulting rate of cost is extended to all food imports. The result is a net cost of £650 million at the prices ruling at the beginning of 1977. At the time the estimates were prepared, an increase in prices, of products protected by levy, of 15 per cent was under discussion and this, according to McFarquhar *et al.*, would have added a further £250 million to the cost of British membership of the EEC. After the article was published, a much smaller price increase was agreed which suggests that a total net cost of £700 million would have probably been more appropriate.

Such sums may seem large but, compared with Josling's pre-entry estimate of cost, they are still modest. These estimates must be compared carefully, however, because of differences in method. In particular Josling's estimates allow for a response of consumers to higher food prices, which would somewhat reduce the cost of entry. Since McFarquhar *et al.* do not make such an allowance, their estimates of cost would tend to be higher than Josling's. The other important difference is that Josling's is a predictive study – his estimates are *ex ante* whereas McFarquhar *et al.* were working with recent actual data and were thus less at risk from forecasting errors.

Despite these difficulties, if we take the two estimates and compare them as money prices, they suggest a massive increase in the cost to British of membership of EEC (from £355 million in 1970 to £700 million in 1976). However, such a comparison would be quite inappropriate, even if the calculations were on the same basis, because of the massive rate of inflation over the period between them. If we crudely allow for this by deflating the McFarquhar *et al.* estimate by the retail price index, this produces an estimate in real terms which is less than Josling's. In other words, the effect of the commodity price boom of the early 1970s has been to reduce the cost of British membership. This cost is now rising as world commodity prices fall below those set inside the EEC. Clearly these estimates would not represent all of the implications of British membership of the EEC. If we actually withdrew, much wider effects, many of them beyond the scope of calculation, would follow.

The increase in commodity prices in 1972 was indeed a major

event for consumers, farmers and for agricultural policy-makers. It was hailed by many commentators as 'the end of the era of cheap food' – an expression which is not easily translated into the formal language of economics. The question it raised, which was very basic to policy formation, was whether the increase in prices should be expected to persist, or whether it was merely a chance disturbance of an established long-term trend. If the former interpretation was correct, then Britain would be acting in her own best interests to encourage the expansion of domestic agriculture. If the increase was merely a random event, then no long-term change in policy was called for. In fact the British Government has recently produced a medium term policy statement, in the White Paper *Food from Our Own Resources* (MAFF 1975), which is based firmly on the assumption that commodity price levels would remain high throughout the five-year period to 1980.

A broadly based survey of commodity prices was published by Harris (1974) shortly after the price boom of 1972. After lengthy discussion of all the factors determining commodity prices in 1972, Harris concluded that special conditions in that year promoted the price rise and that a return to pre-1972 relative price levels was to be expected. The special conditions he cited were: a delayed farmer response to depressed prices in 1970 and 1971, the coincidence of normal cyclical price movements for several commodities, adverse seasonal conditions in producing areas (particularly in the USSR) and a sharp upswing in world economic activity. Strikingly, he draws attention to the fact that prices of commodities, although dramatically higher than the previous year or two were not, *in real terms* (that is after allowing for inflation) notably different from their levels at the end of the 1940s. In each of the two harvests since Harris's article, there have been markedly unusual weather conditions and short harvests in Europe. Had these not occurred, there is a strong presumption that commodity prices would by now be even closer to the level of the late 1960s and early 1970s than they actually are.

An important effect of the commodity price boom will have been to remind policy-makers that such events can have a dramatic impact on policies. In the light of Harris's conclusions, the British Government policy of expanding agriculture seemed misguided. Nevertheless, short harvests over two years of the five-year period to which it relates will have made the results of such a policy less disastrous. Thus policies which seem quite appropriate with the wisdom of hindsight, are often much less certain of success at the time of their initiation. One of the main uncertainties underlying agricultural policies has been, and will remain, the level of commodity prices.

11   Rural settlement
patterns

Theories describing and attempting to explain the pattern of settlement were developed over a century and a half ago. Their rigorous
application is still a recent phenomenon, however, and many
empirical and data problems will have to be surmounted before
optimal solutions to settlement problems can be identified. This
chapter starts with a review of settlement theories developed mainly
by geographers. Then follows a discussion of the economic factors
determining settlement patterns. A particular feature which
underlies much of the proposed re-ordering of settlements is the
question of scale economies; the theoretical and empirical implications of this are discussed in the next section. This is followed by a
listing of present regrouping procedures, and then the possibility of
economic appraisal of settlement policies is reviewed in the context
of empirical studies.

Optimal settlement patterns

The development of a rural settlement pattern takes place over time
within a changing economic and social setting and is subject to
spatial market forces leading towards efficient location. Lösch
(1940) suggested that firms would seek a location at which revenue is
maximized: individually, they would locate at the place where

maximum profits would be earned, that is, where total revenue exceeds total costs by the greatest amount. He further argued that perfect competition would gradually reduce the size of sales areas until, ultimately, they became hexagonal in shape as all space is ` filled. Of all the geometrical forms that could fill space (hexagons, triangles, squares), the hexagon most nearly resembles a circle. It has the highest demand per unit area and minimizes total distance from its centre to all points within the market area, as Christaller (1933) demonstrated (Smith, 1971; Haggett, 1965). The hexagon provides the most economical form for the equal division of an area between a number of points. It can also be shown that the centres of these hexagons must form a regular triangular lattice to conform with the same minimum energy requirements. Lösch, further argued that as different goods are produced, a system of hexagons will arise for each industry, with the size of the market area varying from industry to industry, according to the nature of the product. Lösch then showed how concentrations of settlements will occur in certain parts of a uniform plane: where the greatest coincidence of production sites exist, the maximum number of purchases can be made locally, and transport costs are minimized. This is the spatial arrangement of economic activity which fulfulls equilibrium conditions.

Lösch provided the economic theory to supplement the earlier notion of settlements arranged in this regular triangular fashion, which was developed by Christaller in 1933 in his original development of central place theory. Christaller's work contains the classic statement of central place theory, developed as a 'general purely deductive theory' to explain the 'size, number and distribution of towns' in the belief that 'there is some ordering principle governing the distribution'. Christaller considered that his theories 'could also be designated as the theory of location of urban trades and institutions' to be placed beside von Thünen's (1826) theory of the location of agricultural production and the theory of location of industries developed by Weber (1909).

Central places vary in importance. Those of higher order dominate larger regions than those of lesser order, exercise more central functions, and therefore are said to have greater centrality. For all, however, the sum of the distances which rural residents travel to the central place is the smallest conceivable sum. Higher-order places offer more goods, have more establishments and business types, larger populations, tributary areas and tributary populations, do greater volumes of business, and are more widely spaced than lower-order places. Low-order places provide only low-order goods to low-order tributary areas; these low-order goods are generally necessities requiring frequent purchasing with little consumer travel. Moreover, low-order goods are provided by establishments with relatively low conditions of entry. Conversely, higher centres provide not only low-order goods, but also high-order goods sold by high-order establishments with greater conditions of entry. The higher the order of goods provided, the fewer are the establishments providing them, the greater the conditions of entry and trade areas of the establishments, and the fewer and more widely spaced are the towns in which the establishments are located.

Every type of good has its special range, which differs at different central places and is not the same in all directions from the same centre, but varies according to objective and subjective economic distance. More basically, range is determined by:

(1) size and importance of the centre and the spatial distribution of population;
(2) the price-willingness of purchasers;
(3) subjective economic distance;
(4) quality and price of the good at the central place.

The range is actually a ring with an upper limit beyond which a good can no longer be obtained from a centre, and a lower limit which is determined by the minimum amount of consumption which is necessary before production (or offering the central good) will be profitable.

There is a system of central places comprising several size types, determined in general by the spatial effects of upper and lower limits to the range of central goods. In this system the relations between size, spacing, functions and hierarchical interdependence in the system of central places are determined precisely. This strict mathematical scheme is, of course, as imperfect as the simplifying assumptions from which it is deduced, and reality may be approached by recognizing spatial differences in population distribution costs of production and services.

Many deviations from the hexagonal pattern which are not explainable by these models can nevertheless be explained by economic forces. For example:

(1) the whole system may be raised to a higher or lower level with general wealth and a dense population or general poverty and a sparse population;
(2) spacing may be enlarged or compressed by the relative strength of any one system and adjacent systems;
(3) depending upon the economic base of the area in question there may be more or less centres of any order.

Deviations may result from local spas, mining towns, for example, from political, religious and physical conditions or from military necessity.

What would be the optimum form of rural settlement patterns, if somehow the slate could be wiped clean, and a new settlement pattern emerged which is optimal for technological, economic, social and political conditions of the present? Unless the slate is considered as wiped clean, any optimum pattern will be strongly affected by the present pattern, because most present settlements would be costly to replace completely. They represent large investments whose value (effectively their replacement cost) can be realized only by their continued use. Settlement viability thus becomes a matter of the relative cost of providing residential and other settlement services from the existing pattern or producing these services from some other pattern. Farm size, location, roads, schools, villages, services and many other aspects of rural settlement were established long ago. What patterns would be optimal now? This can be answered by looking at locational forces within the farm, and between the farm and outside markets and services.

The optimum location of the farmstead in relation to farm area, and size of total farm area, depend on the types of enterprise on the farm and the physical conditions of production. In general, intra-farm locational forces are vastly weaker than they once were – with modern farm equipment distance travelled is a far less important cost component than formerly, and there is comparatively less advantage in having the farmstead near the centre of the farm. Similarly economic factors associated with inputs to and outputs from farms have changed. The costs of marketing farm products are relatively less a locational factor than they once were. It is increasingly cheap, with modern transport and storage equipment, to pick up farm products at the farm gate and move them direct to a central market or processing plant. However, in the case of inputs there has been an increase in the cost of bringing farm and domestic requisites from the town to the farmstead. Farms today purchase a substantially larger proportion of total inputs from the non-farm sector than they did thirty years ago. The greatest increase has been in domestic requirements – fresh meat and vegetables, electricity, water, telephone and social and technical services. All of these costs and quality of service considerations argue for farmsteads nearer small urban centres.

The costs in money and time of different homestead locations with respect to fields and livestock will vary widely, but are measurable, as are the inter-farm relations with service centres. The combined effect of all these forces could be used to design an optimum rural intra-settlement pattern. Chisholm (1962) cites examples of the integration of settlements and farm organization (see Fig. 12.2, p. 249). The settlement patterns established in practice were those which gave more social contact and minimized inter-farm location costs. Although intra- and inter-farm costs are measurable in principle, few empirical studies have been undertaken and no detailed costing has been done. The high cost of data collection and analysis in relation to the possible gains from within-settlement relocation may account for this neglect.

Although there has been a rich development of theories to explain settlement patterns, it may be questioned whether these have great practical significance. Situations where optimal settlement patterns are to be determined irrespective of the existing pattern are generally rare and, in Britain, nonexistent. However, there are policies which aim at modifying the pattern of settlement, often in a highly specific way, and these policies derive their rationale mainly from arguments about economies of scale in service provision.

As with many government decisions, the objective function dictated by the administrative framework, namely cash cost minimization, may bear little relationship to the welfare maximizing objective. An exception to this general rule will be discussed at the end of this chapter. We therefore discuss the theoretical aspects of identifying optimum scale and then review some empirical work as a preliminary to examining regrouping procedures currently applied.

Economies of scale may be defined in terms of the classical theory of the firm. Most producing units, including those producing community services, will be subject to economies or diseconomies of scale if they are operating at any but the lowest point of their U-shaped long-run average cost curve. Shapiro (1963) found evidence of a U-shaped pattern in local government expenditures, with high *per capita* expenditures in both the smallest and largest communities.

This is not really an indication of the economies or diseconomies of size, because quality of service was not held constant and the number actually served would be expected to be a function of the age and occupational distribution of the population. Hirsch (1965), in an analysis of refuse collection in the USA, tried to allow for this by identifying two aspects of quality – convenience to the individual household, in terms of frequency and location of pickup, and to the community, in terms of method of treatment of the collected refuse. Similarly, in order to overcome this problem of quality, Riew (1966), in an inquiry into education, limited the observations in his sample to those schools which were accredited, eliminating those schools with exceptionally high teacher salaries, and including in his cost function such quality indicator variables as average teacher's salary, number of credit units offered and number of courses taught per teacher.

Farm, rural and small town areas are generally thought to be in the steeply-falling phase of the U-shaped cost curve for most goods and services. Rarely will scale be such that unit costs are minimized and it is unlikely that demand will be large enough for operation in the rising cost phase. In the theoretical case of a single firm, producing X units of a single homogeneous good, its total costs of production depend upon the level of output. In the short run, the firm has fixed costs attributable to its scale of plant but, in the long run all costs are variable as the scale of the plant can be adjusted to that producing X at minimum cost per unit. The function

$$Y = aX - bX^2 + cX^3$$

describes long-run *total* cost and yields a U-shaped *average* cost function

$$\frac{Y}{X} = a - bX + cX^2$$

whose minimum point is the long-run 'optimum' rate of output.

This analysis can be applied to spatial units and settlements to determine the optimum settlement size for different services. There may be special reasons for a settlement having higher or lower costs than its scale of output would indicate, for example differences in demographic structure of population, or location. The cost function may be modified to

$$\frac{Y}{X} = a - bX + cX^2 + d_1Z_1 + \ldots d_nZ_n$$

where Z variables indicate the environment within which the settlement operates.

Using this approach Gupta and Hutton (1968) studied the economies of scale in local government services, by fitting a regression function of the form

$$Y = a + \beta_1 X_1 + \gamma_1 X_1^2 + \beta_2 X_2 \ldots \beta_n X_n$$

where X_1, the population of the local authority area, is polynominal and the other variables are fitted linearly. If β_1 is negative and γ_1 positive, the function is U-shaped with respect to X_1. The 'optimum' population for the particular activity and type of authority might be said to lie at the minimum point of the U-shaped curve.

In an analysis of housing, highways and health services, Gupta and Hutton looked at the economies and diseconomies of scale at a county council, county borough, non-county borough, urban district council and rural district council level. Rural districts had diseconomies of scale in the provision of housing, urban councils economies and higher-order settlements diseconomies. Highway economies were mainly found at a county council level.

Some evidence on the high costs of public services in rural areas is provided by two recent government reports. Because of distance and sparsity of population, one would expect the current cost per head of the population of providing many public services to be greater in rural areas than elsewhere. This is true for the services listed in Table 11.1. Information from the main public utilities confirms this picture. The Treasury Report (1976) quotes electricity authorities running operating deficits in the rural areas they studied, ranging from £10 per head per year, to the extreme case of £49 per head per year in Sutherland. For gas, the figures ranged from a small surplus per head in Roxburgh, to an estimated deficit per customer of nearly £130 in Sutherland (1971 prices). This general picture is confirmed by a Yorkshire and Humberside Economic Planning Board (1976)

Sutherland							
current	77.5	0.6	67.0	7.1	13.2	10.8	
capital	2.9	7.6	5.5	1.9	0.1	—	
Roxburgh							
current	10.5	1.6	33.7	6.9	7.5	9.9	
capital	0.6	0.6	12.0	0.8	0.3	—	
Wigtown							
current	12.9	0.3	42.4	5.7	11.0	9.7	
capital	2.9	0.4	6.2	0.4	0.6	—	
Treasury study area average							
current	19.6	1.6	45.4	6.1	9.8	10.2	92.7
capital	3.1	3.8	5.2	0.5	1.3	—	13.9

Source: HM Treasury (1976).

report on the Pennine Uplands in Yorkshire. This report noted the high costs of education in rural areas due mainly to staff costs (i.e. low pupil – teacher ratio) and transport costs. In the West Riding Education Authority, the total cost of school transport was over £2350 per 1000 population in the Settle Division in 1970–1, compared to the West Riding LEA average of £660. The bulk of this expenditure arose from the extensive network of special school bus services. Postal services tend to be of lower quality in rural areas and also relatively expensive. The Yorkshire study noted the uneconomic nature of post offices from the the fact that two-thirds of them in the study area received only the minimum scale payment, and that costs in the area in 1971 were above the national average for rural areas, as defined by the Post Office, by more than 35 per cent per item. Similarly, almost all telephone boxes in the Pennine study area were uneconomic, and several had receipts of under £10 per year in 1971, compared to the average running cost per call box of £300 per annum. Of course, receipts are low because a high proportion of premises in rural areas have private telephones: in the less accessible parts of the uplands in the north part of the Bradford Telephone area, 60 per cent of tenancies had telephones, compared to a 34 per cent average for the North Eastern Telecommunications Region in 1971.

Not only are costs per head higher where population is sparser, one would also expect that they would tend to increase as depopulation continued. The Treasury (1976) were not able to get estimates, for most public services, of the effect which any given change in the population might have on costs per head. The Gas Board produced some estimates. For example, in Wigtown a 5 per cent fall in population with no increase in charges would, it was estimated, raise costs per consumer there by about £2 per year. In mid-Wales, it was thought that a change of 5 per cent in the population in either direction would not have much effect on unit costs, provided that the change in the population was spatially uniform. If the population were concentrated in one or two towns, there would be a significant fall in unit costs.

But how can the study of individual cost functions indicate size optima for settlements embodying a range of activities? The efficient solution might be identified by combining this information into an aggregate long-run cost curve for all services. The lowest point on such a curve would then be the optimum for a given mix of services.

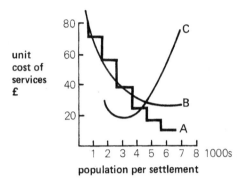

Figure 11.1

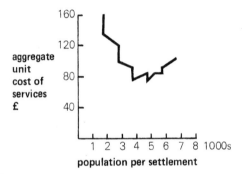

Figure 11.2

The shape of such a curve has been the subject of some research which has produced some general rules of thumb, though rigorous analysis has yet to be done. The analytical problem may be seen in the simple example in Fig. 11.1. Suppose settlements *had to* have three services *A*, *B* and *C* in order to stay in existence. Under such conditions, settlements would have to be greater than 1.7 thousand.

The curves specified are hypothetical, although they do indicate possible relationships. The stepped curve, *A*, relates to a service which can only be supplied in discrete units, *B* offers economies of scale over the whole range depicted, whereas *C* offers first economies and then diseconomies. The optimum settlement size can be identified by summing the three curves and observing its lowest position. The different behaviour of the individual cost curves produces a markedly stepped aggregate function in Fig. 11.2, where clearly-defined thresholds (vertical sections) can be seen. It is emphasized that this example is a theoretical one which is likely to be much simpler than the real world.

In postulating an optimum settlement size, we imply some mix of services which *must be* available. However, if this constraint could be relaxed, a more flexible approach to optimum settlement size would be appropriate. Institutional rigidity of service provision in rural areas would result in some services being more costly than they need be. In fact, it is virtually impossible to provide an identical standard of services for all communities and there is some flexibility in provision. However, there can be little doubt that the quality of services provided for rural communities often surpasses the standard they are willing to pay for. If decisions as to the level and quality of provision are taken centrally there is considerable danger of over-provision. Such over-provision might be regarded as a cost inherent in running an equitable social system, but there would be grounds for questioning how much regrouping of rural settlements its existence would justify.

The question of a true optimum settlement size is thus difficult to establish. On the cost side, the production functions for each service might give an indication of optimum scale if they could be combined together. This would require aggregation of the marginal cost functions so that the minimum cost situation could be identified. Also there would have to be some consideration of the demand for services taking account of variation due to demographic structure and to the provision of competing alternatives as a result of location. Generally speaking, there will be less alternative provision the more remote the community. It should also be borne in mind that production functions shift as new techniques are evolved and this applies in social services too. It is not therefore possible to identify a unique optimum size of settlement which will hold for any length of time or have general validity.

In view of the theoretical difficulty of defining an optimum settlement size, we should beware of unfairly criticising existing procedures. It follows from what has already been said that local authorities seeking to reorganize settlement patterns will find it difficult to do so except on a rough and ready judgemental basis. Our concern here is with the possibility of improving the information available for such decisions rather than with finding the one 'best' solution.

The majority of planning authorities in England recognize a need to regroup the population in areas of rural decline. Normal development control procedure has to be based on judgements and assumptions which may be ill-supported by research. Criteria such as assessed cheapness of service provision, proximity to workplace, shops and leisure facilities, transport connections, the 'character' of existing villages, the avoidance of traffic congestion and assumptions as to people's locational preferences may all enter into decisions, and it is not surprising that the results may seem irrational.

County councils, such as Northumberland, have undertaken village surveys (Northumberland County Council, 1968) to identify and assess the quality of facilities in settlements. Researchers have also used threshold analysis as a method of identifying settlements. It is hypothesized that depopulation in rural areas lowers the community toward economic and social thresholds. The nature of thresholds is such that they separate communities which change in different ways. Generally, the implication is that irreversible change sets in below the threshold level of 'viability'. Thresholds relate to the size of population served, which justifies the provision of an economic or social service within the area. Social thresholds relate to numbers required to maintain community institutions in existence, and economic thresholds the numbers required to maintain economic services, such as public transport, distributive and personal services. Many rural communities are already below a population size which justify banking and legal services or consumer durable shops. Others are tending downward to a level where public transport and food distribution services are in danger of being withdrawn. Edwards (1971), after looking at the relationship between population, function and social provision in the 1950s, advanced the following thresholds for size of settlement:

(1) Below a settlement size of 90 adults (120 persons) there was a sharp break in social provision and a rapid rise in the loss of production;

(2) settlements between 90 and 120 adults (120–160 persons) were below the threshold for population growth;

(3) but settlements with 120 to 140 adults (160–180 persons)

proved resilient with social provision. This was regarded as a minimum size for regrouped settlements;
(4) settlements above 180 persons have had mixed histories in North-east England, but from 450 adults (750 persons) there was a general growth in the 1950s with adequate social provision.

Threshold analysis in this simple form ignores many social and economic factors in community life. The threshold approach to the problem can identify sites within the region which have potential for future growth, i.e. it enables one to choose a limited set of 'efficient' locations and to rule out patterns of development that are not feasible on cost grounds. The technique concentrates on the settlement itself and not its relations with surrounding areas, emphasizing development costs and ignoring other costs, such as operating costs and the social cost of congestion and the benefits of alternative patterns of settlement (Richardson, 1971).

Economic appraisal of settlement patterns

Can we develop criteria which will help choose between settlement alternatives? This appears to be a much under-researched area, although related problems have received attention. These are discussed first and then a major empirical study of the question of settlement alternatives is reviewed.

Work relevant to the economic appraisal of settlements is Lichfield's (1970) outline of his planning balance sheet approach. Lichfield distinguishes the process of testing a plan from evaluation. Broadly, the result of the testing phase is a conclusion as to the feasibility of a particular proposal and, in evaluation, the consequences of a plan are measured in money terms as far as possible; where cash values cannot be applied, the physical consequences are noted in the balance sheet. This approach to evaluating alternatives may thus be preferred, in that it produces an exhibit for the decision-taker which enumerates all of the foreseeable consequences of a plan, whereas cost-benefit procedures produce a ranking index which can be compared with similarly calculated indices for other projects. The essence of the planning balance sheet is thus that it leaves more for evaluation by the decision-maker. However, the difference between the two techniques is slight in practice. Lichfield

(1970) sums it up as follows:

> In brief, where a cost-benefit analysis is carried out in a comprehensive manner, that is comprehensive in relation to the systems and sectors which are of interest in urban and regional planning, such analysis becomes in effect a Planning Balance Sheet. Put alternatively, although it must be recognized that the failure to measure costs and benefits leads to difficulty in interpretation of the results, a Planning Balance Sheet applies cost-benefit analysis as far as it can be taken in the absence of full measurement.

It may well be that in the planning context, where mutually exclusive ways of achieving one narrowly-defined objective are under consideration, the planning balance sheet approach is the best technique to use. Cost-benefit analysis, however, is a more appropriate tool for allocating a fixed total sum amongst competing investment projects: that is, where a ranking function is needed.

How then do we measure the costs and benefits of alternative settlement policies? The cost side of the calculation, in terms of public outlays, may be determined from information on cost curves of the type discussed above. It is more difficult to measure the benefits of each strategy, but it could be argued that these will be partly transferred to property values by the market. The benefit side of the calculation is a great deal more difficult, as the information about the demand for housing is not sufficiently refined for alternatives to be distinguished. Strictly speaking, a knowledge of the demand curve for residence in different types of community would be needed if the benefits were to be measured. Lichfield (1970) lists some of the difficulties of this approach in the urban renewal context. The main problem in settlement choice would appear to be empirical measurement of demand. These problems are made worse by imperfections in the land and housing markets, and they are probably sufficiently serious to prevent measurement of benefits from demand studies.

An alternative to a full cost-benefit appraisal would be a cost-minimization calculation. This would take the demographic characteristics of a region as given and compare settlement plans on the basis of social cost. It should perhaps be emphasized that it is social cost not public expenditure which is to be minimized. This is particularly relevant to existing resettlement plans which give a strong impression of a hierarchy of objectives, in which the goal of expenditure minimization comes well before that of maximum welfare. This is a case where the established institutions work imperfectly because they have inappropriate objectives set for them by the political framework in which they operate.

An interesting attempt to apply cost-benefit analysis to the re-grouping of dwellings and settlements was undertaken by Warford (1969) to a small area, South Atcham in rural Shropshire. The study originated because it had been observed that as successive water schemes were implemented, the areas remaining unserved tended to be the more remote, and this was reflected in a sharp increase in cost – and subsidy – per potential consumer. To pipe water to the existing settlements would be costly and it was, therefore, thought worth-while to consider other policy options. Other policy options might have been to

    (1) do nothing and accept the status quo
    (2) improve supplies from private wells, streams and roof catchments.

However, since the Government regard meeting the health hazard as an absolute constraint and because this can only be done by giving people access to mains water, the only real alternative of taking mains water to people was taking people to mains water. Thus, this lengthy report presents a thorough appraisal of the social costs and benefits of regrouping the population of various parts of the defined study area, so that scale economies of water distribution could be realized.

The study area was divided into four sub-areas (A, B, C, and D). The borehole and principal storage reservoir for the whole of the study area were to be located in sub-area A. Consequently, it was con-cluded that no relocation should occur from sub-area A. Thus, the relocation alternatives were a 'do nothing' solution (i.e. provide access to mains water to all properties in the study area); relocation from B alone, from C alone, from D alone, from $B + C$, from $B + D$, from $C + D$, and from $B + C + D$. The impact of each of these relocation alternatives was then appraised with respect to water supply, sewage, disposal, telephones, postal services, electricity, schools, housing, agriculture, travel to work and miscellaneous transport effects, e.g. mobile libraries, school transport, mobile shops and so on.

For all but two of these activities, benefits could be measured in terms of the cheapest alternative means of achieving the same result.

R_1 – two-year re-employment lag.

R_2 – zero re-employment lag.

T_1 – value of non-working time taken as ¾ value of working time.

T_2 – value of non-working time taken as zero.

H_1 – is the maximum estimate of value of abandoned houses.

H_2 – is the minimum estimate of value of abandoned houses.

Net benefit is calculated as the social cost of *no* relocation minus the social cost of each relocation option.

Table 11.3 Present worth of budgetary costs of relocation at 8 per cent (£ thousands)

	Area relocated							
	None	B	C	D	B + C	B + D	C + D	B + C + D
Total cost	2,717	3,423	3,018	3,274	3,720	3,973	3,574	4,276
Net cost		706	301	557	1,003	1,256	857	1,559

Source: Warford (1969).

Assumptions R_2 and the sample mean of house values were applied in obtaining these estimates. Net cost is the cost, of each relocation option, in excess of the 'none' case.

Options ranked on the basis of:

Decreasing Net social benefit (corresponding with $R_2 T_2 H_2$)	Increasing Budgetary cost
B + C + D	C
B + D	D
B + C	B
B	C + D
C + D	B + C
D	B + D
C	B + C + D

Agriculture was one exception in that different benefits would flow from different relocation options. To estimate the net social gain of each pattern of output entailed removing the subsidy element from the value of inputs and outputs, and pricing farmers' own services at their social opportunity cost. The other exception was housing, where some simplifying assumptions had to be made, for example, that value in use is equivalent to market value. It is probably that the market value of many existing properties understates their value to current occupiers, and the fact that the turnover rate of property in these areas is typically low supports this assertion. The existence of this 'consumers' surplus' would suggest that all values of property used in the study are too low as estimates of occupants' valuation of the stream of services provided by their homes.

The report of the South Atcham study contains a wealth of information and it is only possible to provide the barest impression of the results here. The costs and the benefits were all discounted over a thirty year period and a range of interest rates were used. Furthermore, because of uncertainty about some of the implications, ranges of assumptions were used. Sensitivity analysis revealed that the assumptions about house values and the appropriate discount rate were major elements in determining the outcome of the study. The preceding tables summarize the results of the calculations using an 8 per cent discount rate and two alternative sets of assumptions. The net benefit of a particular relocation policy is arrived at by reference to the policy of no relocation, i.e. providing access to mains water to all at existing locations. Ideally, projects or policies are usually adopted where the present value of the gross benefits minus gross costs is greatest. In this case, however, net benefits are measured in terms of reductions in social cost (or net benefit forgone elsewhere in the economy) of adopting an alternative policy. Thus, in Table 11.2 any of the relocation possibilities shows a social gain (all net benefits are positive). Raising the discount rate to 10 per cent, eliminates one or two of the options and to 12 per cent a few more, depending on the assumptions about R (re-employment lag), T (value of non-working time), and H (sampling error in the value of abandoned houses). Generally speaking these calculations lend strong support to relocation policies: the costs of maintaining the existing settlement pattern exceed those incurred in providing similar facilities by relocation.

Of course, since Warford could obtain no satisfactory evidence to indicate that the health record of rural areas without mains water was significantly different from those with such water, it is tempting to conclude that the benefits must be negligible and the whole policy should be abandoned anyway. Indeed Warford's measure of net benefits from relocation is also small. Since the costs of relocation are considerable, taxpayers might well argue or suggest that the next round of effort might more profitably be expended on redefining the 'feasibility' limit of the health hazard as an absolute constraint.

The South Atcham report also contains some subsidiary calculations of the budgetary cost of the various relocation options considered. These are summarized in Table 11.3 where it can be seen that in contrast with the social cost situation, any amount of relocation involves extra budgetary cost. It is stressed that the costs in Table 11.3 are measured in cash terms and must not be added to the social cost in Table 11.2. The implications of basing decisions on these different criteria are highly significant. Ranking the options in descending order of net social benefit gives almost the reverse of ranking by decreasing budgetary cost. The implication of this is that, if an agency was required to pursue minimum cost location policies (perhaps because of pressure to keep taxes low), it would be likely to choose an option which would be less than optimal on a net social benefit criterion. If it was given a fixed budget for relocation and told to allocate it on the basis of budgetary cost the chosen option could also be sub-optimal. For example, if the budget constraint was just enough to allow implementation of $C + D$ this would be chosen on the basis of budget cost. But the ranking on net social benefit indicates that B is preferred to $C + D$ and is also attainable within the budget constraint. Thus a misallocation involving a loss of social benefit of (£283 thousand minus £248 thousand) £35 thousand and an extra budgetary cost of (£857 thousand minus £706 thousand) £151 thousand would result.

The importance of this distinction between budgetary cost and social cost can hardly be over-emphasized. The South Atcham example demonstrates this very clearly because it allows the comparison to be made.

12 Transport in rural areas

The chief purpose of transport is to minimize the problem of movement between areas and settlements; recently, the demand for transport facilities has increased as a result of the growing popularity of travel as a pleasure in itself. Transportation planning is concerned in general with four fields, of which we shall consider the first three. These are the recognition of any shortcomings in the existing transportation system and the estimation of future transport demands; the design of alternative transportation plans which accord with community aims and objectives; the evaluation of alternative transportation systems in socio-economic terms to derive the optimum solution; and the implementation of the chosen transportation plan.

Rural transport problems

Migration from rural to urban areas has brought serious problems to the countryside, the chief of these being a reduction in total population size and an unbalanced age-sex structure. Both have consequences for transport. Population densities are generally too low to support mass transit public transport systems. The excess of older population in the countryside – pensioners rarely ride motor cycles, relatively few can afford cars and perhaps 50 to 60 per cent are physically unfit to drive (Bracey, 1970) – leads to greater dependence upon public transport, which is often inadequate. As in towns, growing affluence has led to greater mobility for most, but less mobility for a significant group (Thompson, 1965).

Thomas (1963) has argued that steps have been taken to maintain an active and prosperous rural economy in Britain. Agriculture is directly and indirectly subsidized. Post and telephone, roads, power, water, all cost more than the price charged to rural dwellers, being cross-subsidized by profits from urban areas. Other services, such as education, health and libraries, are made available in rural areas as a right and are provided at less than economic cost. Transport has stood as an exception to direct financial help. It has relied upon cross-subsidies: profits on main routes and urban routes have been used to cover rural ones. But transport is becoming more competitive, especially between sectors – rail, bus, car, etc. It is becoming increasingly difficult to raise charges on profitable routes to cover rural ones; operators have lost business to undertakings which concentrate on profitable routes and incur no rural losses or to another transport sector such as the private motor car. Part of the problem has been due to the historical evolution of the industry – profitable territory has become distributed indiscriminately among operators. Many services such as electricity and post office are virtual monopolies and can price urban services to cover rural ones without any (or much) loss. Transport has no such monopoly: high fares on inter-city railway lines to cover rural losses persuade the traveller to go by road where no contribution is exacted to cover secondary lines.

Transport objectives

Having briefly discussed some transport issues in rural areas, what are or should be the main objectives in transport policy? Foster (1963) argued that marginal cost pricing and the investment policy associated with it was not an acceptable basis for policy, principally because of politically undesirable effects on income distribution. He suggested two alternatives: transport undertakings should be required to maximize profits, subject to some constraint on the amount of profit they are allowed to make, or transport should be run in the consumers' interest. These were applied to specific types of transport, but little was said on objectives of the overall transport system. Yet not only should overall transport objectives be considered, the policies should also be evaluated in terms of transport's effect on other sectors os the rural economy.

Broad economic goals and evaluation criteria might be concerned with two effects: economic efficiency and distributional efficiency. We may wish to maximize aggregate consumption of the community (net user benefit) and assist in a more equitable real income distribution among its members. Economic evaluation of transportation is primarily concerned with changes in aggregate economic welfare and changes in the distribution of benefits. A re-allocation of resources is desirable in a distributional sense if changes in real income distribution are in the direction of the distribution desired by the community. This must find expression through the decision processes. Wilson and Kirwan (1969) have discussed basic problems of measuring net-user benefit in terms of such variables as money cost of travel, time in travel and in interchange, accident risk, comfort and noise, but found the outstanding shortcoming of all existing methods was a failure to take account of income effects.

Goals of maximization of aggregate consumption may be resolved into sub-objectives:

(1) maximize aggregate accessibility provided by the system;
(2) maximize aggregate environmental quality of the rural area;
(3) maximize achievement of desirable long-term rural development (settlement and production) patterns.

These objectives are broader than the aims which generally underlie discussions of rural transport.

Conflict between objectives may be seen in the elasticity of demand for transport. In the short run, with a given technology, the demand for transport (both freight and passenger) is inelastic – it takes a long time for human activities to resettle in different places. There are many ways of providing the same transport service, so that in relation to transport costs, the demand for particular forms of transport tends to be highly elastic in the short run. The long-run elasticity of demand would create few problems if it were not for the fact that much transport depends on the provision of an infrastructure which is extremely costly and long-lived. Much of the pattern of our lives is determined by decisions made to locate roads, railways and ports in particular places.

Transportation systems are important determinants of development patterns and can be modified to satisfy criteria other than economic ones. Moreover, existing systems may no longer be optimal in any other sense than that they already exist. This has been pointed out by Harris (1968), who argues that the external effects on industry, agriculture, and services of the location decisions of transport routes are rarely considered and do not adequately influence the behaviour of transport decision-makers. Even if present externalities are properly accounted for by shadow prices and considered in a behavioural system and in economic aims, the effects of current decisions are frozen in capital works. As time passes and conditions change, these decisions not only may be no longer optimal but they may generate new externalities as their effects are propagated through the economic system.

Networks

Little evaluation has taken place of whole transport systems as distinct from individual routes or media. Routes form the fragments of systems and are amenable to development or closure. Simple networks and routes will be discussed first and we shall then consider the integration of the transportation complex into the fabric of society.

The intuitive solution to a route location problem between two settlements is to join them by a straight line. In the real world, with few exceptions routes follow complex paths rather than straight lines. Haggett (1965) has discussed some problems of route location in terms of negative and positive deviations. Wellington's work, *The Economic Theory of the Location of Railways (1877)*, is cited as an example of positive deviation or route lengthening in order to collect more freight. Here the problem is to optimize the relationship between length of railway (the shorter the better in terms of building costs) and the amount of traffic (the greater the better until marginal cost exceeds marginal revenue). Negative deviation in a route occurs from the need to avoid certain barriers, such as mountain ranges, or to minimize the distance travelled through high-cost areas. In rural areas, unless a road is of major importance, a road bridge spans a railway line at or near a right angle, deviating from its general direction on either side of the bridge. This is the result of strong refractive bridge-construction costs on the alignment of the route.

Bunge (1962) has used topology to illustrate network characters

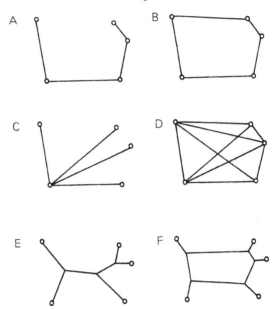

Figure 12.1 Alternative definitions of minimum-distance networks, after Bunge (1962).

(see Fig. 12.1). *A* is the minimum distance for starting at a particular point and travelling to all others in the shortest mileage; *B* is the shortest distance around the five points (travelling salesman problem); *C* is a hierarchy connecting one point to all others; *D* is a complete network connecting any point to all others; but the shortest set of lines connecting all five points contains none of these elements – it is represented by *E*. *F* shows a general network attributable to Beckmann (1952). *D* represents the least cost network from the point of view of the user (in time and distance); *E* the least cost for the transport builder (short-network). Least cost to user patterns are likely to predominate in urban areas (or some ratio of user to builder cost); but in rural areas, where traffic is generally light and sparse, least cost to builder patterns predominate.

The integration of communication systems with settlements and farm organization has been discussed by Chisholm (1962) with reference to areas where new farm settlements are being planned, as in the reclaimed Dutch polders. Here attempts are made to minimize internal distance within the farm from buildings to fields and

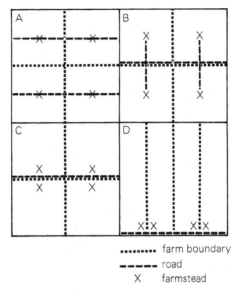

.... farm boundary
—————— road
X   farmstead

Figure 12.2 Rural road patterns, after Chisholm (1962).

external distance from buildings to public services such as roads, water, electricity. In the examples given in Fig. 12.2, in *A* and *B* farm units are square and the distance is minimized for the farmers (buildings are optimally cited in relation to fields), but this requires two miles of service road to connect all four farmsteads in the square mile block. *C* represents a movement from the optimal location of buildings in relation to farm area, but service lengths are halved to one mile. In *D* internal farm organization is far from optimal, but service lengths are located on the southern edge of the road. This latter solution provides more social contact, farm costs are increased but service costs decreased. More complex combinations result if we introduce size of farmstead cluster to be maximized. This social contact principle, which is evident in *C* and *D* but not in *A* and *B*, gives modified alternatives. Each move away from *A* and *B* increases farm costs, but decreases service provision costs and provides increased social contact.

We can therefore see that transport and network studies have a vital role in the development of an 'undeveloped' area and perhaps in the readjustment of existing rural areas. The so-called development problem in rural areas in Britain is of the latter type – a readjustment problem involving contraction and selected expansion, given changes in production, distribution and efficiency.

Many of the interesting problems of optimal network synthesis arise from the subtle trade-offs between construction and travel costs. MacKinnon and Hodgson (1970) have used an algorithm which attempts to minimize the sum of all inter-modal shortest path distances subject to the constraints that a predetermined total 'construction mileage budget' is not exceeded, and that the resulting network is a connected network.

Other problems arise from attempting to establish a framework to estimate transportation demand relationships for a given transport system and between different transport systems. Manufactured goods constitute a disproportionately large share of transport revenue, forest and agricultural products are poor contributors, while animal products barely cover out-of-pocket expenses. This is partly a response to raise increased charges on items with inelastic demand for transport services. Rural area products thus have high elasticities of demand for transportation.

The elasticity of demand can be measured by

$$\frac{dQ_i}{dP_i} \cdot \frac{P_i}{Q_i} = \frac{d(\log Q_i)}{d(\log P_i)} \tag{1}$$

and the substitutability of two competitive services by

$$\frac{d(Q_i/Q_j)}{d(P_i/P_j)} \cdot \frac{P_i/P_j}{Q_i/Q_j} = \frac{d(\log Q_i/Q_j)}{d(\log P_i/P_j)} \tag{2}$$

where i and j refer to two goods or services and Q and P are quantities and prices respectively (Perle, 1965).

These may be formulated in terms of least-squares; for example (2) becomes,

$$\log(Q_i/Q_j) = \log A + b_{ij} \log(P_i/P_j) + e$$

This can be disaggregated spatially and separately for different transport types, for example

$$\log Q_m = a_m + b_m \log P_m + \sum_{i=1}^{n} c_m R_i + \sum_{j=1}^{t} d_m T_j$$

$$\log Q_r = a_r + b_r \log P_r + \sum_{i=1}^{n} c_r R_i + \sum_{j=1}^{t} d_r T_j$$

where R_i are regions, T_j are years, m refers to road transport and r to railways, c_i are regional shift variables and d_j temporal effects, a the intercept, and b the price elasticities of demand.

Inter-network substitution can be specified by a model such as

$$\log(Q_m/Q_r) = a + b \log(P_m/P_r) + \sum_{i=1}^{n} c_i R_i + \sum_{i=1}^{t} d_j T_j$$

where b is the least-squares estimate of the elasticity of inter-modal substitution.

In this model only tons of freight originating in the region of a given commodity is required as an input (this can be derived from production figures). There is generally a complete lack of statistics on destinations of commodity shipments. This is not too serious a problem since one can still look at regional demands for transport services. In any expanded model, however, destinations would require specification.

Little measurement of demand elasticity has been undertaken on British transport systems and, consequently, the pricing policy of motor and rail transport has never effectively been based on strictly economic criteria, so that optimal allocation of transport resources between transport sectors has never been achieved. Motor transport has been capturing larger shares of the transport service market over time, and there is now great competition in long hauls over 200 miles between road, rail and air. Yet research on transport economics for goods indicates that for hauls over 150 miles, railroads are low-cost carriers (Meyer *et al.*, 1960).

Attention has usually centred on modal split models as a method of allocating total number of person trips between different methods or modes of travel. Procedures are based on the competitiveness of each mode of transport in relation to others, and this competitiveness is usually measured by characteristics of person making journey (car ownership, income, socio-economic position), characteristics of the journey to be made (length, time, purpose), and characteristics of transport system (travel time, cost, accessibility, comfort). Some theoretical work on trip distribution, mode split and route split has been undertaken in Britain by Wilson (1969) and practical studies are beginning to emerge.

We now turn to the problem of allocating traffic along routes of a network. The elements of a transportation problem may be defined as a certain amount of some (homogeneous) commodity available at each of a number of sources, a certain amount required at each of a number of destinations, where the total amount available altogether equals the total amount required altogether. The cost of supplying each destination from each source (as so much per unit) is given and the cheapest way of meeting these requirements has to be found. This is a typical linear programming model. Linear programming may be used to analyse changes in transport costs and proposed developments. The simplex solution is rarely used now in the transportation problem: generally the model has total requirements exactly equal to the restrictions, so that more efficient methods can be applied.

The problem is to maximize

$$x_0 = - \sum_i \sum_j c_{ij} x_{ij}$$

subject to $\sum_j x_{ij} = a_i$ & $\left[\sum_i x_{ij} = b_j . \right]$

It is assumed that $\sum_i a_i = \sum_j b_j$

where x_{ij} is the number of units sent from source i to destination j

    c_{ij} is the cost of sending one unit from source i to destination j

    a_i is the amount available at source i

    b_j is the amount required at destination j.

It is also possible to specify that some destinations cannot be supplied from specified origins, that when supply exceeds demand fictitious destinations can be specified and imports created when demand exceeds supply. Inventory costs can also be added to transshipment costs, and the whole system treated as a multi-time-period problem with storage costs etc.

However, a simple problem will be given by way of illustration. Transport costs in the £s per unit of material from settlements A, B and C to destinations at settlements D, E, F are

	D	E	F
A	7	4	1
B	6	9	10
C	10	6	8

8, 7 and 9 units are available at A, B and C respectively and 6, 8 and

10 units are required at D, E and F respectively. The problem is to devise a transport network to achieve the lowest total transport costs.

One method of solution is to use the 'north-west corner rule' (Heady and Candler, 1958). As much as possible is supplied from the first source to the first destination until either the source has used all its supply or until the destination has received its full requirement. This would give

	Destination	D	E	F	Transport
	Amount required	6	8	10	cost
Source	Amount Available				
A	8	6	2	0	£186
B	7	0	6	1	
C	9	0	0	9	

This can be modified to reduce costs – route AF looks promising. One unit sent on this route would have the following cost changes:

$$1(AF) - 4(AE) + 9(BE) - 10(BF) = -4, \text{ a saving of £4.}$$

The resulting matrix would have the form

	D	E	F	Transport
A	6	1	1	cost
B	0	7	0	£182
C	0	0	9	

It should be noted that one unit is the maximum possible amount to divert along this route. The next possible cost saving solution is along BD which would cost for one unit change:

$$6(BD) - 7(AD) + 4(AE) - 9(BE) = -6, \text{ a saving of £6.}$$

A maximum of 6 units could be sent along this route, with a saving of £36. Thus we now have

	D	E	F	Transport
A	0	7	1	cost
B	6	1	0	£146
C	0	0	9	

Further cost economics may be found by exploring routes CD and BF.

The optimum solution is

	D	E	F	Transport
A	0	0	8	cost
B	6	0	1	£110
C	0	8	1	

The 'north-west corner rule' is apt to produce a very poor initial solution, since it pays no attention to cost. In practice a modified 'north-west corner rule' is used in which the next destination considered is chosen as the one with the smallest cost from the source being considered. Looking at the cost matrix a reasonable guess at the solution might be

	D	E	F
A	0	0	8
B	6	1	0
C	0	7	2

which is very close to the optimal solution.

A more difficult multi-period-time example is given by E.M.L. Beale (1968) in *Mathematical Programming in Practice*, to which the reader is referred.

One of the deficiencies in current methods of network analysis is that procedures for optimizing network configuration are only weakly developed. Few attempts have been made to generate entirely new, optimized, physical networks linking together a given set of nodes. Scott (1967) has considered optimizing networks where gross supply and demand at each point are known, and the origin and destination as well as the path through the generated network of each flow are to be determined. Domanski (1967), commenting on Scott, has noted two significant problems relevant in development studies:

(1) simultaneous determination of the spatial pattern of transportation network and settlement pattern;
(2) simultaneous determination of the spatial pattern of transportation network complexes (e.g. road network and rail network).

It is insufficient to consider how to determine an optimal transportation network linking a given set of settlements; an inverse dependence exists – the spatial pattern of settlements is conditioned by a transportation network. Both transportation networks and settlement patterns should then be determined simultaneously. Domanski quotes some mathematical models as steps towards possible solutions of these problems, and the reader is referred to these.

Railways

Fogel's (1964) econometric study of American railroads and their effect on economic development in terms of cost of transport, availability on natural resources, social savings of railroads, and their lead to technical innovations in other sectors of the economy, cast doubt on the value of their tranditional role. Allowing for the cost of more canal construction, with resulting increased inventory costs, Fogel estimated that railways were of marginal significance in terms of the extra area of agricultural land they opened up. His detailed study of the effect of railroads on the rest of the economy, including foreign capital investments and timing of the advent of the motor vehicle, revealed that the US economy would only be one and a half years behind its present position had the rail system not been developed. A later study repeating the analysis for Britain (Hawke, 1970) estimated that in the first 30–40 years railways contributed about 10 per cent of national income, and overall had a very much larger impact on the economy than in the USA. In Britain, the linkage of railways to agriculture was much weaker than that to manufacturing and mining, but the social rate of return to investments in railways was high.

The main problems facing railways in rural areas were the existence of low traffic regions, competitive duplication, and the hostility of landowners to the construction of lines across their land with concomitant financial strains. Many rural railway routes were built as branches to serve largely rural areas, the majority in the latter half of the nineteenth century after the railway had become fully established and had achieved a virtual monopoly of land transport. They were built to feed traffic into the main line, but many did not yield an economic return even in their Victorian heyday (Nock, 1957). The traffic from them helped to swell that on trunk routes to greater proportions, but their role as traffic feeders was vulnerable to the development of effective road transport. The feeder lines in the Northern dales are an example of this transport situation.

Other parts of the railway system were unnecessary because of competitive duplication. The unbridled competition between railway companies in the nineteenth century resulted in many lines being built solely to further competition with other companies, often leading to a duplication of facilities that was scarcely justified even at the time of construction. Stretton (1907) cites the Midland Railway as one of the most blatant railway imperialists of the nineteenth century. In 1876 it opened a parallel but independent route through the Pennines, rather than depend on the rival London and North Western Railway to forward its traffic north of Ingleton to Scotland. The line cost £3¼ million, carried virtually no local traffic and only a small proportion of the total Anglo-Scottish through traffic.

The effects on railway construction of landowners' objections have been documented by Appleton (1966). The Midland Railway line through Wyedale (Derbyshire) to Manchester, passes through the Duke of Rutland's Haddon Estate, but one condition for its development was that it should not pass too close to the Hall. The line, therefore, plunges into the side of a hill and re-emerges after it has passed the precincts of the Hall. Such engineering exacted by landowners considerably added to costs. £35,000 was paid in 1846 to the Duke of Cleveland to overcome his objections to a line through Raby Castle Estate from Bishop Auckland to Tebay, in addition to the value of the land. The Northern Countries Union Railway, through paying this sum and others for the withdrawal of landowners' opposition, found itself unable to build the railway.

The specialized route system and its high fixed cost characterized the railway system in the mid-twentieth century and formed the chief problem to be tackled by Beeching. The Beeching Report (British Railways Board, 1963) stated:

Railways are distinguished by the provision and maintenance of specialized route systems for their own exclusive use. This gives rise to high fixed costs. On the other hand, the benefits which can be derived from possession of this route system are very great. Firstly, it permits the running of high capacity trains, which themselves have very low movement costs per unit carried. Secondly, it permits dense flows of traffic and, provided the flows are dense, the fixed costs per unit are also low. . . .

The total cost of providing the route system . . . amounts to nearly a quarter of the railways' total revenue. This is a fixed cost, in the full sense of the term, all the while the route system remains unchanged, and its high level emphasizes the necessity for matching the railway system to available traffic so as to ensure a high average level of loading.

Rural areas do not give rise to dense traffic flows, and it was inevitable even before the 'Beeching axe' that some contraction should take place in such routes. But three courses of action were open to British Rail to reduce the unit cost of the system:

(1) expand output – increase freight and passengers carried;
(2) length of route system could be reduced to remove low-density routes – the solution adopted in general;
(3) reduce the level of expenditure on the least profitable part of the system – about one-third of the entire system in 1963.

Joy (1964) argued that cost per unit mile on British Rail was higher than necessary even on the lowest estimate of BR's nine different categories of type of line maintenance costs. He stated that many routes were low density and therefore should only be single track and costed as such. Permanent way costs may be varied at short notice, by varying the number of tracks, subject to a minimum of one, laid along the desired routes. The cost of providing each one of these tracks might be inelastic to changes in traffic density, but the number of tracks on each route can easily be adjusted downward to match a fall in traffic density or, in conjunction with modern signalling equipment, to carry the same traffic over fewer tracks. With a limiting section of ten miles, which, Joy argued, was four times the then average distance between BR's stations, and an average train speed of only 20 miles per hour, a single track route would have a theoretical capacity of forty-eight trains per day. This would have been adequate for many routes then equipped with double track. It has been felt that although the opportunity to reduce routes from multiple to single tracks has always been present, BR has always allowed traffic densities to fall to uneconomic levels without taking up the option of adjusting the amount of track facilities to reduce the route system costs. Between 1948 and 1961, 30.9 per cent of route mileage closed without BR having explored single-track economy.

However, despite these criticisms, the fact remains that, for the majority of rural branch lines and duplicated main lines, traffic generated is not sufficient to justify even single-track operations. Beeching may have been superficial in his analysis and devious in parts of his logic, but within his terms of reference (to design a profitable non-subsidized system) he arrived at a defensible conclusion.

Since 1964 there has been increasing emphasis in Great Britain on the idea that proposals to withdraw railway services should not be decided purely on financial criteria, but rather on broader economic and social grounds. The 1966 White Paper on Transport Policy stated there were some railways services 'which have little or no prospect of becoming directly remunerative, in a commercial sense, on the basis of revenue from users . . . . yet their value to the community outweighs their accounting cost to the railways'. Thus cost-benefit analysis has come into vogue to attempt to evaluate the social costs and benefits associated with the withdrawal of a railway service.

Ray and Crum (1963) looked at the social costs as well as financial savings from Beeching proposals, under the recommendations for improved methods of working, increased charges to particular users, savings from closing commuter lines and savings from rural closures. The first proposal represents a social as well as financial saving but the latter two may represent smaller social savings given that they may lead to more road congestion in cities, more road accidents, lengthier journeys in rural areas etc. The overall result of Beeching, however, seems to have been a substantial social saving in real terms, even if not quite as large as the financial saving.

Other studies have looked at individual routes in the network. Clayton and Rees (1967) undertook the first cost-benefit study of a rural railway line, the Central Wales line from Craven Arms to Llanelli, 80 miles long and passing through a sparsely populated area which is generally deficient in public transport facilities. On the basis of a one week survey in 1964 of all passengers travelling on the line, Clayton and Rees calculated the benefits accruing from the traffic to be £16,319, and the costs as £40,000. Thus the annual social costs of operating the line exceeded the annual social benefits by £23,681. This implied that closure would be justified unless the annual intangible benefits of retention were judged to be worth an amount at least equal to this figure. By 1970, the Swansea-Llanelli-Shrewsbury line was operating on the basis of an Exchequer grant of £370,000 per annum. The service is still operated, though as a through service of five trains per day each way between Shrewsbury and Swansea.

Two other cost-benefit studies of rural lines are of note. A study of the Cambrian coast line from Machynlleth to Pwllheli was undertaken by the Ministry of Transport Economic Unit (1969). The discounted net social cost over social benefit of retaining the line over a 10 year period was £695,500 (if it was closed after 10 years, thus reducing the need for expenditure on replacement), or between £748,500 and £927,500 (if the line was to remain open indefinitely). These figures were estimated by discounting costs and benefits back to 1968 at 8 per cent. On the basis of this study, Ministerial consent for closure was given, but the line was reprieved in the summer of 1974. Foot and Starkie (1970) undertook a cost-benefit study of the 26 mile Ashford-Hastings line. They concluded that the average net cost of retaining the line, discounted at 10 per cent per annum over 10 years, was £189,500. Closure would, they thought, lead to some intangible costs but these did not appear to be large, so it appeared that closure of the line was justified. This line was also reprieved in 1974.

Many rural lines are financed with the aid of central Exchequer subsidies. This is justifiable on efficiency grounds where social benefits are greater than social costs. However cost-benefit studies of the three rural lines quoted above indicate that social costs exceed social benefit on some rural rail lines, and that considerable social savings would be effected if such lines were closed. The extent to which losses on public transport are reduced when a rail line is closed will partly depend on the quality of the alternative bus service that is provided, and the assumptions made about this can have a major impact on the results of the cost-benefit study. For example, in the Ministry of Transport's study of the Cambrian Coast line, the costs of the alternative bus service accounted for 77 per cent of the benefits of complete retention of the line.

Since the justification for keeping such lines open cannot be made in terms of social efficiency, can a case for their retention be made in terms of equity? As well as considering social efficiency, governments are also interested in the distribution of costs and benefits between different income groups and between areas. Pryke and Dodgson (1975) have argued that personal expenditure on rail travel is heavily weighted towards the highest income group, with just over 50 per cent of personal rail expenditure contributed by the top 20 per cent of households, although they account for only one-third of all expenditure. In contrast, the poorest 20 per cent of households accounted for only 5 per cent of personal expenditure on rail travel, although their share of all expenditure is around 8 per cent. Again, season ticket holders account for half of the passenger miles travelled on the loss-making services, and the richest 20 per cent of householders accounted in 1972 for 57 per cent of the total expenditure on season-ticket travel. Thus Pryke and Dodgson argue that if non-business demand for rail travel were to double because no fares were charged and if none of this extra demand came from the richest 20 per cent of households, then the richest 20 per cent, which accounted for 51 per cent of £215 million personal expenditure on all BR passenger services in 1972, would gain £109.65 million if rail transport were provided free. The benefits to other income groups would be £105.35 million to those already travelling; plus benefits for extra journeys by this income group, if the demand curve were linear, of £107.5 million of consumers' surplus. The total gains in consumers' surplus would, therefore, come to £322.5 million. If this were so, the richest 20 per cent would still enjoy 34 per cent of the efficiency benefit, which is almost exactly the same as their proportion of total consumers' expenditure. Thus, Pryke and Dodgson argue, even on assumptions which are heavily loaded against the richest 20 per cent, extra subsidization would not make the distribution of income any more equal. Moreover, it seems clear that the existing subsidies contribute to inequality. In rural areas, this statement may be true to a greater or lesser extent depending on any possible difference in the income distribution of rail users from the national situation. But it implies that subsidization cannot be readily justified on grounds of promoting income equality. In addition, if the government has spatial distribution and efficiency goals, it still implies that this subsidy should be applied to some other transport sector in the area, or another industry or service altogether.

Road transport: public

The decline in rural bus services is a relatively recent phenomenon compared to railway problems. Expansion occurred in rural bus services in the 1930s and in the immediate post-war period, the latter as a result of petrol rationing and restriction on private transport.

The high level of demand persisted until 1955-6, when passenger journeys fell on public omnibus services and the number of vehicle miles operated fell the following year. This decline may have started as early as 1952 in rural areas, but the combined urban-rural figures do not permit this to be distinguished. The decline in the 1950s was about 3.4 per cent per year.

In 1961 the Jack Committee (Ministry of Transport, 1961) was set up to investigate rural bus services. They considered the main cause of decline in services to be the growth of private transport. Another important factor in causing a decline in the number of bus passengers was thought to have been the rapid spread of television, which it is estimated reduced cinema trips by half. Contributory factors were the changing geographical distribution of population, increasing concentration in towns and villages, higher fares and mobile shops. Difficulties have been aggravated by rising costs and by far the greatest factor in this rise is the increasing cost of labour which represents about two-thirds of overall bus operating costs compared with 9-12 per cent for fuel tax. Increasing costs and declining traffic do not present problems, of course if they can be covered by fare increases. Experience has shown, however that when fares have been raised, the number of passenger journeys has dropped and the net result has sometimes been a fall in total receipts instead of a rise. Country people have, in general, been unwilling or unable to pay increased fares more in line with the full cost of providing rural services, and passengers on other services have not yielded enough revenue to meet the losses on rural routes by way of cross-subsidy. In remote areas of mid-Wales, Northumberland and Scotland the majority of services are operated by small companies, probably because the large companies (which could cross-subsidize operations) have not wished to acquire services which, because of the extremely sparse population of the area, have always had low receipts. Thomas (1963) illustrates some of the exceptional difficulties which small operators face in remote rural areas.

Profits of bus operators follow a downward tendency as services become more rural. This has been shown by Beesley and Politi (1969) who constructed an economic model to estimate average profits per seat. The model was of the form

$$\pi/S = k(M/B) + f(P/S) + \text{constant}$$
$$\text{where } k > 0$$

where π = profit per year (revenue minus costs)
          S = number of seats.
Dividing π by S standardizes for differences in size of total assets by companies.
          P = number of passengers carried per year
          f = average fare per passenger paid
          M/B = mileage per bus (a cost variable).

The revenue term $f(P/S)$ is represented in the equation by passengers per seat P/S, since no information on f for individual companies exists, but it varies according to type of service and length of journey. No detailed data are available on costs (particularly capital assets), but since one of the main determinants of cost per seat is intensity with which the stock of buses of a company is used, it was postulated that C/S (where C = costs) is negatively related to mileage per bus.

$$C/S = k(M/B) + \text{constant } k < 0$$

Table 12.1 shows average profit per seat of companies in four different rural groupings for given years.

The model was used to provide results for rural services for stage routes only and for companies with a specialization in stage services to 75 per cent or more of operations, i.e. express, tours and contract work is excluded.

Profits derived from more urban services are not only higher than profits from more rural ones but they are entirely predictable in terms of bus mileage and/or more passengers per seat. The model used estimated that a company with rural operations exceeding 75 per cent and not a member of a holding company group had a profit of £3.4 per seat 1965–6. This indicates that a sizeable subsidy would be required to bring profits in this class of operations up to the level of those in the non-controlled sector (£6.6) should licensing authorities abandon their policy of intra-stage cross-subsidization. The apparent increase in profits in the heavily rural areas is due to the influence of one company which has shown a phenomenal growth. This company's activities could also account for the divergence between average profit and predicted profit in this group.

The Jack Committee, considering what assistance might be given to rural companies, argued that the amount of financial assistance should not be measured by the difference between operators' average costs and their receipts per mile, because receipts per mile vary so

Table 12.1   Profits per seat by degree of rurality (£)

	All companies	0–25 per cent rural	26–50 per cent rural	51–75 per cent rural	Over 75 per cent rural
1960–1	10.6 (63)*	12.4 (29)	10.9 (21)	6.8 (6)	5.1 (7)
1962–3	9.5 (70)	11.1 (32)	9.2 (21)	6.7 (9)	4.0 (8)
1964–5	9.1 (74)	10.6 (33)	9.9 (22)	6.5 (10)	4.3 (9)
1965–6	8.3 (76)	9.4 (35)	8.0 (23)	6.7 (9)	5.8 (8)

Source: Beesley and Politi (1969).

*Figures in brackets refer to number of observations.

much depending on population density and size of company. Any solution involving financial assistance should be related to the circumstances of each case and not based on any general formula of costs per vehicle mile.

Some of the recommendations of the Jack Committee were subsequently augmented in the 1968 Transport Act. The committee argued against tax reliefs, such as fuel tax, as indiscriminate, and argued for financial help from outside the industry in the form of direct financial aid, the cost of the aid to fall partly on the Exchequer and partly on the County Councils. Under the 1968 Transport Act, the Ministry of Transport provided 50 per cent of such a grant if local authorities found the remainder. Few local authorities made extensive use of the grants offered under this Act.

Other proposals have been made from time to time to alleviate the problems of public road transport in rural areas. It has been suggested that operators might give more attention to the possibility of expanding their parcel traffic, and that the Post Office should be invited to reconsider the extent to which mail at present carried in Post Office vans could be passed over to buses, and the possibility of allowing fare-paying passengers to travel in Post Office vans. These proposals have never been seriously considered for England and Wales by the Post Office, but some integration occurs in the Highlands and Islands of Scotland.[1]

---

[1] In July 1972 the Scottish Traffic Commissioners granted the Post Office a licence to operate a bus passenger service in Barra. Since that date post buses have begun operating in some parts of rural England.

Road transport: private

The chief determinant of the demand for public transport is the level of car ownership in rural areas. Public transport demand is now largely a residual of private transport. It is, therefore, important to determine the level of private car ownership in rural areas. Little research in Britain has been undertaken to build mathematical models to express automobile density in rural areas as a function of socio-economic variables. However, an elementary model has been built in Finland to investigate rural automobile density as a function of basic socio-economic variables (West 1966).

The principal equation in the model with the smallest set of residuals was

$$\log y = -0.02 + 0.79 \log I + 0.20 \log R + 0.10 \log A + 0.37 \log B$$
$$\text{with } R^2 = 0.56$$

where I = 100 x total income tax units/number of inhabitants
   R = length of public roads/land area
   A = number of farms whose cultivated area is equal to or greater than 15 hectares/100 inhabitants
   B = number of persons employed in business/number of inhabitants.

About half of the automobile density is due to the income variable and the influence of road density and farming variables together equal about 25 per cent of the density. The logarithmic expressions show that the sum of the regression coefficients is greater than one. It is typical of this type of function, that if the sum of the exponents is greater than one, the function itself grows faster than the variables describing it, that is, automobile density is growing faster than the economic variables upon which it depends. If this is so, then the demand for public transport will inevitably decline in the future, and that for private transport will continue to grow at a rate greater than the growth in income. Demand for private transport in rural areas has indeed continued to grow despite the fact that oil (a non-renewable natural resource – see Chapter 8) is being depleted too slowly: the world is using too little oil rather than too much because of overpricing by the oil cartel OPEC. Because of demand in-elasticity for oil, it is quite likely that losses arising from monopoly are very large (Kay and Mirrlees, 1975) and some of these losses are clearly sustained by rural residents.

Table 12.2 Annual cost per head of capital and current spending on rural roads, 1971 (£)

	Great Britain	Rural Northumberland	Merioneth and Montgomery	Rural Carmarthan	Sutherland	Roxburgh	Wigtown
Current	5.7	17.9	24.0	14.6	77.5	10.5	12.9
Capital	4.4	5.4	2.2	2.6	2.9	0.6	2.9

Source: HM Treasury (1976).

What is generally not realized, however, is that while capital spending on roads in rural areas is below the national average, current spending is very much above the national average. This is because rural roads are very expensive to maintain – see Table 12.2. There must be a real question over whether such an extensive system of rural roads as we have at present is economically justified, and whether they should all be maintained to their present standards. Small villages in the less accessible parts of rural areas are served by 'B' and 'C' class roads. They are frequently of poor alignment, width and visibility. Most carry only local traffic and would not justify road improvements in the majority of instances, although there may be a case for improvement on selected roads to improve access to some villages and urban centres and to enhance road safety. Road improvements are more likely to be economically justified where there is a heavy seasonal recreational traffic and in cases where heavy lorries transport minerals from quarries. The latter often give rise to considerable controversy because of the environmental conflict they create. On the other hand, there is the environmental argument that improved roads do not fit as easily into the landscape as the traditional narrow and winding routes. The point is taken up in the recent Sandford Report on the national parks, where it is urged that all changes in the width and alignment of roads should be subject to planning permission. In the case of recreation there needs to be careful consideration of what constitutes a realistic level of investment to deal with what is an occasional rather than a constant problem.

Current decision-making framework

Rationalization in public transport in rural areas continues to occur, as in the ever-present competition among transport media: rail, bus, and passenger car. Competition between rail and bus services has given way to competition between bus and private cars. Solutions to transport problems will not be easily found or universally accepted. One factor common to nearly all the possibilities however, is the direct or indirect involvement of the relevant local authority.

Sections 202 and 203 of the Local Government Act 1972 place a duty on local authorities to develop policies that promote the provision of efficient and co-ordinated systems of public transport and gives power to support them financially. Such support was provided, for example, for all bus routes in the Sedbergh area in West Yorkshire (Yorkshire and Humberside Economic Planning Board, 1976). However, this bus subsidy system changed after the introduction of the new transport grant system which came into effect on 1 April 1975 (DoE Circular 27/74). Instead of schemes being considered individually for specific central government grants, local authorities receive an annual supplementary block grant for all transport expenditure which is not tied directly to particular projects. This means that although the amount of the Transport Supplementary Grant will reflect the total programme the local authority decides to undertake each year, decisions on the relative priority of schemes, both in respect of one highway scheme against another and one sector of the transport field against another, are for the local authority to take. The final decision on whether and when a particular scheme should proceed is a matter for the county council. One of the main aims of the new system is to encourage local authorities to plan the transport of their areas in an integrated and comprehensive way by looking at both their road programmes and their public transport policies together. This is in fact required of local authorities by the annual submission of Transport Policies and Programmes (TPPs) to the Department of the Environment. The TPP takes stock of the existing situation by forecasting main trends and problems leading to the formulation of objectives, identifying the range of realistic policy options, testing alternatives and evolving a preferred plan, and taking decisions on phasing and implementation as the basis for an expenditure programme. This process is envisaged as a continuing one. Once a medium-long term strategy has been completed, future work will be concerned with amending the planning horizon, updating existing forecasts, monitoring the progress of policies and programmes already in operation and translating the results of these exercizes into new or modified expenditure programmes. Policy instruments distinguished in TPPs are highway investment, traffic management and pedestrianization measures, public transport investment, public transport revenue support, parking controls and pricing. In undertaking studies on transport expenditure proposals, local authorities are required to bear in mind the likely availability of resources over the period to be considered and the proportion of these funds which may reasonably be allocated to transport. Of course, TPPs and structure plans are required to be mutually consistent: structure plans should provide an essential link between the transport sector and the broader objectives towards which all local policy is directed. It is, however, too early yet to assess the impact of this new system on rural transport.

Specific action can be taken as, for example, under the Heavy Commercial Vehicles (Controls and Regulations) Act 1973. This places on county authorities a duty to prepare written proposals for the control of heavy commercial vehicles on the basis of a survey. They were required to publish, by 1 January 1977, Draft Traffic Regulation Orders for the use of roads in their area by heavy commercial vehicles, so as to preserve or improve amenity. They now have permissive powers to specify through routes for heavy commercial vehicles.

The Department of the Environment recommend that transportation plans be evaluated on economic principles and on environmental and operational grounds. A full economic evaluation requires the use of cost-benefit analysis techniques to compare the benefits accruing to transport users and other sections of the community from the changes included in the various alternative plans and policies with a base situation: it is necessary not only to show that option A is better than B, but also that the resources are worth committing to the strategy or project at all. Department of the Environment instructions (Dawson, 1968) require a consideration of capital costs, user costs (value of travellers' time and vehicle operating costs), accident costs, highway maintenance costs and any generated traffic, all estimated over the whole life of the project (usually taken as thirty years) and discounted to obtain the net present value. A full discounting analysis has the advantage that it establishes both the ranking of alternative options and their absolute worth. No single measure of the effect of transport on the environment is available and no specific recommendations are made, although quantification of the effects is urged wherever possible. Operational appraisal is primarily concerned with technical/engineering relationships to ensure that the transport system proposed in the various alternatives will function and provide a specified standard of service: operational evaluation will ascertain where adjustments are necessary in the capacity provision and check the internal consistency of the system.

Finally, the contribution of transport to wider planning objectives may need to be considered and also the trade-off between economic efficiency and equity considerations. Simple efficiency solutions ignore many social problems: for example, many aged people in rural areas cannot drive. Although as many journeys in rural areas are made in other people's cars as are made by bus services, there is a need for public transport in rural areas for those who do not have cars – the young, the elderly and housewives. This is mainly a distributional problem. A number of courses of action could be advanced to improve this current situation. The removal of legal impediments and institutional constraints to achieve a more efficient use of existing resources, such as car sharing, is one policy option. In this context the Government has promised legislation to permit, in selected rural areas, the carrying of fare paying passengers in private cars. Further subsidization of existing public transport could be introduced, but this would imply a further urban-rural transfer of income. Since rural areas are already heavily subsidized by urban areas, an alternative solution might be to encourage people to move from specific rural areas by offering compensation. The size of compensation would be partly a matter of equity, but an upper limit could be set by the net savings to society from transport (plus the net savings in all other subsidies received by that particular rural area). The solution to the rural transport problem does not lie in transport itself, but in the general field of rural economic policy. It is intimately bound up with social objectives and planning policies, such as the concentration of population in certain areas and industrial and recreational developments. Transport needs to be evaluated, not in isolation, but as a component in the general rural economy.

13 A cautionary
case study

In this chapter, we conclude the book with a case study of a bitterly
contested public decision, made in 1966, relating to the construction
of a reservoir at Cow Green. The facts leading up to the decision are
taken from the excellent account by Gregory (1971), also published
in Smith (1975). As there was little formal economic analysis undertaken in connection with this decision, we then go on to discuss
whether such work might have contributed to the decision.

In 1964, ICI decided to construct a chemical plant at Billingham
which would use a new chemical process to make ammonia out of
naphtha. At that time, the fertilizer industry was suffering from one
of its periodic bouts of excess capacity. Overseas production, based
on natural gas, was holding down prices and rendering ICIs coal-
based production uncompetitive. This decision to switch to naphtha
was the first move in what has since become known as the Cow
Green affair. For the process itself, ICI needed large volumes of
water which would require extra supply capacity by 1971, that is,
within seven years of the decision. The effect of the decision to
proceed with the new plant was made more dramatic because ICI had,
in August 1963, told the Tees Valley and Cleveland Water Board
that their plans did not indicate an increase in expected water requirements in the immediate future. The Water Board were then faced
with unexpected industrial demands for a drastic increase in water

supply in a short period. In 1964, the amounts of extra water needed was 158 m³ of water per day, an increase of more than 150 per cent on previous expectations.

The available means of generating such an increase in supply were reviewed. They included:

(1) a large impounding reservoir from which water could be piped to point of use;
(2) a storage reservoir filled by pump from the river nearer to the point of use;
(3) extraction from an aquifer, by borehole;
(4) a further regulating reservoir in the Upper Tees which would store the winter's rainfall and release it in summer, thus allowing abstraction further downstream.

The further possibilities of an estuarine barrage and desalination are not mentioned by Gregory, perhaps because the technology available in 1964 was not sufficiently developed to make them worth considering.

At this stage, (1) could be rejected on grounds of cost in relation to yield, particularly the cost of pipeworks. (2) was rejected because it would have involved flooding a substantial area of good quality agricultural land. The borehole did not find favour because it was uncertain whether it would produce enough water. A pilot project taking some years would be needed to establish whether it would yield sufficient water. The regulating reservoir, on the other hand, would not require expensive pipeworks, nor would it require better quality agricultural land and it could be brought into production comparatively quickly.

Thus, at this early stage, it was decided to proceed with a river-regulating reservoir. Having reached this conclusion, particular requirements for the project could be set down. They were first, that an adequate yield should be available and, secondly, that access for construction should be possible at reasonable cost. Thirdly the geology of the site should be such that leakage would be within tolerable limits. Fourthly, ICI and the Water Board were aware of the over-riding requirement to produce a sufficiently non-controversial proposal to avoid provoking opposition and hence delay.

The Water Board then commissioned a survey of all possible sites which identified and compared 17 reservoir sites including Cow

Green. At this stage, they consulted the Nature Conservancy and invited its reaction to the list. The Board indicated its preference for Cow Green to the Conservancy, who were thought to be in favour of it too. The Conservancy then commissioned an ecological survey of the area which was not available until late in 1965. The survey report argued that part of the site (Widdy Bank Fell) was of very special scientific interest, because of its ecological complexity, and that the loss of even 10 hectares of such ground would be a very serious matter. Nevertheless, the Board decided to proceed and submitted a Draft Order to the Minister of Housing and Local Government.

The Minister invited the newly formed Water Resources Board to produce a report on the range of possibilities jointly with the Tees Valley and Cleveland Water Board. Gregory tabulates their findings as in Table 13.1.

This tabulation clearly indicates the attractions of the Cow Green site. It would be completed in the shortest time and would cost much less than the other sites, both in total and in terms of capital cost per cubic metre per day. The dam at Cow Green would be relatively small, yet it would yield enough water to supply expected demand. All of the other sites would take two years longer and only one of them, Middleton, would yield more water. Middleton is an interesting site, costing nearly three times as much, but yielding more than twice as much as Cow Green. Middleton would provide a very substantial excess capacity in the region until well into the 1980s and the construction cost per m^3 from this source was only slightly greater than that at Cow Green. Against Middleton was the loss of agricultural land involved (about 400 hectares) and the important fact that more than 100 properties of all kinds would be wholly or partly submerged. Middleton was thus not promising if public controversy was to be avoided.

Over-riding all other factors, from the point of view of ICI, was that of timeliness, and on this criterion Cow Green was undoubtedly the best option. The Water Board was therefore strengthened in its resolve to go ahead with it. However it had now been discovered that the Cow Green site included about 120 hectares of common land. This meant that more stringent and complex legal procedures must precede a change of use. Had there been no common land, the Water Board could have acquired the land by compulsory purchase. Acquisition of Common Land, however, required proceeding under a mixture of ancient and modern legislation and the outcome was unpredictable both in substance and timing. An alternative to this

Table 13.1   Comparison of eight river-regulating sites

Site	Capacity ($10^6 m^3$)	Yield ($10^3 m^3$ a day)	Length (m)	Height (m)	Cost (£ millions)	Water area ($10^6 m^2$)	Disturbance	Intended completion date
Cow Green	40.5	157.5	525	22.0	2.0–2.5	3.3	area of SSSI	1969
Upper Cow Green	35.1	130.5–135.0	1550	46.4	6.0	3.4	nature reserve	1971
Cronkley	36.0	135.0–144.0	518	53.4	4.0	2.0	nature reserve	1971
Upper Maize Beck	24.8	85.5– 90.0	952	48.5	4.0	2.7	nature reserve	1971
Lower Maize Beck	24.8	81.0– 90.0	1180	56.1	4.5	1.2	nature reserve	1971
Middleton	81.0	337.5	1180	54.0	6.0	4.0	farmland, roads, houses	1972
Harwood	36.0	135.0–144.0	1310	43.6	5.0	1.4	area of SSSI, agricultural land, houses, roads	1971
Eggleston	36.0	135.0–144.0	1010	58.6	5.3	1.7	road diversion	1971

Sources: Water Resources Board, quoted by Gregory (1971), and Smith (1975).

would be to promote a Private Members Bill in the House of Commons. In favour of the Private Bill would be the fixed timetable which would determine its rate of progress through Parliament. Against it would be the risk of the reservoir becoming a political *cause célébre* and the case being decided on the basis of lobbying, rhetoric and emotion. The alternative, of using established legal procedures, offered the attraction of a more considered outcome, but brought with it the risk of delay while the Minister reached a decision. In the event, it was decided to proceed with a parliamentary private members bill. The Bill was laid before Parliament on 27 November 1965.

However the resistance to Cow Green has now begun to crystallize. Prime movers in this were a group of botanists interested in the rare flora of Upper Teesdale. The flavour of the debate can be judged from the following letter which appeared in *The Times* on 2 February 1966:

Sir, – The announcement in your columns on January 26 that the Nature Conservancy have agreed, without prejudice, to trial borings by the Tees Valley and Cleveland Water Board to test the feasibility of a 650-acre reservoir at Cow Green in Upper Teesdale does little to quieten the grave anxiety which many scientists have felt since December 8, when the Water Board announced in the press their plans to construct a reservoir there.

The valley of the Tees above High Force is an area of unique scientific value in Britain, recognized as such by the creation of two National Nature Reserves and the designation of the remaining area as a Site of Specific Scientific Interest. The saving of its remarkable complex of plant communities dependent upon unusual geological formations must rank as the most urgent conservation issue in Britain at the present time.

Upper Teesdale is not merely a site of national importance; the scientific research on the valley, actively progressing and already embedded in more than 100 publications, has given the Teesdale vegetation, with its extraordinary floristic assemblage of rare and local species, an outstanding international reputation. As an irreplaceable open-air laboratory it must be protected from gross interference and destruction such as would inevitably result from the construction of a reservoir and the impounding of the headwaters of the River Tees.

Whilst we are not unmindful of the claims in an expanding economy, we cannot believe that the values of our society are so crudely materialistic that we shall consciously permit the destruction of such a splendid heritage, for what can be, at best, only a short-term solution of the problem of industrial water.

We must strengthen the hand of the Nature Conservancy and declare that we are firmly opposed, on scientific grounds which will be stated in detail at a public inquiry or elsewhere as appropriate, to the construction of any reservoir in the main valley of the Tees above High Force. A public appeal for support is being prepared.

Its signatories were all eminent botanists and some had detailed research experience of the Cow Green Site. However, they were also mostly based away from the region of the reservoir. In this they were different from the supporters of the reservoir most of whom lived in the same region. The botanists had already indicated their determination in July 1965, by rejecting an offer of £100,000 from ICI, for an intensive research programme before the valley was flooded.

Amenity interests had also joined the opposition to Cow Green, though their case rested less on the uniqueness of the site than that of the scientists. The Council for the Preservation of Rural England and the Ramblers Association and many similar organizations also joined the fracas. Their case rested on arguments such as to the visual intrusion of the proposed dam and reservoir and its impact on the recreational use of the area.

Proponents of the reservoir included many Northern Eastern industrialists, trade unionists and MPs; four of the five relevant Government departments also supported it. Eventually, following the usual conventions, all departments accepted it, the last to agree being the Department of Education and Science which had reservations about the scientific interest of the site.

The Bill was given its First Reading on 26 January 1966. Its Second Reading was unopposed on 1 February and it was then referred to a Select Committee of four MPs (two Conservative; two Labour). The Committee took evidence for twelve full days over three weeks. The cross-examination of the botanists stressed their unfamiliarity with the area and the lack of detailed knowledge of the site. During the debate the borehole to raise ground-water was again put forward as a serious option.

After considering the mass of evidence which had been presented the Select Committee found in favour of the Bill. However, the vote was not unanimous: there was one vote against the Bill, partly in support for the scientific lobby and partly on the grounds that to give way on Cow Green would quickly be followed by capitulation at Middleton. Following presentation of the report, there was further lobbying of MPs before the Bill was put through its Report Stage on 28 July 1966. A free vote at the end of the debate passed the Bill by 112 to 82. Most of those for the Bill were Labour supporters, the majority of those against were Conservatives, but a substantial group of Labour MPs and most of the Liberals voted against the Bill.

The Bill's passage through the House of Lords provided another opportunity for the opponents of the reservoir to state their case. Enough opposition was expressed for another Select Committee to be set up. This time the Committee numbered seven and they spent nineteen days receiving evidence. Further technical information, much of it favourable to Cow Green, was now available. A young botanist came forward to dispute the 'exaggerated claims' of his eminent colleagues. Meanwhile, the objectors changed the strategy of their attack, focusing on the advantages of Middleton, which were relatively quantifiable, rather than on the disadvantages of Cow Green, which were not. As a result of this shift of emphasis, the proponents of Cow Green had to divert some effort to spelling out the disadvantages of the Middleton site. Thus the option of developing a reservoir at Middleton became much more remote.

The Select Committee concluded (unanimously) that Cow Green would be the appropriate site. The Bill was given its Third Reading on 23 February 1967: it was passed without a division. The Bill received the Royal Assent on 22 March 1967, nearly twenty-eight months after the Water Board had formally announced its intention to proceed. Ten years later, we may reasonably ask two questions. First, were the consequences of the decision accurately forecast at the time it was taken? And secondly, can we improve the public decision-taking process from what we have learnt about this one?

Clearly some of the forecasts at the time of the decision must have been wrong, in that mutually exclusive scenarios were portrayed by those for and against the reservoir. We must therefore check individual points to see whether they were correct or not. There has not been a full re-examination of the reservoir issue and we must rely on fragmentary evidence.

The forecasts advanced before the decision related to the demand for water and the extent to which Cow Green would satisfy the demand on the one hand, and, on the other the environmental and ecological consequences of the reservoir. The water supply and demand aspects of the reservoir have recently been assessed by Aponso (1976) who found that the yield of the reservoir, over its first few years, had been slightly better than expected. Furthermore, the problems of seepage and the need for expensive grouting to prevent it, which had been predicted before the Bill was passed, did not materialize. Another problem which has arisen is that of wave erosion of the sugar limestone of Widdybank Fell. This metamorphic rock is a feature of particular interest in the area. It is very soft and the strong winds across the water surface can whip up substantial waves which are eroding the rock along a one mile stretch of shore-line.

The ecological impact of the reservoir is, predictably, must more difficult to assess. ICI did contribute £100,000 towards research and this has now been spent. Before the site was flooded, some tons of soil and many collections of plants were moved to artificial reconstructions of the Upper Tees (Hillaby, 1974). So far, the inundation of 10 hectares of this rare ecosystem does not appear to have affected the rest. The climatic changes forecast are not yet fully detectable although, according to Harding (forthcoming) there are fewer and less severe frosts. The changes so far have not been great enough to affect vegetation. The physical construction of the dam did not bring much environmental damage with it. Opponents of the reservoir were correct in predicting a drastic increase in visitors to the site: according to Aponso, the growth has been from 2000 per annum to 60,000 per annum. We must thus return an open verdict on the environmental impact at this stage.

How then can we improve public decisions as a result of studying these events? In the format of Chapter 2, we may itemize the benefits and costs associated with the Cow Green decision as follows:

Benefits	*Costs*
Water	Construction costs
Jobs	Ecological losses
Recreation	Amenity losses
	Transactions cost

Their precise evaluation is more difficult. Demand relationships for water are not easily established because it is not, generally, priced to consumers. Aponso calculates an implicit net price of water, (which would just produce enough revenue to cover costs discounted at 10 per cent) at Cow Green of 2.19p per thousand gallons. This compares favourably with Middleton, where the implicit price at 10 per cent was 3.94p per thousand gallons. However, the essence of the case for Cow Green was timeliness: that is, there was a particularly strong demand for water in 1970–2 which had to be met. During the progress of the Bill, it was estimated that the value of ICI output which might be lost in the event of Cow Green not being constructed and 1970–2 being dry years was between £8.5 million and £33 million, depending on the severity of the drought. These estimates would provide a basis for evaluating the benefits from Cow Green, which could be obtained by deducting from them the social opportunity cost of the other resources which would be used elsewhere if ICIs production had been cut due to shortage of water. The main benefit here, water, is available for the whole life of the project – in effect, for all time. This contrasts with the letter to *The Times* quoted above which refers to a 'short-term solution of the problem of industrial water'. In these terms, the only *long-run* solution would be to prevent industrial expansion – a solution which is unlikely to attract wide support at present levels of affluence in this country.

An important non-efficiency benefit was the reduction in unemployment on Teesside, due to the industrial development made possible by the reservoir. Note that these benefits are quite separate from the efficiency benefits due to increased output from low-opportunity-cost labour. Recreation benefits from this reservoir arise from the vastly increased number of visitors the area now receives. However, we must avoid the 'before/after' comparison here and convert the trend in a visitor numbers to a 'with/without' basis, in order to establish the effect of the reservoir alone. This would undoubtedly involve a smaller increase than the 2000 to 60,000 mentioned by Aponso.

On the cost side, we now have the advantage of hindsight in that the actual cost of construction is a matter of fact. The ecological losses are much more difficult to evaluate. So far, they may seem negligible, but they might well take several decades to appear. It is tempting to suggest that the £100,000 ICI contributed to research on the site would provide a useful approximation of how the scientists themselves valued the site. However, such reasoning would be far-fetched, because the scientists were not able to negotiate this figure. It has a thoroughly arbitrary look about it and we should not assume that it will represent an equilibrium between those for and those against the reservoir.

The broader class of costs, labelled amenity losses, are even more difficult to evaluate. Those who knew the valley before the dam was built may well claim that the amenity they can now enjoy has been sharply reduced. However, the remaining (new?) amenity is now enjoyed by very many more people. From the visitor numbers quoted by Aponso, we might infer that the value to visitors before construction of the dam would have to exceed the value to visitors after the dam by a factor of more than 20 for an aggregate loss in amenity to have occurred. There has in any case been a substantial transfer of welfare, from the small number who must now seek solitude in other places to the large number who now find pleasure in visiting Cow Green.

At Cow Green there is no doubt that the botanists and environ-mentalists were substantial losers. The public at large, and particu-larly those who would (without it) have to pay for more expensive water and higher levels of unemployment, were the immediate bene-ficiaries. The difference between the value of total benefits and total costs would give a sensible upper limit to the amount of compensa-tion which the beneficiaries would have chosen to pay rather than forego the reservoir. Part of this money might have been put into scientific research to compensate the losers. If such compensation could have been determined early in the decision-taking process, the scientists would have been able to decide whether an extended campaign would yield them better terms. Effective public admini-strators would have the difficult task of judging the amounts which were just likely to be accepted and the transactions cost, in terms of extra administrative effort, of offering less than such amounts.

Perhaps the likelihood of another Cow Green affair has been some-what reduced by changes in the organization of the water industry. The procedures now operating might, by ensuring wider considera-tion of the strategic aspects of water provision, have identified an acceptable alternative to the Cow Green site at the time it was proposed. This argument is by no means certain however, because the number of sites in any region which can be developed quickly is necessarily limited. Such decisions will remain marginal, individually, and the case for any particular site will not necessarily be changed by introducing wider scale planning.

The cost of such decision-making procedures would be further reduced by making a fuller analysis of all of the implications available at an early stage in the procedure. In this case, the lack of firm scientific information on the site would have slowed the decision, a point which emphasizes the importance of environmental inventories in making the case for conservation.

Perhaps the most interesting item here is the transactions cost of the reservoir. Many months of high-cost professional time, and many days of the politicians who served on the select committees, were taken up in choosing Cow Green. Another consequence of the procedures followed here is the effect on future development of water in the region. The level of agitation about Cow Green has been sufficient to discourage those responsible for providing water in the region from siting reservoirs in the Tees valley. Indeed, it could be argued that part of the transactions cost of Cow Green was to close off these options. In fact the next major water investment in the region, after Cow Green, has been on the River North Tyne at Kielder. This is a massive reservoir which will supply water to three industrial concentrations on Tyneside, Wearside and Teesside. The extent to which that choice was influenced by the level of opposition to Cow Green cannot be precisely gauged but may nevertheless be substantial. It should be mentioned that the water industry has been re-organized since the Cow Green affair, and the strategic aspects of water supply are now more systematically considered on a regional basis.

It remains an open question how much of this time, effort and resources put into choosing Cow Green would have been saved if a more explicit formal analysis of the costs and benefits had been available. From what we have seen, it is virtually certain that it would have indicated the same decision, although this would probably have been evident at an early stage. Furthermore, it might well have speeded the passage of the Bill through the House of Lords, because it should have made clear the broad magnitudes of the efficiency/distribution/employment implications of the alternatives. By obliging the protagonists to be explicit and precise about the implications of their proposals, such an analysis would have reduced the heat and passion that was expended on this decision. It would probably also have saved more resources than were required to undertake it.

Such a conclusion may be true of the Cow Green affair but we recognize that there are some public decisions which are quite beyond the reach of economic analysis. Equally, there are many which could be much improved if the issues were spelt out rigorously and publicly. Insistence on the availability of such information offers one means of providing an effective democratic check on the public sector.

References

Adams, R. L., Lewis, R. C., Drake, B. A. and Vogely, W. A. (1973)
Appendix A: An economic analysis, in *Outdoor Recreation: A Legacy for America*. Washington, DC: Department of the Interior, Bureau of Outdoor Recreation.

Agricultural Adjustment Unit (1968) *Farm Size Adjustment*. Bulletin No. 6. Agricultural Adjustment Unit, University of Newcastle upon Tyne.

Anderson, T. W. (1958) *An Introduction to Multivariate Statistical Analysis*. New York: Wiley.

Annual Review of Agriculture (1977) *Annual Review of Agriculture*. Cmnd 6703. London: HMSO.

Aponso, M. C. D. V. (1976) *Report on the Re-Appraisal of Cow Green and Derwent Reservoirs*. Dissertation for M.Sc. in Water Resources. University of Newcastle upon Tyne.

Appleton, J. (1966) Transport and the landscape of northern England, in J. W. House (ed.) *Northern Geographical Essays*. University of Newcastle upon Tyne: Oriel Press.

Archer, B. H. (1973) *The Impact of Domestic Tourism*. Cardiff: University of Wales Press.

Armstrong, J. S. and Grohman, M. C. (1972) A comparative study for long-range forecasting. *Management Science*, 19, 211–21.

Ashton, J. and Rogers, S. J. (eds) (1967) *Economic Change and Agriculture*. Edinburgh: Oliver & Boyd, published for Agricultural Adjustment Unit, University of Newcastle upon Tyne.

Ashworth, W. (1954) *The Genesis of Modern British Town Planning*. London: Routledge & Kegan Paul.

Barlow Report (1940) *Report on the Royal Commission on the Distribution of Industrial Population*. Cmnd 6153. London: HMSO.

Bayliss, D. (1968) *Some Recent Trends in Forecasting*. Working Paper 17. London: Centre for Environmental Studies.

Beale, E. M. L. (1968) *Mathematical Programming in Practice*. London: Pitman.

Beckmann, M. (1952) A continuous model of transportation. *Econometrica*, 20, 643–60.

Beesley, M. E. and Politi, J. (1969) A study of the profits of bus companies 1960–66. *Economica*, 36, 151–71.

Bell, F. W. (1967) An econometric forecasting model for a region. *Journal of Regional Science*, 7, 109–27.

Bellerby, J. R. (1956) *Agriculture and Industry Relative Income*. London: Macmillan.

Bellerby, J. R. (1960) International conditions affecting farm income policy. *The Farm Economist*, IX, No. 8, 339–52.

Benjamin, B. (1968) *Demographic Analysis*. London: George Allen & Unwin.

Ben–Shahar, H., Mazor, A. and Pines, D. (1969) Town planning and welfare maximisation: a methodological approach. *Regional Studies*, 3, 105–13.

Best, R. H. (1976) The changing land use structure of Britain. *Town and Country Planning*, 44, No. 3, 171–6.

Bloxsidge, R. (1975) The local authority contribution: a bibliographic note. *Town Planning Review*, 46, 466–80.

Bloxsidge, R. (1976) Conservation reports and studies: continuation list and commentary 1975–1976. *Town Planning Review*, 47, 398–417.

Boudeville J.-R. (1966) *Problems of Regional Economic Planning*. Edinburgh: University Press.

Boulding, K. E. (1973) *The Economy of Love and Fear: A Preface to Grant's Economics*. Belmont, California: Wadsworth.

Bourque, P. J. and Cox, M. (1970) *An Inventory of Regional Input*-Output Studies in the U.S. Seattle: Graduate School of Business Administration, University of Washington.

Bowers, J. K., Cheshire, P. C. and Webb, A. E. (1970). The change in the relationship between unemployment and earnings increases: A review of some possible explanations. *National Institute Economic Review*, 54 (November) 44–63.

Box, G. E. P. and Jenkins, G. M. (1968) Some recent advances in forecasting and control, Part I. *Applied Statistics*, 17, 91–109.

Box, G. E. P. and Jenkins, G. M. (1970) *Time-Series Analysis, Forecasting and Control*. San Francisco: Holden Day.

Bracey, H. E. (1958) Some aspects of rural depopulation in the United Kingdom. *Rural Sociology*, 23, 385–91.

Bracey, H. E. (1970) *The People and the Countryside*. London: Routledge & Kegan Paul.

British Railways Board (1963) *Reshaping British Railways* ('The Beeching Report'). London: HMSO.

Bromley, D. W. (1971) The use of discriminant analysis in selecting rural development strategies. *American Journal of Agricultural Economics*, 53, 319–24.

Brown, W. G. and Nawas, F. (1973) Impact of aggregation on the estimation of outdoor recreation demand functions. *American Journal of Agricultural Economics*, 55, No. 2, 246–9.

Brown, W. G., Singh, A. and Castle, E. N. (1964) *An Economic Evaluation of Oregon Salmon and Steelhead Sport Fishing*. Technical Bulletin No. 78. Oregon Agricultural Experiment Station, Corvallis, Oregon.

Brownrigg, M. (1973) The economic impact of a new university. *Scottish Journal of Political Economy*, 20, 123–9.

Bunge, W. (1962) Theoretical geography. *Lund Studies in Geography, Series C, General & Mathematical Geography 1*. University of Lund.

Burton, T. L. (1970) Current trends in recreational demands, in Burton, T. L. (ed.) *Recreation Research and Planning*. London: George Allen & Unwin.

Catlow, J. and Thirlwell, C. G. (1975) *Environmental Impact Analysis Study: Draft and Interim Report*. London: Department of the Environment.

Central Statistical Office (1969) *National Income and Expenditure*. London: HMSO.

Central Statistical Office (1976) *Annual Abstract of Statistics 1975*. London: HMSO.

Central Statistical Office (1976a) *National Income and Expenditure 1965–75*. London: HMSO.

Central Statistical Office (1976b) *Social Trends*. London: HMSO.

Centre for Agricultural Strategy (1976) *Land for Agriculture*. CAS Report 1. University of Reading.

Chadwick G. F. (1971) *A Systems View of Planning*. London: Pergamon.

Champion, A. G. (1974) Competition for agricultural land, in A. M. Edwards and A. W. Rogers (eds) *Agricultural Resources*. London: Faber.

Champion, A. G. (1975) *An Estimate of the Changing Extent and Distribution of Urban Land in England and Wales, 1950–1970*. Research Paper No. 10. London: Centre for Environmental Studies.

Chapman, H. (1975) The machinery of conservation: finance and planning problems. *Town Planning Review*, 46, 365–82.

Chisholm, M. (1962) *Rural Settlement and Land Use*. London: Hutchinson.

Christ, C. F. (1966) *Econometric Models and Methods*. New York: Wiley.

Christaller, W. (1933) *Die zentralen Orte in Suddeutschland*. Jena: Gustave Fischer Verlag. Translated by C. W. Baskin (1966) as *Central Places in Southern Germany*. Englewood Cliffs, New Jersey: Prentice-Hall.

Clawson, M. (1959) *Methods of Measuring the Demand for the Value of Outdoor Recreation*. Reprint No. 10. Washington, DC: Resources for the Future Inc.

Clayton, G. and Rees, J. H. (1967) *The Economic Problems of Rural Transport in Wales*. Cardiff: University of Wales Press.

Cobbett, W. (1821–32) *Rural Rides*. London: J. M. Dent & Sons, 1925.

Country Landowners Association (1970) *The Changing Uplands*. London: CLA.

Countryside Commission (1976) *The Lake District Upland Management Experiment 1969–76*. Cheltenham: Countryside Commission.

Countryside Commission (1976) *Eighth Report, 1974–5*. London: HMSO.

Countryside Commission (1977) *Ninth Report, 1975–6*. London: HMSO.

Cowie, W. G. and Giles, A. K. (1957) *An Inquiry into Reasons for 'The Drift from the Land'*. Selected Papers in Agricultural Economics, University of Bristol.

Cowling, K., Metcalf, D. and Rayner, A. J. (1970) *Resource Structure of Agriculture: An Economic Appraisal*. London: Pergamon.

Cox, P. R. (1970) *Demography*. Cambridge: University Press.

Craig, J. (1970) Estimating the age and sex structure of net migration for a sub-region: a case study of North and South Humberside 1951–1961. *Regional Studies*, 4, 333–47.

Czamanski, S. (1972) *Regional Science Techniques in Practice: The Case of Nova Scotia*. Lexington, Massachusetts: D. C. Heath.

Dasgupta, A. K. and Pearce, D. W. (1972) *Cost Benefit Analysis: Theory and Practice*. London: Macmillan.

Dawson, R. F. (1968) *The Economic Assessment of Road Improvement Schemes*. Technical Report No. 75. Road Research Laboratory, HMSO.

Demsetz, H. (1966) Some aspects of property rights. *Journal of Law and Economics*, 9, 61–70.

Department of Employment and Productivity (1957 *et seq.*) *Family Expenditure Surveys*. London: HMSO.

Department of the Environment (1972) *Documentation of Resource Aspects of Structure Plans*. Structure Plan Note 6/72. London: DoE, Marsham Street.

Department of the Environment (1972) *Evaluating Alternatives in Structure Plan Making*. Structure Plan Note 7/72. London: DoE, Marsham Street.

Department of the Environment (1973) *The Use of Evaluation Matrices for Structure Plans*. Structure Plan Note 8/72. London: DoE, Marsham Street.

Department of the Environment (1974) *Structure Plans*. Circular 98/74. London: HMSO.

Department of the Environment (1974) Statistics of decisions on planning applications 1973, England and Wales, No. 6 in *Statistics for Town and Country Planning, Series 1: Planning Decisions*. London: HMSO.

Department of the Environment (1974) *Transport Supplementary Grant: More Details of the New System*. Circular 27/74. London: HMSO.

Department of the Environment (1975) *The Generation of Alternative Strategies in Structure Planning*. Draft Structure Plan Note No. 6. London: DoE, Marsham Street.

Department of the Environment (1976) *Report of the National Parks Policies Review Committee*. Circular 4/76. London: HMSO.

Department of the Environment (1976) *Local Government Finance: Report of a Committee of Enquiry*. London: HMSO.

Development Commission (1972) *Mid Wales: An Assessment of the Impact of the Development Commission Factory Programme*. London: HMSO.

Development Commission (1977) *Thirty-fourth Annual Report 1973–6*. London: HMSO.

Diehl, W. D. (1964) *Farm — Nonfarm Migration in the South-East: A Costs-Return Analysis*. Ph.D. Thesis, North Carolina State University.

Domanski, R. (1967) Remarks on simultaneous and anisotropic models of transportation network. *Papers of the Regional Science Association*, 19, 223–8.

Dorset County Council (1970) *Milton Abbas Conservation Area*. Dorchester: County Planning Officer.

Duffield, B. S. and Owen, M. L. (1970) *Leisure and Countryside*. Department of Geography, University of Edinburgh.

Dunlop, J. (1976) The examination of structure plans; an emerging procedure. *Journal of Planning and Environment Law* (January 1976), 8–17; (February 1976), 75–85.

Durkheim, E. (1964) *The Division of Labour in Society*. Glencoe, Illinois: The Free Press. (First published in French in 1893.)

Dye, A. O. (1973) Upland sub-regional planning model using a simulation model. *Journal of Environmental Management*, 1, 169–99.

East Lothian County Council (1974) *County Planning Policy*. Reference to Gifford Conservation Area.

East Sussex County Council (1975) *East Sussex County Structure Plan*. Lewes: County Planning Office.

Economic Development Committee of Agriculture (1968) *Agriculture's Import Saving Role*. London: HMSO.

Economic Development Committee for Agriculture (1977) *Agriculture in the 1980s: Land Use*. London: National Economic Development Office.

Economic Trends (May 1965) *Projecting the Population of the United Kingdom*. London: HMSO.

Edwards, A. (1974) Resources in agriculture: land, in A. M. Edwards and A. W. Rogers (eds) *Agricultural Resources*. London: Faber.

Edwards, J. A. (1971) The viability of lower size-order settlements in rural areas: the case of north-east England. *Sociologia Ruralis*, 11, 247–76.

Fairbrother, N. (1972) *New Lives, New Landscapes*. Harmondsworth: Penguin.

Flowerdew, A. D. J. (1971) Cost benefit analysis in evaluating alternative planning policies for Greater London, in M. G. Kendall (ed.) *Cost Benefit Analysis*. London: English Universities Press.

Fogel, R. W. (1964) *Railroads and American Economic Growth*. Baltimore, Maryland: The Johns Hopkins University Press.

Foot, D. H. S. and Starkie, D. M. N. (1970) *Ashford-Hastings Railway Line*. University of Reading Geographical Paper No. 3.

Forrester, J. W. (1971) *World Dynamics*. Cambridge, Massachusetts: Wright Allen Press Inc.

Forestry Commission (1977) *Fifty-sixth Annual Report and Accounts 1975-6*. London: HMSO.

Foster, C. D. (1963) *The Transport Problem*. London: Blackie.

Fox, K. A. (1963) The food and agricultural sectors in advanced economics, in T. Barna (ed.) *Structural Interdependence and Economic Development*. Proceeding of an international conference on input-output techniques, Geneva. London: Macmillan.

Frankenberg, R. (1966) *Communities in Britain*. Harmondsworth: Penguin.

Friend, J. K. and Jessop, W. N. (1969) *Local Government and Strategic Choice*. London: Tavistock.

Funck, R. (1970) Welfare solutions and regional policy decisions. *Papers of the Regional Science Association*, 24, 157-62.

Gasson, R. (1970) Structural reform and the mobility of the small farmer. *Land Reform*, No. 2, 1-20. FAO.

Gasson, R. (1974) *Mobility of Farm Workers*. Occasional Paper No. 2. Department of Land Economy, University of Cambridge.

Geddes, M. (1971) Review of Yorkshire and Humberside regional strategy. *Official Architecture and Planning*, 34, 60.

Gibbs, R. S. and Harrison, A. (1974) *Landownership by Public and Semi-Public Bodies in Great Britain*. Miscellaneous Study No. 56. Department of Agricultural Economics and Management, University of Reading.

Gibbs, R. S. and Harrison, A. (1977) *Institutional Landownership in the United Kingdom*. Centre for Agricultural Strategy, University of Reading.

Gibbs, R. S. and Whitby, M. C. (1975) *Local Authority Expenditure on Access Land*. Research Monograph No. 6. Agriculture Adjustment Unit, University of Newcastle upon Tyne.

Glickman, N. J. (1971) An econometric forecasting model for the Philadelphia region. *Journal of Regional Science*, 11, 15-32.

Gregory, P. (1971) *The Price of Amenity*. London: Macmillan.

Greig, M. A. (1971) The regional income and employment multiplier effects of a pulp mill and paper mill. *Scottish Journal of Political Economy*, 18, 31-48.

Greig, M. A. (1972) *A Study of the Economic Impact of the Highlands and Islands Development Board's Investment in Fisheries*. Inverness: Highlands and Islands Development Board.

Grieve, R. (1972) Problems and objectives in the Highlands and Islands, In J. Ashton and W. H. Long (eds) *The Remoter Rural Areas of Britain*. Edinburgh: Oliver & Boyd.

Gupta, S. P. and Hutton, J. P. (1968) *Economies of Scale in Local Government Services*. Institute of Social and Economic Research and

Royal Commission on Local Government in England, Research Studies No. 3. London: HMSO.

Haggett, P. (1965) *Locational Analysis in Human Geography*. London: Arnold.

Hamilton, R. N. D. (1975) *A Guide to Development and Planning*. Sixth Edition. London: Oyez Publishing.

Hampshire County Council (1973) *South Hampshire Structure Plan*. Winchester: Hampshire County Council.

Harris, B. (1968) Problems in regional science. *Papers of the Regional Science Association*, 21, 7–16.

Harris, S. (1974) Changes in the terms of trade for agriculture: new plateau or new precipice. *Australian Journal of Agricultural Economics*, 18, No. 2, 85–99.

Harrison, A. (1976) Owner occupiers, their wealth and capital taxes, in A. Harrison (ed.) *Farming, the Land and Capital Taxation*. Department of Agricultural Economics, University of Reading.

Haveman, R. H. (1972) *The Economic Performance of Public Investments: An Ex Post Evaluation of Water Resources*. Baltimore, Maryland, and London: Johns Hopkins University Press.

Hawke, G. R. (1970) *Railways and Economic Growth in England and Wales 1840–1870*. Oxford: Clarendon.

Heady, E. O. (1957) *Economics of Agricultural Production and Resource Use*. Englewood Cliffs, New Jersey: Prentice-Hall.

Heady, E. O. and Candler, W. (1958) *Linear Programming Methods*. Ames, Iowa: Iowa State Univerity Press.

Heal, G. (1975) Economic aspects of natural resource depletion, in D. W. Pearce (ed.) *The Economics of Natural Resource Depletion*. London: Macmillan.

Heath, C. E. and Whitby, M. C. (1970) *The Changing Agricultural Labour Force*. Bulletin No. 10. Agricultural Adjustment Unit, University of Newcastle upon Tyne.

Henderson, D. M. (1975) *The Economic Impact of Tourism: A Case Study in Greater Tayside*. Tourism and Recreation Research Unit, University of Edinburgh.

Hepworth, N. P. (1976) *The Finance of Local Government*. Third Edition. London: George Allen & Unwin.

Hill, M.(1968) A goals-achievement matrix in evaluating alternative plans. *Journal of American Institute of Planners*, 34, 19–29.

Hillaby, J. (1974) Teesdale revisited. *New Scientist*, 62, 632.

Hirsh, G. P. (1969) Planning for development of rural areas – a criticism of present practice. *Report of the Proceedings of the Town and Country Planning Summer School*. University of Nottingham.

Hirsch, W. Z. (1965) Cost-functions of an urban government service: refuse collection. *Review of Economics and Statistics*, 47, 87–92.

HM Treasury (1972) *Forestry in Great Britain: An Interdepartmental Cost/Benefit Study*. London: HMSO.

References 289

HM Treasury (1976) *Rural Depopulation: Report by an Interdepartmental Group*. London: HM Treasury.

Hodge, I. D. (1976) Social cost and modern agricultural practice: some possible approaches to their evaluation. *Journal of Environmental Management*, 4, 225-40.

House, J. W. (1965) *Rural North-East England*. Papers on Migration and Mobility in Northern England No. 1. Department of Geography, University of Newcastle upon Tyne.

House, J. W. and Knight, E. M. (1966) *People on the Move: The South Tyne in the Sixties*. Papers on Migration and Mobility in Northern England No. 3. Department of Geography, University of Newcastle upon Tyne.

House, J. W. and Willis, K. G. (1967) *Northern Region and Nation: A Short Migration Atlas 1960-61*. Papers on Migration and Mobility in Northern England No. 4. Department of Geography, University of Newcastle upon Tyne.

Hyder, K. and Maunder, A. H. (1974) The price of farms. *Oxford Agrarian Studies*, III, No. 1, 3-14.

Irving, R. W. and Fearn, H. A. (1975) *Green Money and the Common Agricultural Policy*. Centre for European Studies, Wye College.

Isard, W. (1960) *Methods of Regional Analysis*. Cambridge, Massachusetts: Massachusetts Institute of Technology Press.

Isard, W., Langford, T. W. and Romanoff, E. (1966) *Philadelphia Region Input-Output Study*. Philadelphia, Pennsylvania: Regional Science Research Institute.

Jackson, V. J. (1968) *Population in the Countryside: Growth and Stagnation in the Cotswolds*. London: Frank Cass.

Jensen, R. C. (1969) Some characteristics of investment criteria. *Journal of Agricultural Economics*, XX, No. 2, 251-68.

Joint Working Party (1974) *Report of the Energy Working Party*. Report No. 1. Joint Consultative Organization for Research and Development in Agriculture and Food.

Josling, T. E. (1970) *Britain's Trade Policy Dilemma*. London: Trade Policy Research Centre.

Josling, T. E. (1974) Agricultural policies in developed countries: a review. *Journal of Agricultural Economics*, XXV, No. 3, 229-64.

Josling, T. E. and Hammway, D. (1972) Distribution of costs and benefits of farm policy, in *Burdens and Benefits of Farm-support Policies*. London: Trade Policy Research Centre.

Journal of Planning and Environmental Law (1974) Building operations requisite for the use of land for the purpose of agriculture; permission under class VI of General Development Order. *Journal of Planning and Environmental Law*, 483-5.

Joy, S. (1964) British Railways' track costs. *Journal of Industrial Economics*, 13, 74-89.

Kalter, R. J. (1968) *An Inter-industry Analysis of the Central New York*

Region. Ithaca, New York: Department of Agricultural Economics, Cornell University Press.

Kalter, R. J. and Allee, D. J. (1967) *Recreation and Regional Development.* Ithaca, New York: Department of Agricultural Economics, Cornell University Press.

Kay, J. and Mirrlees J. (1975) The desirability of natural resource depletion, in D. W. Pearce (ed.) *The Economics of Natural Resource Depletion.* London: Macmillan.

Kinsey, A. C., Pomeroy, W. B. and Martin, C. E. (1948) *Sexual Behaviour in the Human Male.* Philadelphia, Pennsylvania: W. B. Saunders Co.

Kneese, A. V., Ayres, R. V. and D'Arge, R. (1970) *Economics and the Environment: A Materials Balance Approach.* Baltimore, Maryland: Johns Hopkins University Press.

Krutilla, J. V. (1967) Conservation reconsidered. *The American Economic Review*, 57, No. 2, 777–86.

Layard, R. (ed.) (1972) *Cost Benefit Analysis.* Harmondsworth: Penguin.

Layfield Committee (1976) *Committee of Enquiry into Local Government Finance Report.* Cmnd 6453. London: HMSO.

Lee, E. S. (1966) A theory of migration. *Demography*, 4, 47–57.

Leicestershire County Council (1974) *Leicester and Leicestershire Structure Plan: Written Statement.* Leicester: County Planning Officer.

Lewis, R. C. and Whitby, M. C. (1972) *Recreation Benefits from a Reservoir.* Research Monograph No. 2. Agricultural Adjustment Unit, University of Newcastle upon Tyne.

Lichfield, N. (1969) Cost benefit analysis in urban expansion: a case study, Peterborough. *Regional Studies*, 3, 123–55.

Lichfield, N. (1970) Evaluation methodology of urban and regional plans: a review. *Regional Studies*, 4, 151–65.

Lindsey County Council (1973) *Communities in Rural Lindsey.* Lincoln: County Planning Office.

Lipsey, R. G. (1975) *An Introduction to Positive Economics.* London: Weidenfeld & Nicolson.

Lipsey, R. G. and Lancaster, K. (1956) The general theory of second best. *Review of Economic Studies* (November), 11–32.

Lösch, A. (1940) *Die räumliche Ordnung der Wirtschaft.* Translated by W. H. Woglom as *The Economics of Location.* New Haven: Yale University Press.

McFarquar, A., Godley, W. and Silvey, D. (1977) The cost of food and Britain's membership of the EEC. *Economic Policy Review*, 43–6.

McGuire, M. C. and Garn, H. A. (1969) The integration of equity and efficiency in criteria in public project selection. *Economic Journal,* LXXIX, No. 316, 882–93.

McInerney, J. P. (1976) The simple analytics of natural resource economics. *Journal of Agricultural Economics*, XXVII, No. 1, 31–52.

McIntosh, F. (1969) A survey of workers leaving Scottish farms. *Scottish Agricultural Economics*, 19, 191–7.

McKean, R. N. (1968) The use of shadow prices, in S. B. Chase (ed.) *Problems of Public Expenditure Analysis.* Washington, DC: The Brookings Institution.

Mackel, C. J. (1975) A survey of the agricultural labour market. *Journal of Agricultural Economics*, 26, 367–81.

MacKinnon, R. D. and Hodgson, M. J. (1970) Optimal transportation networks: a case study of highway systems. *Environment and Planning*, 2, 267–84.

Malthus, T. R. (1798) *First Essay on Population.* Facsimile Edition, 1966. London: Macmillan.

Mansfeld, N. W. (1971) Estimation of benefits from recreation sites and the provision of a new facility. *Regional Studies*, 5, 55–69.

Marshall, A. (1884) The housing of the London poor: 1. Where to house them. *Contemporary Review*, 45, 224.

Martin, A. (1959) A comment on J. R. Bellerby's 'Explanation of the Level of Income in Agriculture'. *The Farm Economist*, 9, 271–84.

Masser, I. (1972) *Analytical Models for Urban and Regional Planning.* Newton Abbot: David & Charles.

Mathur, V. K., McGuire, M. C. and Garn, H. A. (1971) The integration of equity and efficiency criteria: an interchange. *Economic Journal*, LXXXI, No. 324, 929–33.

Meadows, D. H. *et al.* (1972) *The Limits to Growth.* London: Pan Books.

Meyer, J. R. *et al.* (1960) *The Economics of Competition in the Transportation Industries.* Cambridge, Massachusetts: Harvard University Press.

Miles, J. C. (1972) *The Goyt Valley Traffic Experiment.* London: Countryside Commission and Peak Park Planning Board.

Ministry of Agriculture, Fisheries and Food (1966) *Agricultural Land Classification.* Technical Report of the Agricultural Land Service No. 11. London: HMSO.

Ministry of Agriculture, Fisheries and Food (1968) *A Century of Agricultural Statistics, Great Britain 1866–1966.* London: HMSO.

Ministry of Agriculture, Fisheries and Food (1975) *Food from Our Own Resources.* Cmnd 6020. London: HMSO.

Ministry of Agriculture, Fisheries and Food (1975a) *Agricultural Statistics 1974, United Kingdom.* London: HMSO.

Ministry of Town and Country Planning (1945) *National Parks in England and Wales.* (Dower Report.) Cmnd 6628. London: HMSO.

Ministry of Town and Country Planning (1947) *Report of the National Parks Committee (England and Wales).* (Hobhouse Report.) Cmnd 7121. London: HMSO.

Ministry of Transport (1961) *Rural Bus Services: Report of the Committee.* ('The Jack Committee'.) London: HMSO.

Ministry of Transport (1969) *The Cambrian Coast Line.* London: HMSO.

Munton, R. C. J. (1975) The state of the agricultural land market, 1971–3: a survey of auctioneers' property transactions. *Oxford Agrarian Studies*, IV (new series), No. 2, 111–30.

Nalson, J. S. (1968) *Mobility of Farm Families*. Manchester: University Press.

Nath, S. K. (1973) *A Perspective of Welfare Economics*. London: Macmillan.

National Opinion Polls (1969) *Outdoor Recreation in the Northern Region*. Northern Economic Planning Committee.

National Park Policies Review Committee (1974) *Report*. London: HMSO.

Nature Conservancy Council (1977) *Nature Conservation and Agriculture*. London: HMSO.

Naylor, T. H., Seaks, T. G. and Wichern, D. W. (1972) Box-Jenkins methods: an alternative to econometric models. *International Statistical Review*, 40, 123–37.

Nelson, P. (1959) Migration, real income and information. *Journal of Regional Science*, 1, 43–74.

Newby, H. (1977) *The Deferential Worker: A Study of Farm Workers in East Anglia*. London: Allen Lane.

Newby, H. *et al.* (1978) *Property, Paternalism and Power: A Study of East Anglian Farmers*. London: Hutchinson.

Nock, O. S. (1957) *Branch Lines*. London.

Nordhaus, W. D. (1973) World dynamics: measurement without data. *Economic Journal*, 83, 1156–83.

North Regional Planning Committee (1969) *Outdoor Leisure Activities in the Northern Region*. Newcastle upon Tyne: NRPC.

North Riding County Council (1973) *The North Riding of Yorkshire Structure Plan: Draft Policies and Proposals*. Northallerton: North Riding County Council.

Northern Economic Planning Council (1966) *Challenge of the Changing North*, London: HMSO.

Northumberland County Council (1967) *Rural Northumberland, Background Report*. Newcastle upon Tyne: County Planning Office.

Northumberland County Council (1968) *Rural Northumberland Village Household Survey*. Newcastle uponTyne: Northumberland County Council.

Northumberland County Council (1969) *Rural Northumberland: Policy for Growth and Concentration*. Newcastle upon Tyne: Northumberland County Council.

Nottinghamshire County Council (1966) *Rural Nottinghamshire: 1. East Retford District*. Nottingham: County Planning Office.

Nottinghamshire County Council (1969) *Plan for Rural Nottinghamshire: 5. Central Nottinghamshire*. Nottingham: County Planning Office.

Office of Population Censuses and Surveys (1975) *Population Projections 1974–2014*. Series PP2, No. 5. London: HMSO.

Openshaw, S. and Whitehead, P. T. (1975) A decision optimising technique for planners. *Planning Outlook*, 16, 19–33.

Openshaw, S. and Whitehead, P. T. (1977) Decision-making in local plans. The DOT methodology and a case study. *Town Planning Review*, 48 29–41.

Open University (1975) *Planning and Pollution Areas of Concern*. Unit 16 of Course PT 272, Environmental Control and Public Health. Milton Keynes: The Open University.

Oxfordshire County Council (1976) *Draft Structure Plan for Oxfordshire*. Oxford: County Planning Office.

Passmore, J. (1974) *Man's Responsibility for Nature*. London: Duckworth.

Pearce, D. W. (1971) *Cost-Benefit Analysis*. London: Macmillan.

Pearce, D. W. (1976) *Environmental Economics*. London: Longman.

Pennock, J. R. (1962) 'Responsible government', separated powers and special interests. *American Political Science Review*, 56, 621–33.

Perle, E. D. (1965) Estimation of transportation demand. *Papers of the Regional Science Association*, 15, 203–15.

Peters, G. H. and Eckford, J. C. (1976) The impact of capital transfer tax on agriculture: a preliminary assessment. *Oxford Agrarian Studies*, V, 35–65.

Price, C. (1973) To the future: with indifference of concern? The social discount rate and its implications in land use. *Journal of Agricultural Economics*, XXIV, No. 2, 393–7.

Pryke, R. W. S. and Dodgson, J. S. (1975) *The Rail Problem*. London: Martin Robertson.

Ray, G. F. and Crum, R. E. (1963) Transport: notes and comments. *National Institute Economic Review*, No. 24.

Redfield, R. (1955) *The Little Community: Viewpoints for the Study of a Human Whole*. Chicago, Illinois: University of Chicago Press.

Redford, A. (1964) *Labour Migration in England 1800–1850*. Manchester: University Press.

Registrar General (1967) *Decennial Supplement. England and Wales (1961) Area Mortality Tables*. London: HMSO.

Registrar General (1968) *Statistical Review for England and Wales. Part 2: Population*. London: HMSO.

Reynolds, J. P. (1975) Heritage year in Britain: the aims and objectives of conservation. *Town Planning Review*, 46, 335–64.

Ricardo, D. (1817) *The Principles of Political Economy and Taxation*. 1957 Edition. New York: Dutton, Everyman.

Richardson, H. W. (1971) *Urban Economics*. Harmondsworth: Penguin.

Riew, J. (1966) Economies of scale in high school operation. *Review of Economics and Statistics*, 48, 332–8.

Robinson, J. N. (1972) *Planning and Forecasting Techniques*. London: Weidenfeld & Nicolson.

Rodgers, J. (1974) *Quantitative Techniques for Forecasting: A Review with Applications to New Zealand Wool Prices*. Research Report No. 69. Agricultural Economics Research Unit, Lincoln College, University of Canterbury, New Zealand.

Rose, D., Newby, H., Saunders, P. and Bell, C. (1977) Land tenure and official statistics: a research note. *Journal of Agricultural Economics*, XXVIII, No. 1, 69–76.

Roskill, The Hon. Mr. Justice (1970) *Committee on the Third London Airport. Report*. London: HMSO.

Ross, G. (1976) Capital taxation and structural policy: some EEC and UK issues, in A. Harrison (ed.) *Farming, the Land and Capital Taxation*. Department of Agricultural Economics, University of Reading.

Rowley, C. K. and Peacock, A. T. (1975) *Welfare Economics: A Liberal Restatement*. London: Martin Robertson.

Royal Town Planning Institute (1974) *The Land Question*. Planning Paper No. 4. London: Royal Town Planning Institute.

Samuelson, P. A. (1976) *Economics*. Tenth Edition. New York: McGraw-Hill.

Saville, J. (1957) *Rural Depopulation in England and Wales 1851–1951*. London: Routledge & Kegan Paul.

Schneider, J. R. L. (1956) Local population projections in England and Wales. *Population Studies*, 10, 95–114.

Schultz, T. W. (1953) *The Economic Organization of Agriculture*. New York: McGraw-Hill.

Scitovsky, T. (1941) A note on welfare propositions in economics. *Review of Economic Studies*, 9, 77–88. Reprinted in K. Arrow and T. Scitovsky (eds) (1969) *Readings in Welfare Economics*. London: Allen & Unwin.

Scott, A. J. (1967) A programming model of an integrated transportation network. *Papers of the Regional Science Association*, 19, 215–22.

Secretary of State for Wales (1973) Cambrian Mountains National Park Proposal. Letter to the Chairman of the Countryside Commission. Reprinted in Countryside Commission (1974) *Sixth Report 1972–3*. London: HMSO.

Self, P. (1975) *Econocrats and the Policy Process*. London: Macmillan.

Self, P. and Storling, H. (1962) *The State and the Farmer*. London: Allen & Unwin.

Sengupta, J. K. (1963) Models of agriculture and industry in less developed economies, in T. Barna (ed.) *Structural Interdependence and Economic Development*. London: Macmillan.

Shapiro, H. (1963) Economies of scale and local government finance. *Land Economics*, 39, 175–86.

Sinden, J. A. (1974) A utility approach to the valuation of recreational and aesthetic experiences. *American Journal of Agricultural Economics*, 56, No. 1, 61–72.

Sjaastad, L. A. (1962) The costs and returns of human migration. *Journal of Political Economy*, 70, 80–93.

Smith, D. M. (1971) *Industrial Location*. New York: Wiley.

Smith, R. J. (1971) The evaluation of recreation benefits: the Clawson method in practice. *Urban Studies*, 8, No. 2, 89–102.

Smith, R. J. (ed.) (1975) *The Politics of Physical Resources*. Milton Keynes: The Open University.

Speare, A. (1971) A cost-benefit model of rural to urban migration in Taiwan. *Population Studies*, 25, 117-30.

Spiegelman, R. G., Baum, E. L. and Talbert, L. E. (1965) *Application of Activity Analysis to Regional Development Planning: A Case Study of Economic Planning in Rural South Central Kentucky*. Technical Bulletin No. 1339. Washington, DC: Department of Agriculture.

Squire L. and Van Der Tak H. G. (1976) *Economic Analysis of Projects*. Baltimore, Maryland, and London: Johns Hopkins, Worldbank Research Publication.

Staffordshire County Council (1973) *Staffordshire County Structure Plan: Policies and Proposals*. Staffordshire County Council.

Stevens Committee (1976) *Report on Planning Control over Mineral Workings*. London: HMSO.

Stoakes, R. (1972) The effects of government support payments on income distribution in a sample of farms from the Northern Region between 1961 and 1970. Dissertation submitted in partial fulfilment of the requirements for the degree of M.Sc. in Agricultural Economics at the University of Newcastle upon Tyne.

Stone, R. (1971) *Demographic Accounting and Model Building*. Paris: OECD.

Stretton, C. E. (1907) *The History of the Midland Railway*. London.

Surrey, A. J. and Page, W. (1975) Some issues in the current debate about energy and natural resources, in D. W. Pearce (ed.) *The Economics of Natural Resource Depletion*. London: Macmillan.

Tarver, J. D. (1961) Predicting migration. *Social Forces*, 39, 207-13.

Thomas, D. S. (1938) *Research Memorandum on Migration Differentials*. New York: Social Science Research Council.

Thomas, D. St John (1963) *The Rural Transport System*. London: Routledge & Kegan Paul.

Thompson, W. R. (1965) *A Preface to Urban Economics*. Baltimore, Maryland: Johns Hopkins University Press.

Thomson, K. J. and Whitby, M. C. (1976) The economics of public access in the countryside. *Journal of Agricultural Economics*, XXVII, No. 3, 307-20.

Tintner, G. (1952) *Econometrics*. New York: Wiley.

Tönnies, F. (1955) *Community and Association*. London: Routledge & Kegan Paul. (First published in German in 1877.)

Tracey, M. (1964) *Agriculture in Western Europe: Crisis and Adaptation since 1880*. London: Jonathan Cape.

Tyler, G. J. (1972) Factors affecting the size of the labour force and the level of earnings in UK agriculture 1948-65. *Oxford Agrarian Studies*, 1, No. 1, 20-45.

Vickerman, R. W. (1975) *The Economics of Leisure and Recreation*. London: Macmillan.

Von Thunen, J. H. (1826) *Der isolierte Staat in Beziehung auf Landwirtschaft und Nationalökonomie.* Hamburg. For a brief account see M. Chisholm (1962) *Rural Settlement and Land Use.* London: Hutchinson.

Wagle, B. Rappoport, J. Q. G. H. and Downes, V. A. (1968) A program for short term forecasting. *The Statistician,* 18, 141-7.

Walters, A. A. (1970) *An Introduction to Econometrics.* London: Macmillan.

Ward, P. (1968) *Conservation and Development in Historic Towns and Cities.* University of Newcastle: Oriel Press.

Warford, J. J. (1969) *The South Atcham Scheme: An Economic Appraisal.* London: HMSO.

Weber, A. (1909) *Ueber den Standort der Industrien.* Part 1: *Reine Theorie der Standorts.* Tübingen. Translated by C. J. Friedrich (1928) as *Alfred Weber's Theory of the Location of Industries.* Chicago, Illinois: University of Chicago Press.

Weisbrod, B. A. (1968) Income redistribution effects and benefit-cost analysis, in S. R. Chase (ed.) *Problems in Expenditure Analysis.* Washington, DC: The Brookings Institute.

Wellington, A. M. (1887) *The Economic Theory of the Location of Railways.* New York.

West, L. (1966) *Automobile Density in Rural Finnish Communes.* Publications Institute Geographici Universitatis Turkuensis No. 40. Turku.

Westmacott, R. and Worthington, T. (1974) *New Agricultural Landscapes.* Countryside Commission. London: HMSO.

Whitby, M. C. (1977) Subsidy shifts across the Store Sheep Market. *Journal of Agricultural Economics,* XXVIII, No. 1, 1-10.

White Paper (1965) *The Development of Agriculture.* Cmnd 2738. London: HMSO.

White Paper (1972) *Forestry Policy.* London: HMSO.

White Paper (1974) *Land.* Cmnd 5730. London: HMSO.

Wibberley, G. P. (1959) *Agriculture and Urban Growth.* London: Michael Joseph.

Wibberley, G. P. (1976) Rural resource development in Britain and environmental concern. *Journal of Agricultural Economics,* XXVII, No. 1, 1-18.

Wibberley, G. P. and Edwards, A. M. (1971) *An Agricultural Land Budget for Britain 1965-2000.* Studies in Rural Land Use No. 10. Wye College.

Williams, W. M. (1956) *The Sociology of an English Village: Gosforth.* London: Routledge & Kegan Paul.

Willis, K. G. (1971) *Models of Population and Income: Economic Planning in Rural Areas.* Research Monograph No. 1. Department of Agricultural Economics, University of Newcastle upon Tyne.

Willis, K. G. (1973) *Economic Policy Determination and Evaluation in the North Pennines.* Research Monograph No. 3. Agricultural Adjustment

Unit, Department of Agricultural Economics, University of Newcastle upon Tyne.

Willis, K. G. (1974) *Problems in Migration Analysis*. Farnborough: Saxon House.

Wilson, A. G. (1969) The use of entropy maximising models in the theory of trip distribution, mode split and route split. *Journal of Transport Economics and Policy*, 3, 108–26.

Wilson, A. G. and Kirwan, R. (1969) *Measuring the Benefits of Urban Transportation Improvements*. Working Paper 43. London: Centre for Environmental Studies.

Wolfe, J. N. and Caborn, J. M. (1973) *Some Considerations Regarding Forestry Policy in Great Britain. An Inter-disciplinary Report*. Forestry Committee of Great Britain.

Wolpert, J. (1966) Migration as an adjustment to environmental stress. *Journal of Social Issues*, 22, 92–102.

Woodruffe, B. J. (1976) *Rural Settlement Policies and Plans*. Oxford: University Press.

Worcestershire County Council (1975) *Worcestershire Structure Plan*. Worcester: County Planning Office.

Worksett, R. (1969) *The Character of Towns: An Approach to Conservation*. London: Architectural Press.

Yorkshire and Humberside Economic Planning Board (1976) *The Pennine Uplands: Socio-economic Interactions and Opportunities in the Yorkshire Pennines*. London: HMSO.

Index

Printed in the United States
by Baker & Taylor Publisher Services